The Data Webhouse Toolkit

Advance Praise for
The Data Webhouse Toolkit: Building the Web-Enabled Data Warehouse

"In a world glutted with commercial Web server log analysis tools, Kimball's new book is as refreshing as his first. Kimball's brilliant dimensional model for clickstream data proves that a standard RDBMS plus a better-than-standard brain is what the world's e-commerce sites need."

—Philip Greenspun, CEO, ArsDigita.com

"Ralph's latest book ushers in the second wave of the Internet. Here companies leverage the Internet beyond just a means of sales, but as a strategic business tool to strengthen customer relationships. Bottomline, this book provides the insight to help companies combine Internet-based business intelligence with the bounty of customer data generated from the Internet to convert 'eyeballs' into profits."

—William Schmarzo, Director Worldwide Solutions
Sales and Marketing, IBM NUMA-Q

"As a society we have come to accept the truth that the Internet truly does change everything. Great organizations are readily embracing this reality and aggressively positioning to capitalize on the Web-based informational asset. This book provides both the vision and the practical advice to enable this journey."

—David Fenton, Vice President,
Business Intelligence and Warehouse
Global Service Line, Oracle

The Data Webhouse Toolkit

Building the Web-Enabled Data Warehouse

Ralph Kimball

Richard Merz

WILEY COMPUTER PUBLISHING

John Wiley & Sons, Inc.
New York • Chichester • Weinheim • Brisbane • Singapore • Toronto

Publisher: Robert Ipsen

Editor: Robert M. Elliott

Managing Editor: Brian Snapp

Associate New Media Editor: Mike Sosa

Text Design & Composition: Rob Mauhar

Library of Congress Cataloging-in-Publication Data:
0471-37680-9

Printed in the United States of America.

10 9 8 7 6 5 4 3 2 1

Contents

Acknowledgments

Both of the authors feel very privileged to be professionally active at such an exciting time in history. We each began our careers when IBM mainframes typically had less than 8K of memory! The changes wrought by the Web are happening at breathtaking speed and it is clear that we are only at the beginning of the Internet Age. So our first acknowledgement is to the Web itself for being such an interesting phenomenon and creating so many opportunities.

This book has been a real pleasure to write, in part because of the wonderful support we have had from Bob Elliott, our editor at John Wiley & Sons. Bob and his staff are the best in this business. We've enjoyed working with Emilie Herman, Susan McCarty, and Brian Snapp at the Wiley office.

Justin Kestelyn, Editor-in-Chief of Intelligent Enterprise Magazine, has been extraordinarily generous in allowing us to adapt material from a few of Ralph Kimball's articles for inclusion in the body of this book.

We'd like to thank Neal Kite and Kent Millington of Verio for their encouragement and support of this project, and to extend special thanks to James Mitchell, Webmaster of Verio's WebCom subsidiary, for rendering many of the illustrations in Chapter 10.

This book, like the previous two Toolkit books by Ralph Kimball, was extensively reviewed before the manuscript was submitted to Wiley. Although such a review step can result in more work just when the authors would like to take a rest, the book turns out much better for the effort. This time we had a marvelous set of reviewers and we thank them all, in alphabetic order: Caroline Ahdab, Maurice Frank, Mike Heathman, Joy Mundy, Margy Ross, Susan Roston, Dick Smallwood, Mark Sweiger, Jerry Tattershall, and Warren Thornthwaite.

We would like to thank Julie Kimball, Ralph Kimball's business partner and wife, for playing an indispensable role throughout the production of this book. Julie negotiated the business contract, made the arrangements with the reviewers, and urged us on.

Finally, Ralph and Richard wish to thank our wives Julie Kimball and Toni Merz for being so positive and enthusiastic during this project, and our grown-up children Sara Hayden Smith, Brian Kimball, Alexey Merz, and Chris Merz for putting up with a couple of distracted dads.

Introduction

In just the past year, the impact of the Web has transformed the mission of IT from supporting legacy applications to delivering content, information, and transaction-processing capabilities, all through browser interfaces. Or so it seems. Never before have IT organizations been under as much pressure to adapt to new ways of thinking and to retool so many of their interfaces.

The Year 2000 problem has been only a temporary pause in pursuing the larger challenge: responding to the demands of the Web. The Web is much more than a technology for connecting distributed computing devices. The Web is a new and cheaper form of communication.

BUILDING THE INFRASTRUCTURE FOR THE REVOLUTION

In our history, there have been a number of revolutions where the cost of communicating has suddenly been lowered. In all of these cases, when this cost dropped dramatically, the volume of communication rose abruptly, people became literate in a new medium, and society was permanently transformed. Consider the following list, also shown in Figure I.1:

- The printing press in the 1500s, which introduced reading and publishing to wide segments of society
- The Penny Post in England in the 1840s, which set the cost of sending a letter anywhere in England to a single penny

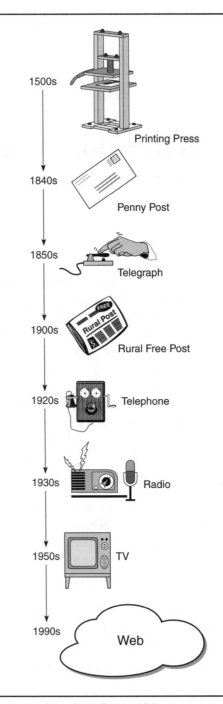

FIGURE I.1   Media That Profoundly Influenced Society

- The telegraph in the 1840s and 1850s in Europe and in the United States, which was the first form of immediate long distance communication
- Rural free postal delivery in the United States in the early 1900s, which brought news, commerce, and personal communication to a far-flung population scattered across a big country
- Telephone in the 1920s, which allowed any citizen to talk instantly with any other citizen
- Radio in the 1930s, which spread news, culture, language, and opinion across the country instantaneously
- Television in the 1950s, which continued the impact begun by radio, but in an even more compelling medium
- The Web in the 1990s, which is a kind of supercharged, high-bandwidth descendant of the post office, the telephone, radio, and television

Perhaps the biggest difference between the Web revolution of the 1990s and the earlier revolutions is the sheer speed at which this latest revolution is occurring. In the space of a half dozen years, a significant fraction of the world has changed how it communicates, how it conducts business, and how it uses information.

This time, it is our turn as IT professionals to build the infrastructure for the revolution. We are expected by our organizations to adapt our primary legacy applications to the Web so that everyone can use the Web ubiquitously for input and output. We are expected to provide Web-enabled interfaces for our customers, our business partners, and our internal employees. We are expected to make available from our "archives" all the forms of multimedia data suggested by the Web, including databases, spreadsheets, unstructured text, images, maps, and maybe even audio and video. At the same time, we are supposed to sort through all the security and confidentiality issues of protecting and appropriately disseminating all this information.

Building this new Web infrastructure is exciting and mind-boggling at the same time. Where do we get started? How can we cut the problem down to size so that it is manageable and so that we can apply our existing system-building skills to this challenge?

The Data Webhouse

During the last decade, before the Web revolution really gathered steam, IT organizations have been learning how to publish the data assets of the organization to internal analysts and to management. This act of publishing is the central task of the data warehouse.

Data warehousing is one of the core responsibilities of IT. In many ways, data warehousing fulfills the promise of "getting the data out" after our OLTP-based systems "get the data in." As a result of our decade of experience with data warehousing, we have a relatively mature understanding of what data warehousing is, and how IT can bring technology to bear in publishing all this data.

The Web revolution has certainly not replaced the need for the data warehouse. In fact, the Web revolution has raised everyone's expectations much higher that all sorts of information will be seamlessly published through Web browser interfaces. The audience for data warehouse data has grown from internal management to encompass customers, partners, and a much larger pool of internal employees. The Web's focus on the "customer experience" has made many organizations much more aware of learning about the customer and giving the customer useful information.

The Web revolution has propelled the data warehouse out onto the main stage, because in many situations the data warehouse must be the engine that controls or analyzes the Web experience. In order to step up to this heightened responsibility, the data warehouse must adjust. The nature of the data warehouse needs to be somewhat different than it has been for the past decade. In Figure I.2 we show the relationship of the customer to the Website and to the Webhouse.

We will call this rebirth of the data warehouse the data Webhouse.

WHAT THIS BOOK IS ABOUT

This book is about data Webhouses. We will define the data Webhouse and show how it differs from the conventional data warehouse. Most important, we will show in detail how to build a data Webhouse, either starting from scratch, or, more likely, adapting and extending the existing data warehouse to make it into a full-fledged data Webhouse.

We will see that the data Webhouse has two personalities, and this is reflected in the two halves of the book. See Figure I.3. The first half describes bringing the Web to the warehouse. The Web itself is an immense source of behavioral data as individuals interact through their browsers with remote Websites. Although this *clickstream* data in many cases is raw and unvarnished, it has the potential of providing unprecedented detail about every gesture made by every human being using

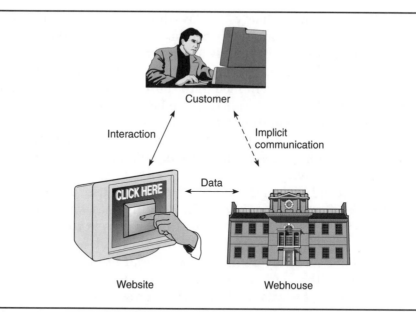

FIGURE I.2   The Customer, the Website, and the Webhouse

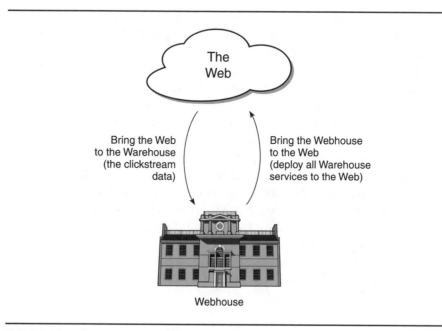

FIGURE I.3   The Two Personalities of the Webhouse

the Web medium. Already the raw data sources for this Amazon-like flow of clickstream data are becoming the largest known text and number databases in existence, dwarfing even the famous large examples from telco and insurance. When we bring the Web to the warehouse, we bring this huge, undisciplined data source into our data Webhouse to be analyzed itself, and alternatively, to be conformed and combined with existing, more conventional data sources.

The entire first half of the book is about understanding and taming the clickstream source so that it can be stored in the data Webhouse and used effectively.

The second personality of the data Webhouse, described in the second half of the book, is bringing the existing data warehouse to the Web. The most succinct way to describe this process is that we are no longer in a client/server environment. We are in a Web-enabled environment, and we have more layers in our architecture than before.

Bringing the warehouse to the Web means making all data warehouse interfaces available through Web browsers. This ranges the gamut from data entry, to simple ad hoc querying, to complex reporting, to serious application development, and finally to database and system administration.

Bringing the warehouse to the Web also means addressing, for once and for all, the issues of a fully distributed environment. The data Webhouse is a profound alternative to the fully centralized data warehouse approach. The data Webhouse can no more be centralized than the Internet itself can be centralized. Somehow, we must adopt a design philosophy that allows separate islands of data warehousing across the Web to see and communicate with each other in an effective way. One of the goals of this book is to show what that means. We will learn how to build and control distributed data Webhouses.

We do not make a big distinction in this book between *intranet* Webhousing and *Internet* Webhousing, because we think the design issues, the technologies, and the exposures of these two kinds of networks are virtually identical. We are convinced that it is practically impossible to limit one's organization to a pure intranet approach. Almost from the outset, people are going to want to use their browsers remotely, connecting via the Web backbone. As soon as that happens, you have all the issues of a full Web deployment. So you may as well address the bigger problem from the outset.

Who the Book Is For

This book is for designers and project managers in IT organizations who have various Web and warehouse responsibilities as described earlier and are going to build some or all of a data Webhouse. If you are such a professional then you or your staff may need to:

- Capture clickstream logs and convert them into database tables for data warehouse analysis
- Merge customer demographic and account information with the clickstream data
- Interpret the paths taken by customers through your company's Website
- Identify sessions that result in "abandoning the shopping cart"
- Identify action sequences on the Website that result in unprofitable behavior
- Use the data warehouse to drive customer responses appearing on your Website
- Help the marketing department tell whether your on-line sales channel is profitable
- Make conventional data warehouse services like querying and reporting widely available to different parties logging in from Web browsers
- Attach unconventional multimedia data types to data warehouse data as part of making the data warehouse available over the Web
- Be responsible for a comprehensive security strategy that makes many different kinds of sensitive data available only to those who need to see it
- Create a project plan for designing, implementing, and deploying a data Webhouse

If any or all of these tasks are your responsibility, then this book has been written for you. If your title isn't project leader, then perhaps you are a database administrator, a data warehouse architect, a system designer, or an application developer. You may be a mainline Webmaster who has been asked to collaborate with an existing data warehouse team to build a data Webhouse. If you are a Webmaster, we hope this book guides you to effectively tag the pages of your Website and to employ cookies judiciously so that the clickstream is made more meaningful. You will also understand what keeps data warehouse designers awake at night.

Other parties who will find this book useful include Web service vendors, especially ISPs and Web measurement houses, because although those parties may create or control the clickstream, they will learn from this book that they can't possibly be the whole data warehouse. The enterprise data warehouse is much bigger than one might think, and the role of the ISP or the Web measurement house is to be a supportive player in the enterprise's overall data warehouse architecture.

Marketing departments interested in implementing 1-to-1 marketing techniques (using data warehouse data to drive the Web interactions) will find much of use in this book. We will show you how to design both your data warehouse and your Web server to make this possible. We also present a detailed design for analyzing the profitability of your Web business.

We have created a Customer Relationship Management (CRM) thread that appears in nearly every chapter of the book. This thread applies the principles developed in each chapter to this important application.

Finally, if you are a higher-level IT manager who needs to understand what a data Webhouse project entails, we think you will find this book very useful.

What You Need to Know

This book cannot possibly be a self-contained introduction to all the perspectives needed to lead a comprehensive data Webhouse project. In this book, we assume that you have a working understanding of:

- **Dimensional modeling as the basis for data warehouse design.** Appropriate introductions to dimensional modeling would be either of Ralph Kimball's previous *Toolkit* books: *The Data Warehouse Toolkit* (Wiley, 1996) or the *Data Warehouse Lifecycle Toolkit* (Wiley, 1998, with Kimball, Reeves, Ross, and Thornthwaite). A good extension of these design concepts, especially for product-based supply chains, can be found in Adamson and Venerable's *Data Warehouse Design Solutions* (Wiley, 1998). Even more than a book-level understanding of dimensional modeling, it would be good if you had actually built some dimensional models. In this book, we will briefly review the basic ideas of dimensional modeling, but we will not present a comprehensive tutorial.

- **Data warehouse project management.** An appropriate introduction, once again, would be the *Data Warehouse Lifecycle Toolkit*, cited earlier. Again, the real-life experience of implementing a working data warehouse is the most valuable background of all.

- **Elementary Webmaster skills.**   You need to be somewhat familiar with the structure of a corporate Website and the layers of firewalls, Web servers, application servers, and databases in your computing environment. Although we discuss all of these in some detail, this book will be hard to relate to if you are completely new to the Web. A good introduction to elementary Webmaster skills is Spainhour and Eckstein's *Webmaster in a Nutshell, Second Edition* (O'Reilly & Associates, 1999).

How to Use This Book

Even if your responsibilities are limited to just analyzing the clickstream, or just making data warehouse queries available over the Web, we think you should read the whole book. In some ways we think the bipartite distinction we have made between bringing the Web to the warehouse and bringing the warehouse to the Web will hold up on a permanent basis, but we have been amazed at the degree to which these two responsibilities are getting incestuously intertwined and more difficult to talk about separately.

If you are analyzing the clickstream data, you are likely to use that very data in its warehouse form to make decisions about customizing the Web-browsing experience of your customers. So the loop will be completed tightly. You need to bring the Web to the warehouse.

Similarly, if you are part of the regular data warehouse team and you are exposing data warehouse functionality over the Web, you won't easily avoid analyzing the behavior of people clicking on your site. Maybe these people will be conventional customers clicking on your commercial pages, or maybe these people will be various kinds of data warehouse users clicking on your data warehouse user interfaces. It would certainly be interesting to analyze the gestures made by a data warehouse user who is legitimately struggling to get results from your data warehouse.

Like the previous *Toolkits*, we have peppered the book with bullets and asides. Our favorite bullet is the light bulb:

    This is a practical design tip.

As part of nearly every chapter, we comment on the application of the ideas in that chapter to customer relationship management (CRM). We label this special section with a CRM bullet:

This highlights how CRM applies to the chapter.

The Purpose of Each Chapter

The next few pages are a map to what is found in this book. It is probably worth reading this section just to allay fears that we aren't going to address a certain topic. There is so much that is new when discussing the Webhouse that "forward dependencies" (using terms that are described more fully later in the book) are difficult to avoid and it is tedious to keep mentioning them in the text, so we have largely left them out.

Part One: Bringing the Web to the Warehouse

1. **Why Bring the Web to the Warehouse?**   The Web is the single most important factor in the commerce revolution that is taking place. Or, it might be more accurate to say that the commerce revolution is part of the larger Web revolution. In any case, Web technology makes it possible to record nearly every gesture made by individuals when they are touring remote Websites. This behavioral information is what marketing analysts die for. Ultimately, understanding the behavioral record drives all marketing responses, whether they are sales promotion programs lasting many weeks or whether they are instantaneous greetings displayed on the user's screen. In all of these cases, the raw behavioral information must be brought to a serious database for analysis. The serious database is, of course, the data warehouse, which we refer to as the Webhouse throughout this book. This chapter draws as many links as we are able to generate between measurable Web activity and the capability of the data warehouse to analyze that activity.

   We conclude the chapter with a brief survey of customer relationship management (CRM) and one-to-one marketing.

2. **Tracking Website User Actions.**   Before diving into the specific details of any of the Web behavior data sources, we need to understand what Web behavior is. We start by discussing the categories of natural Web behavior, including searching, browsing, work, education,

communication, shopping, entertainment, and downloading. We show how many of these categories require the participation of some kind of powerful database.

Several times in this book we divide the world of users into three categories: our customers, our business partners, and our employees. In those places where interpretation of user behavior is noticeably different among these three types, we will point this out.

We analyze the steps of product purchases in detail, because so much of the interest in the Webhouse is in supporting commerce. Since Web data sources often reveal the pathways by which the user entered a given Web page, we dissect the various types of ISPs, portals, bookmarks, referrals, and clickthroughs. We talk in detail about tracking the route a user takes across the Web, but at this point we don't make any guarantees that we will be able to capture this information!

Once we have identified the user's original jumping off point, and the route the user took to get to a certain page, we are starting to have a reasonable handle on behavior. We want to measure how long the user spent on a page, and whether the user returns to that page again.

In this chapter we start tackling the major question of whether we can identify who the user is. We look at anonymous users, authenticated users, and persistent pseudonyms. We try to put cookies in their proper perspective and show why they are necessary and valuable for analyzing and identifying a specific Web visitor.

We show how certain Web service providers, particularly ISPs, have a unique perspective on collecting Web behavior. In many ways, their position on collecting Web behavior is so powerful that they must exercise utmost restraint in order to keep from abusing their connected clients.

Armed with the identity of the user, and perhaps a significant record of where the user has gone, we may be in a position to really tell "what the user is doing." We try to sketch the scientific and ethical boundaries of identifying behavior by associating all the diverse actions that we can observe.

Finally, we conclude this chapter by tightly summarizing the requirements for personalization of a Website. Later, in Chapter 8, we will turn these requirements into an actual architecture for personalization.

3. **Using the Clickstream to Make Decisions.**   Assuming that we have tracked user actions to the extent described in Chapter 2, how do we want to use this information? What decisions does this data drive?

We will see in this chapter that a full analysis of Website behavior has immense economic significance. In certain situations, we want to take a bookkeeper's perspective and keep track of clickthroughs and referrals as a revenue source or a revenue obligation, when there is a contract that calls for payments to be made when a user goes to a site because of a link.

Clickthroughs and referrals are just specific mechanisms for promotions. We show how Web behavior can be interpreted as a response to a promotion. We then link this kind of Web promotion response to classic promotions analysis, including the estimation of "unpromoted volume," which establishes a baseline against which the value of a promotion is judged.

We show how Web behavior can be used to build a simple customer clustering model where recency, frequency, and monetary value of a customer's purchases can be sorted out into 125 quintiles, which is a kind of map of who your customers are.

The highest art form of using Website behavior data is to build a full-fledged profitability model of an enterprise's Web commerce channel. This is one area where the accumulated wisdom of the existing data warehouse industry helps enormously. We propose a series of profitability models that are intended to be developed as a progression over time, gradually adding more detail and more accuracy to the model. The charm of implementing the "Web profitability data mart" incrementally is that some useful results appear early in the implementation, and the model is gradually improved over time.

In this chapter we show how to use the Webhouse to drive customization. We use the Webhouse to help us improve the focus and effectiveness of the Website itself. We figure out which pages are session killers and which pages are abandoned before they have finished painting on the user's screen. We identify those pages that are confusing or do not present the choices users need. And we identify those pages that users return to repeatedly. Return visits are second only in importance to actual product orders. And finally, we discuss the issue of using metatags to lure search engines to our site.

4. **Understanding the Clickstream as a Data Source.**   This chapter gets down to the brass tacks of exactly what is in the clickstream data source. We talk about the problems of stateless protocols, which typify many of the clickstream sources. We show the varieties of the common logging (CLOG) format that you will probably have to deal

with. We squeeze as much information out of the browser IP address and the referrer URL as we can. And we explore the limits of what information is feasible to put in a cookie, whether the cookie is persistent or transient. Using the previous chapter as a base, we push the limits of what can be analyzed from the clickstream data. We figure out how the user got to the site and who the user is. We gather together all page events that constitute a session, and we characterize and classify the different kinds of trips through the Website. We tag each session by type, and we tie in related Web activities such as e-mail and file transfer.

Since analyzing the clickstream is partially done by various third parties, we conclude by commenting on what the advantages and limitations of these kinds of parties are.

5. **Designing the Website to Support Warehousing.**   We show how the Website should be "seeded" with tags and other information specifically meant for understanding Website sessions. We also propose a metadata structure for describing a Website that makes the Webhouse's job much more coherent. The tags and the metadata need to be part of a set of enterprise standards including URL names, cookie contents, user ID assignments, content labeling, activity log content, and look and feel. We discuss the issues of look and feel more deeply as its own topic in Chapter 9.

We tackle the difficult issue of a distributed Website, where the user may not even be aware that they are being transferred from machine to machine as they visit various pages. It takes special care for the Webhouse to be able to reconstruct a single session log from these multiple servers.

6. **Building Clickstream Data Marts.**   Since the clickstream data is at the center of the Webhouse and is often the raison d'être for the merger of the Web with the data warehouse, we develop detailed dimensional models for the various forms of clickstream data. We show fact tables and dimensional tables for customer purchases, support and problem resolution, and information gathering. We conform the clickstream data mart with other existing data marts in the data warehouse in order that they can all be used together in a coherent overall enterprise data warehouse.

Within the clickstream data mart, we go into significant detail about the dimensions and facts unique to Web data. We develop dimensions for IP addresses and Web providers. We define special Web facts, including Web-centric date/time stamps, dwell times, and an array of Web-centric costs, including referral costs, infrastructure costs, and microtransactions. We discuss the issues of allocating these costs all the way down to the Web page click event.

7. **Assembling Clickstream Value Chains.**   We link the clickstream data mart to the other data marts that may be created during the Web visits, such as order entry and customer inquiries. We show four examples of complete value chains, even though one of them is more properly called a value circle. Our examples are drawn from the manufacturing and retail supply chain, insurance company policies and claims, sales pipeline management, and health care treatments and payment processing.

8. **Implementing the Clickstream Post-Processor.**   Once we understand the detailed content of the clickstream, and we understand the target database structures for the clickstream in the Webhouse, we can put the finishing touches on the extract-transform-and-load architecture in the Webhouse back room. The clickstream post-processor is a high-performance multithreaded pipeline system for parsing the huge volume of clickstream data and loading it into the Webhouse.

Part Two: Bringing the Warehouse to the Web

9. **Why Bring the Warehouse to the Web?**   In the second half of the book, we turn our attention to providing all sorts of data warehouse services outward to Web-enabled users. We show how the natural act of publishing the enterprise's data assets leads inevitably to the Web. But then we show how consorting with the Web forces the data warehouse to adjust. The Web raises expectations that cannot be ignored.

10. **Designing the User Experience.**   The design of effective Websites is one of the most exciting areas in all of computing. Many of us user interface designers have watched in frustration as various well-intentioned user interfaces for computer products have never really been judged against the hard crucible of ease of use. The link back from the user's screen to the marketing department's sense of how a product should be improved has never been direct enough. All of that has changed with the Web. If a Web page does not meet the user's needs within a few seconds, the user is gone. And furthermore, we can see that happening.

This chapter draws together the threads of state-of-the-art Website design, and shows both how that feeds the Webhouse, but also how the Webhouse provides the designer with the evidence to improve the design of the site.

We profile the needs and the appropriate design responses of the three types of users. See Figure I.4. A customer will interact with data from the Webhouse much differently than a supply chain partner or an internal employee.

11. **Driving Data Mining from the Webhouse.**   If we have done a good job of capturing the data from the clickstream, we should have a perfect platform for understanding Web visitor behavior. Data mining is an activity that seeks to find meaningful patterns in data. In this book we take the view that the data Webhouse manager is not the analyst who performs data mining, but rather the data Webhouse manager provides the data in the best possible format to make data mining easy. Preparing data for data mining is surprisingly complex, and in some ways can be more work than the data mining itself. In this chapter we briefly survey the main objectives and main

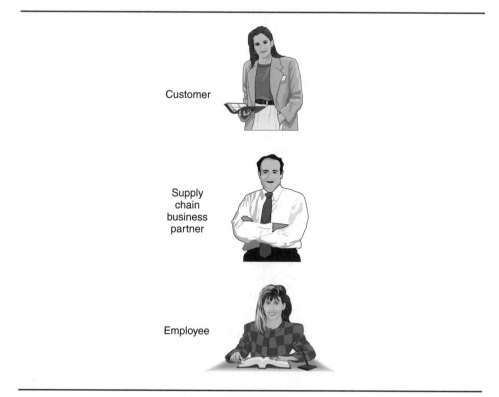

Customer

Supply chain business partner

Employee

FIGURE I.4   The Three Types of Users

tools of data mining, and then we carefully describe the data transformations that you will need to support your data mining clients. We also suggest an architecture for your extract-transform-and-load operation that will be best suited to this task.

12. **Creating an International Data Webhouse.** One of the most powerful aspects of the Web is its lack of geographic boundaries. But effective Websites and effective Webhouses cannot all be in English with American cultural assumptions. In this chapter we address a host of international design considerations, including multilanguage Websites, and the proper treatment of names, addresses, currencies, and calendars. We give a strong argument for converting to a thorough-going UNICODE implementation that will smooth many of the international language and character set issues.

We also tackle the interesting issue of whether the underlying data in the data warehouse can be presented in multilanguage variations, or whether, for reporting consistency and applications coherence, it all needs to be in one language (e.g., English).

13. **Data Webhouse Security.** The Webhouse brings the issues of security to the forefront. The Webhouse has two conflicting mandates: 1) publish the data to everyone, and 2) protect the data from everyone, except those with a legitimate need to know. Strangely, there is an element of good news in this conflicting Web picture. Since we are moving away from client/server configurations into Web-enabled configurations, we actually are creating some new controllable points in our architecture where we can impose security. We can now more easily separate the security challenge into several components, which then work together.

The browser-to-firewall connection should be implemented as a virtual private network. This keeps anyone from eavesdropping. The individual user authenticates themselves with a security token (probably a piece of plastic) at their PC and this authentication is approved by a directory server behind the firewall. Finally, the authenticated user is authorized to view certain Web applications and invoke certain controls on the Web pages of those applications.

We show you how to set up this kind of single login, single console security system for all your Webhouse users, regardless of their profiles. We also think by going to a totally Webhouse perspective, you can simplify and improve the security of your existing data warehouse.

14. **Scaling the Webhouse.** The Web has the potential for explosive changes in demand. You need to be careful if you connect your Webhouse directly to the Website featured in a Super Bowl ad. In this chapter we try to anticipate explosive changes in demand for data warehouse services, and what the critical scaling bottlenecks are in hardware, software, and operations.

     We discuss what to do if your Webhouse also delivers audio or video, and we try to give you some guidance in the granularity tradeoffs you may have to make in analyzing and saving clickstream data.

15. **Managing the Webhouse Project.** If you are building a data Webhouse, you need to be a pretty good project manager, because you have lots of diverse tasks, and you have to manage people with a number of different skills and perspectives. We try to help you plan the design of the Webhouse and the operations of the Webhouse. The operations includes moving from prototype to production, choosing appropriate back room and front room technologies, bringing the Webhouse on-line, making the Webhouse available to a wide audience, building, testing, and releasing applications, and defining and implementing security.

CUSTOMERS, VISITORS, AND USERS

We have tried several times in the course of writing this book to settle on a single name for the person sitting at the computer using your Website. We have revolved around and around with customer, visitor, and user (sometimes end user). Naming this person has proved to be a hopeless task. The most visible person is the *customer,* who is the object of much of the excitement about CRM and clickstream analysis. But many times the person simply isn't a customer in a commercial sense and may never be. A more neutral *visitor* is a generic kind of person who visits Websites and who we are probably interested in.

But we never talk about "visitor relationship management." The commercial interpretation of using a Website really needs to talk about customers.

Finally, we have many situations where the person is a computer *user,* who is accessing a computer server to run an application, like a query or a report.

Obviously, the distinctions among these three roles blur, depending on the situation. So, rather than holding to a foolish consistency, we switch among these three appellations somewhat at will, depending on the situation. We always keep in mind that the person sitting at the personal computer end of our systems is a mixture of customer, visitor, and user.

We suggest a cast of characters for your project team, including Webmasters, Webhouse project managers, clickstream data modelers, extract programmers, database administrators, applications analysts, business sponsors, and of course, end users.

16. **The Future of Webhousing.**   We finish the book by summarizing the main message: the Web and the warehouse are being drawn together like two powerful magnets. The Web needs the warehouse for many of its customer-centric functions, and the warehouse is being transformed by the demands of the Web. We recognize that this book comes at a very early stage in the development of the Web, and that the really big changes in the landscape have only just begun. We try to speculate on what the next ten to twenty years will bring, recognizing that our prognostications will look too aggressive at this point in time, and too timid twenty years from now.

Goals of a Data Webhouse

The data Webhouse is the Web instantiation of the data warehouse. The Webhouse plays a crucial and central role in the operations of a Web-enabled business. To fulfill this potential, the data Webhouse:

- Houses and publishes clickstream data and other behavioral data from the Web that drive an understanding of customer behavior.
- Is conformed to the other distributed data marts in the enterprise data warehouse, and data marts up and down the supply chain, so that all these data marts can be used together.
- Is an adaptive and resilient source of information. As new business questions arise, and as new data sources become available, we insist that the data Webhouse respond gracefully. A graceful response is one that allows old applications to continue to run without interruption and without reprogramming, but allows the new questions and the new data to co-exist.
- Is extensible to the new media of the Web, including still images, graphics, audio, and video.
- Is a secure bastion that publishes data to the customers, business partners, and employees appropriately, but at the same time protects the enterprise's data assets against unintended use.
- Is the foundation for Web-enabled decision making. Again, the data Webhouse must allow its users to make decisions about the Web, as well as make decisions using the Web.

Goals of the Book

We've succeeded with this book, if you—the designers and managers of the data Webhouse—achieve your goals more quickly. You will build an effective data Webhouse that will match the goals of the previous section. Hopefully, you will not reinvent the wheel and rediscover previously owned truths.

We think this book will help you understand the profoundly distributed reality that is the Web. We are convinced that the Web is both the medium of much commercial communication as well as the delivery vehicle that we IT designers must use from here on. The impact of the Web is so profound that it is much more than an "application," it is our new environment. For us (data warehousing professionals), it's "welcome to the data Webhouse."

PART ONE

Bringing the Web to the Warehouse

CHAPTER 1

Why Bring the Web to the Warehouse?

Bringing the Web to the warehouse means bringing behavior to the warehouse. The data warehouse already has many feeds coming to it from transaction processing systems, and some of these feeds come from transactions captured via Web interfaces. But capturing transactions is easy, and it is what we data warehousers have been doing for more than ten years. In the first half of the book, we are trying for a more elusive goal. We are trying to capture, analyze, and understand the behavior of users clicking on our Websites.

The Web presents us with a new and unprecedented data source. We call it the clickstream. This clickstream is literally a log of every gesture made by every visitor to every Website. The clickstream is potentially a much better record of behavior than other more traditional detailed data sources. The famous call detail record (CDR) data from telecommunications companies pales by comparison to the clickstream. CDR data can only show that party A called party B and successfully established a connection for a certain number of minutes. There is no way to know why party A called party B. Was a commercial transaction involved? Were both parties satisfied? Who knows?

Even the very important on-line transaction processing (OLTP) data sources leave out much interesting information. An OLTP data source in a retail environment usually records only the very last step in a relationship that has been building for some time. We certainly see that the sale took place, but we have no idea what led up to that sale. The OLTP data sources represent an accounting and legal perspective, and the marketing analysts usually must peer anxiously over the shoulders of the finance department to get some insight into customer behavior. Even worse, the OLTP system is often interested only in sales transactions. The OLTP system in many cases cannot capture other interactions with the customer, such as inquiries, or visits, or causal factors that led to the customer even approaching the retailer.

The clickstream, on the other hand, is a time series of microscopic actions that can be assembled into sessions. The trajectory of actions that led up to a purchase or to other behavior we are interested in can be analyzed and understood. We can be far more confident how the individual approached us, what their intent was, and what the quality of their experience was. We can be pretty sure what they saw on the screen. We know how long it took them to find the choices they made. We can see direct signs of satisfaction and direct signs of dissatisfaction. We are now in a far better position to respond effectively to the individual customer.

We began this book by declaring that IT needs to build the infrastructure for the Web revolution. The commercial success of the Web will be leveraged in large part by how well commercial Websites respond to their individual visitors. The driver for this personalized style of visitor interaction is the clickstream itself. It's where the content resides. So, a basic mission for IT is to understand the clickstream, capture the clickstream, and get it into a familiar database environment where organizations can use it effectively.

WHY THE CLICKSTREAM IS NOT JUST ANOTHER DATA SOURCE

The clickstream is not just another data source that is extracted, cleaned, and dumped into the data warehouse. The clickstream is really an evolving collection of data sources. There are more than a dozen log file formats for capturing clickstream data. These log file formats have optional data components that, if used, can be very helpful in identifying users, sessions, and the true meaning of behavior. We are in the infancy of this clickstream game, and it is a sure bet that new logging capabilities and new logging formats will become available on a regular basis. Extensible Markup Language (XML) is making the structure of our Web pages far more expressive, and this is bound to affect the clickstream data source.

Because of the distributed nature of the Web, clickstream data often is collected simultaneously by different physical servers, even when the user thinks they are interacting with a single Website. Even if the log files being collected by these separate servers are compatible, a very interesting problem arises in synchronizing the log files after the fact.

Remember that a busy Web server may be processing hundreds of page events per second. It is unlikely that the clocks on separate servers will be in synchrony to a hundredth of a second.

We also get clickstream data from different parties. Besides our own log files, we may get clickstream data from referring partners or from ISPs. We also may get clickstream data from Web watcher services that we have hired to place a special control on certain Web pages that alert them to a user opening the page.

Another important form of clickstream data is the search specification given to a search engine that then directs the user to the Website.

Finally, if we are an ISP providing Web access to directly connected customers, we have a unique perspective because we see every click of the user that may allow much more powerful and invasive analysis of the end user's sessions than can be provided by a single target Website. See Figure 1.1.

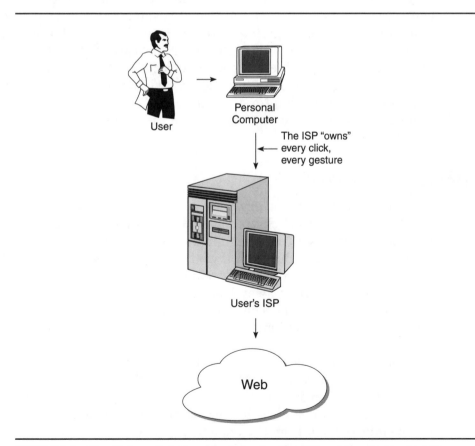

User

Personal Computer

The ISP "owns" every click, every gesture

User's ISP

Web

FIGURE 1.1   The Unique Relationship between the ISP and the Connected User

The most basic form of clickstream data from a normal Website is stateless. That is, the log shows an isolated page retrieval event, but does not provide a clear tie to other page events elsewhere in the log. Without some other kind of context help, it is difficult or impossible to reliably identify a complete user session. In Chapter 2, we discuss this problem in depth, and show how, in many cases, a session can be identified.

The other big frustration with basic clickstream data is the anonymity of the session. Unless the user agrees to reveal their identity in some way, we often cannot be sure who they are, or if we have ever seen them before. In certain situations, we may not even be able to distinguish the clicks of two users who are simultaneously browsing our Website. Again, in Chapter 2, we discuss this problem in depth and show the various ways we can identify the user.

There is tremendous pressure to solve some of these tracking problems, and in particular to make identifying sessions and users much more straightforward. We can anticipate progress by the Web server software vendors, and we can anticipate evolving to more data-rich descriptions of our Web pages delivered to the end user. XML is a follow-on language that is a successor to the original HTML. XML provides a rich capability for tagging Web pages and objects on Web pages. These tags will show up in the clickstream logs and will be very valuable for identifying behavior. In Chapter 4, we snapshot the current status of XML and show how it can be used to improve the content of the clickstream data feed.

ANALYZING BEHAVIOR

It is not enough to put every page event or every user gesture into a database. Such a raw clickstream is not a useful description of behavior because you can't see the forest for the trees. A more useful description of behavior is intent. But even if we think that we recognize intent, we can't just "aggregate" the clickstream up to a small number of intent descriptions and throw away the detail. Behavioral intent has many possible interpretations. The long-term intent of a set of page events may be "Buy a Product," but the short-term intent may be "Get Description of Product."

There are many possible descriptions of intent that we would like to apply to end user behavior. More than one of them might apply to any given set of page events. In this book, we will refer to all descriptions of behavioral intent just as "behavior." Here is a list of behavior types that can be inferred just from the page being viewed:

- General information gathering
- Product feature gathering
- Other information gathering (weather, location, etc.)
- FAQ (frequently asked question) list review
- Specific support question
- Product order
- Service order
- Order status tracking
- Other status tracking (delivery, account, commitment, etc.)
- Searching
- Bidding
- Reading news
- Reading white papers
- Entertainment
- Downloading (purchased products, software patches, documents, etc.)
- E-mail, particularly in response to something on our Website

But there are higher descriptions of behavior that are even more meaningful if we can identify them confidently. These higher descriptions of behavior might include:

- Successful purchase event
- Cancelled, incomplete, or unsuccessful purchase event
- Found information being sought
- Did not find information being sought
- Session killer event (user left the site)
- Incomplete display of information, but user stayed on site (i.e., rapid click to next page)
- Incomplete display of information, and user left site (i.e., user didn't even let the page finish)
- Wrong path taken
- User is angry
- User is happy
- User is reassured

A major goal of this book is to show you how to identify and tag various kinds of behavior. With just a little help from the Website team, we can get the page context behavior described in the first list. We will get as much help from log files, XML metatags, and cookies as we can. But we would like to derive as much of the higher-level behavior as we can. To do this, in many cases we will be stepping up to a more sophisticated form of behavioral analysis than we have done with our databases in the past.

Not only will we identify various types and layers of behavior, but we will show you how to store an open-ended number of these behavior tags in your data warehouse. All of this is what we mean by bringing the Web to the warehouse.

Although tagging of Web sessions with behavior descriptions is certainly interesting in and of itself, the real value of identifying behavior is improving the quality of interaction the user has with our organization. Improving the interaction translates directly into customer loyalty, increased revenues, and increased profits. Patricia Seybold, in her classic book *Customers.com* (Random House, 1998) identifies eight success factors for any business, but especially Web-leveraged businesses. The factors include:

- Target the right customer
- Own the customer's total experience
- Streamline business processes that impact the customer
- Provide a 360 degree view of the customer relationship
- Let customers help themselves
- Help customers do their jobs
- Deliver personalized service
- Foster community

Seybold's success factors are a kind of foundation for customer relationship management (CRM), a major topic in marketing and especially in Web-related marketing. The goals of CRM are to build customer loyalty, increase profit, and seamlessly integrate every customer business function.

In this book, as we learn what a data Webhouse is, we will systematically visit these success factors to show how the data Webhouse can leverage each one.

ENSURING PRIVACY

The issue of privacy is on the mind of everyone who uses the Web. Thanks to the mainstream media, we oscillate between thinking the Web reveals our innermost secrets to everyone, and thinking that the Web is the future of human communication. Probably there is some truth to both positions.

We think the best way to cope with the conflicting feelings about privacy is to use the analogy of a favorite retail store in your city somewhere. As an individual, you are free to make the choice whether to shop at the store, and if you do, whether you want to reveal your personal life to the store in any way. At one extreme, you can perform nothing but cash transactions, never giving your name or any details about yourself. If you go to the store a lot, it's hard to stay completely unnoticed, but it's possible. At the other extreme, you may decide to open a credit account with the store, in which case you voluntarily reveal a lot about yourself. Presumably you do this only after you feel a level of comfort with the store, its products, its service, its people, and its ethics.

In the case of the actual physical retail store, it is very valuable to develop a relationship based on trust, integrity and good will. As a consumer, there are many benefits to a good retail relationship. You can trust the store. They will trust you. You can take back a product that is unacceptable, without too much stress. The store will help you get what you want. They will reassure you in complex situations. You feel like you have a friend.

If the relationship with the store should change for the worse, you can sever your relationship with the store and find somewhere else to shop. If the store has good management, they will notice such defections and try to change in a constructive way.

The goal of an on-line relationship with a business should be the same as an on-the-street relationship with a business. The same judgments, tradeoffs, and end results should pertain, in our opinion. If you wish to remain anonymous on the Web, more power to you. If you wish to trust certain businesses with limited information about yourself, then just like the physical world, you deserve the tangible benefit of good service, as a form of quid pro quo.

On the Web there is certainly a potential for privacy being compromised, but the clear and visible message of the Web is service, and the customer wants to be treated as special. That's what's really the goal. The Web will exhibit a rapid form of Darwinian selection. Those Web businesses who abuse the confidentiality of their customers will be unsuccessful. Word travels fast on the Web. Those businesses that use the clickstream to develop a truly personalized and trusting interface to their customers will be enormously successful.

THE WEBHOUSE ARCHITECTURE

In driving Seybold's eight success factors, the data Webhouse can intervene in real time, or it can play a more contemplative role, supporting marketing decisions and affecting strategy. Although we discuss the system architecture of the data Webhouse in detail in Chapter 12, it is worthwhile at this early stage of the book to point out the main components of the architecture and to make sure that we are all using a common vocabulary. We show physically how the data Webhouse supports both the real time and contemplative roles.

The demands of the Web are forcing us to rethink the architecture of our data warehouses. The data warehouse is being drawn closer and closer to the front line of operational reporting and operational response generation. Ten years ago we thought of the data warehouse as a kind of background resource for management, to be queried in a nonurgent, contemplative mode. But today, the pace of business decision making has increased dramatically. Not only do we want a comprehensive snapshot of the business on a real-time basis, but we are simultaneously asking broad questions about customer behavior.

Let's be sure we understand the implications of this data warehouse evolution. We have managed to make three big technical design factors more difficult, all at once. We have dramatically raised the bar for:

- **Timeliness.** Business results must now be available on a real-time basis. Even as recently as two years ago, we were still trying to accommodate "as of the previous day" reporting. This is no longer sufficient. As we build more and more efficient delivery pipelines with smaller, just-in-time inventories, and as we allow our customers to specify their products and services on an individual basis, we cannot tolerate delays in understanding the demand and managing our responses to that demand.

- **Data volumes.** The big move to mass customization means that we capture, analyze, and respond to every transaction in the business. As recently as two years ago, we saw this coming, but we thought that the impact on the data warehouse would be limited to storing individual sales transactions or individual operational transactions. This looked like a kind of physical limit to the overall volume of possible data. The Web has shown even this to be wrong. The Web, through the clickstream of page events arriving at our Websites, now captures every gesture made by a customer, before and after sales transactions or operational transactions. How many gestures (page clicks) does the customer make before placing an order? There seems to be no upper limit. We are already seeing data volumes coming from the clickstream that dwarf any call tracking database in a telco. For instance, the combined Microsoft-related Websites, which are all analyzed as a single entity on a daily basis, are now seeing busy days where they capture more than one billion events!

- **Response times.**   The Web sends a powerful message demanding fast response times. If something useful doesn't happen in ten seconds, then the visitor is on to another page. Paradoxically, the flakiness and poor response times most of us experienced in the early days of 9.6Kbps modem access to the Web made us more likely to give up quickly. If nothing happened, then we assumed that the system wasn't working. Those of us who run big data warehouses know that many queries will take more than ten seconds. But our pleas to the users to be understanding of performance issues are falling on deaf ears. We are challenged to somehow provide a lot more of our data warehouse services in ten seconds or less.

At the same time as these design factors have become more difficult, we find ourselves supporting a broader continuum of users and a broader continuum of requests. With the increased operational focus of the data warehouse, and the increased ability of anyone anywhere in the world to present themselves at our Website doorstep, we must provide data warehouse services to a widely varying mix of external customers, business partners, and suppliers, as well as internal sales people, employees, analysts, and executives. We must deliver a mixture of query results, top line reports, data mining results, status updates, support answers, custom greetings, images, and downloadable OLAP cubes. Most of these things aren't nice rows from an answer set. They are messy complex objects.

To address these issues, we need to make some adjustments to our data warehouse architecture. We can't just make our single database server more and more powerful. We can't make it deliver all these complicated objects and hope to keep up with the escalating requirements described earlier.

In Figure 1.2 we show a complete high-level view of a commercial system supporting a public Web server and an associated data Webhouse.

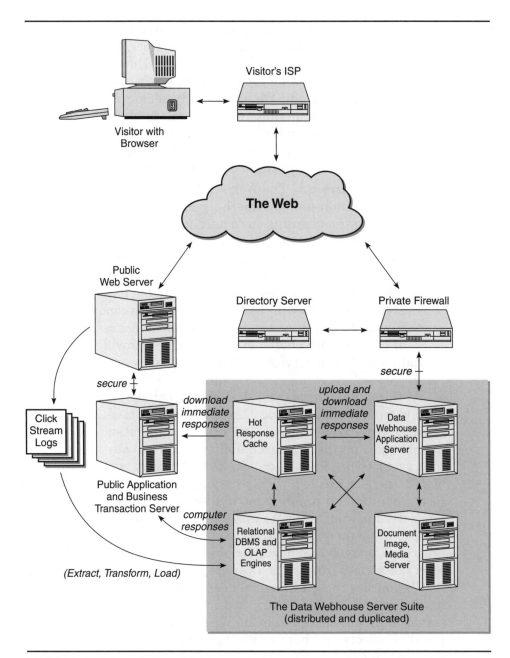

FIGURE 1.2   A Sample Data Webhouse Architecture

Figure 1.2 is intended to illustrate the typical components, and is not to be interpreted as the only possible configuration. For the moment we deliberately omit lots of interesting variations on this architecture such as proxy servers, ad servers, and multiple internal networks. Let's just discuss a simple, typical configuration.

The User and the ISP

At the top of the figure we see the remote user, connected to the Web through an Internet service provider (ISP). We will describe in greater detail the special relationship that the user's ISP has with the user, but for now it is enough to see very clearly that the user's ISP can see absolutely everything that the user does, because the user is hardwired through the ISP.

The Public Web Server and Business Transactions

All of the various components below the Web cloud in Figure 1.2 are assumed to belong to a single commercial entity. We show two important connection points to the Web. One is the public Web server that everyone gets when the URL www.companyname.com or its equivalent is entered into the user's browser. We assume the name of your commercial organization is "companyname."

The public Web server is itself a complex system. It must be able to generate all the possible static and dynamic page images and other information payloads that users request over the Web. In Figure 1.2, we show connections to two of the important and logically distinct services that the Web server needs to conduct effective e-commerce.

We assume that one of the capabilities of the Web server is to take orders for products from the company, or to perform some other kinds of meaningful business transactions. Whenever serious business transactions are being performed, a business transaction server is also needed. The business transaction server is shown immediately below the public Web server in Figure 1.2.

The job of the business transaction server is to record the business transactions in a legally and financially responsible way, and to never lose these transactions. The business transaction server function is very different from the Web server function, and in any serious business, these two servers must be logically and physically separated. We show all the connections from the public Web server to other servers as being highly secured connections, so that if hackers from the Web compromise the public Web server, they are less likely to gain access to the other servers. We'll describe how to secure these connections in Chapter 11.

The Hot Response Cache

One way to take pressure off the main database engines is to build a powerful hot response cache. See Figure 1.2. The hot response cache is built to anticipate as many of the predictable and repeated information requests as possible. The hot response cache is an adjunct of the application servers that feed the public Web server and the private firewall entry point for employees. The data in the hot response cache is created in a series of batch jobs running in the main Webhouse application server. Once stored in the hot response cache, the data objects can be fetched on demand through either a public Web server application or a private firewall application.

The items fetched from the hot response cache are complex file objects, not low-level data elements. The hot response cache is therefore a file server, not a database. Its file storage hierarchy will inevitably be a simple kind of lookup structure, but it does not need to support a complex query access method.

Security in the hot response cache is the responsibility of the requesting application server, not the cache itself. The application servers should be the only entities capable of accessing the hot response cache directly, and they make their security decisions based on centrally administered named roles. This security architecture is described in detail in Chapter 10.

The hot response cache is more than the "operational data store" (ODS) that we built in the early part of the 1990s. The ODS was built most often when legacy operational systems were incapable of responsively reporting status on individual accounts. The hot response cache not only provides this original ODS function, but also provides:

- Custom greetings to Web visitors consisting of both text and graphics
- Cross-selling and up-selling propositions to Web visitors perhaps based on data mining applications looking for other cohort members of the Web visitor's demographic cluster or behavior cluster
- Dynamically chosen promotion content to Web visitors
- XML-based structured forms content to business partners (we used to call this EDI) who are requesting delivery status, order status, hours

supply in inventory (we used to measure *days* supply, but this is becoming obsolete), and critical path warnings in the delivery pipeline

- Low-level FAQ-like answers to problems and support requests
- Midline reports to customers and business partners in the delivery pipeline needing a moderate amount of integration across time (last ten orders, last ten shipments, last ten payments, last ten returns, last ten problems) or across business function (manufacturing, inventory, orders, shipments, delivery, payments)
- Top-line reports to management needing significant integration across time (multiple year trends) or across customers, product lines, or geographies, all delivered in three interchangeable formats including page-oriented report, pivot table, and graph, and accompanied in many cases with images
- Downloadable pre-computed OLAP cubes for exploratory analysis
- Data mining studies on near-term and long-term bases showing the evolution of customer demographic and behavior clusters, and the effects of decisions about promotion content and Website content on business done through the Web
- Conventional aggregations that enhance query performance when drilling up through standard hierarchies in the major dimensions such as customer, product, and time

The hot response cache must be managed to support the needs of the application servers. Ideally, the information object needed by the application server has been computed and stored in advance by a batch job. All applications need to be aware of the existence of the hot response cache and should be able to probe the hot response cache to see if the answer they want is already there. There are two distinct modes of use of the hot response cache, depending on the nature of the visitor session requesting the data.

The *guaranteed response time* request must produce some kind of answer in response to a page request being serviced by the Web server, usually in less than a second. If the requested object (such as a custom greeting, a custom cross-selling proposition, an immediate report, or an answer to a question) has not been precomputed and hence is not stored, then a default response object must be delivered in its place, all within the guaranteed response time.

The *accelerated response time* request hopes to produce a response to the Web visitor's request but will default to computing the response directly from the underlying data warehouse if the precomputed object is not found immediately. The application server should optionally be able to warn the user that there may be a delay in providing the response in this case. The Web server needs to be able to alert the application server if it detects that the user has gone on to another page, so the application server can halt the data warehouse process.

Note that this strategy of seeking a pre-computed answer and defaulting if necessary to the base data is exactly the way conventional aggregates have always worked in the data warehouse. The data warehouse aggregate navigator has always searched for aggregates to answer portions of an overall report query. If the navigator finds the aggregate, it uses it, but if it doesn't find the aggregate, it gracefully defaults to computing the answer slowly from the base data. Viewed this way, the hot response cache is a kind of supercharged aggregate navigator.

Any time we design something that will be used with the Web, especially if used in conjunction with the public Web server, we must pay special attention to scaling and to explosive surges in demand. The nature of the hot response cache is that it is an I/O engine, not a compute engine. It is, after all, a file server. The scalability bottleneck for the hot response cache, therefore, is not compute power, but I/O bandwidth. In periods of peak demand, the hot response cache must provide a flood of large file objects to the requesting application servers.

Building a hot response cache is not a panacea. It introduces another server in what is already a complex architecture. The hot response cache implies administrative support and a particular disciplined application development style. But it is still worth it. The hot response cache takes enormous pressure off of the database management systems and the application systems when they are faced with the timeliness, data volume, and response time requirements that are so typical of the Web.

It is important to understand why the hot response cache is not the public Web server and is not the business transaction server. The job of the public Web server is to manage a large number of simultaneous browser connections, not to be a high-performance database. The job of the business transaction server is to capture and safeguard a river of business transactions. In a very real sense, the business transaction server is the cash register of the company. Nothing should slow down the main cash register. So we don't require it to be a responsive database engine in addition to its main responsibilities.

At the left edge of Figure 1.2 we see that the public Web server makes clickstream logs available. Both these logs and copies of the business transactions are extracted, transformed, and loaded into the company's data Webhouse.

The Data Webhouse System

The four servers in the lower right part of Figure 1.2 logically comprise the data Webhouse. All four of these servers are serious back-room engines equipped to store and deliver the company's data, whether this data is in traditional text and number format, or consists of documents, images, maps, audio, or video.

The best way to think about the data Webhouse is that it is a Web-enabled data warehouse devoted to publishing the company's data assets appropriately. In our opinion, the publishing metaphor is very apt. A publisher of a traditional magazine or newspaper or book has a relationship with the readers based on trust. The publisher endeavors to make the publication as accessible and as readable as possible, and puts his or her name on the masthead of the publication to make sure everyone knows where the buck stops. The publisher works hard never to damage the trust with the readers. In the same way, the manager of the data Webhouse (and any data warehouse, really) has the same relationship with the users of the data, whether they are the company's customers, business partners, or employees. Throughout this book, our designs will be based on maximizing the effectiveness of this publishing mandate we think all data warehouses have.

The four server types in the data Webhouse play distinctly different roles. As we have discussed, the hot response cache is a kind of ODS that can instantly respond to the needs of the public Web server. It can be thought of as a cache of results ready to be displayed by the Web server. In general, the hot response cache does not have time to execute complex queries. It is the job of the data Webhouse application server and the relational database engines to prepare many of the hot results needed for real-time information retrieval, and to upload them to the hot response cache. In Chapter 8, we will discuss the thresholds for query complexity that distinguish queries executed in real time versus queries that are run off-line in order to populate the real-time databases.

Thus far we have only discussed the responsibility of the data Webhouse in supporting the needs of the public Web server. But the Webhouse is the master information publishing resource of the company.

The Webhouse is also available through the private firewall to qualified users from the Web. These users would usually be employees and business partners of the company. The private firewall is a serious security barrier. In Chapter 11 we discuss the details of this firewall and how it implements security. But briefly, a qualified user usually connects to the firewall through a virtual private network (VPN) connection. The firewall unscrambles the encrypted VPN connection and checks with the company's directory server (shown to the left of the private firewall in Figure 1.2). If the user can be authenticated, then the user is connected to the Webhouse application server, which is a Web server devoted to applications serving the qualified users. These applications would include ad hoc querying, status reporting, data mining, and all forms of decisions support.

The data Webhouse application server is the switchboard for all the activities of the qualified users. It is capable of accessing the hot response cache, all the relational database engines, and the other document and multimedia servers. The Webhouse application server delivers everything in browser-compatible format. It doesn't matter whether the user is within the walls of the company, or is actually remotely located on the Web. From the point of view of architecture and administration, we don't distinguish these cases. Above all, in order to keep security administration under control, we don't let any users access the information server, the relational database engines, or the multimedia servers directly. All qualified users must run the standard security gauntlet through the directory server and its authentication function, and then they are connected to the application server.

In Figure 1.2 we have noted but not emphasized that the data Webhouse is actually a fully distributed system, all of whose components are duplicated multiple times in a typical large organization. In reality there are multiple physical hot response caches, application servers, relational DBMSs, and multimedia servers. In Chapter 8, we will show how the data warehouse bus architecture makes it possible to build these servers in such a distributed manner.

SUMMARY

In this chapter we have described how the Web is brought to the warehouse. Bringing the Web to the warehouse is bringing the clickstream to the warehouse. The clickstream is far larger, messier, and more expressive of customer behavior than other data sources we are used to. We have also insisted that the applications environment in which we use the clickstream is much closer to the front line of business transactions than we are used to. Computing a custom greeting may seem like a database query, but the results may have to be delivered within a guaranteed three-second time window. We sketch the new architectures that are required to meet these needs.

Now that we have described why the Web should be brought to the warehouse, and we have sketched the basic architecture of where that data goes and how it is used, we are ready in Chapter 2 to dive into the details of tracking user behavior through the clickstream.

CHAPTER 2

Tracking Website
User Actions

A customer enters a retail store. He walks down an aisle, looks at the coffee display, selects a 4-ounce jar of Taster's Choice decaf, and puts it in his shopping basket. Then he looks over various kinds of cocoa mixes but passes the opportunity to buy. Eventually he completes his shopping and wheels his basket to the checkout stand. In a brick-and-mortar retail setting the customer is identified and his purchases are recorded only after he has completed the entire shopping trip.

In a Web-based retail setting we have an opportunity to follow the customer through the entire shopping trip—to identify the customer before he sees even the first page of our site and to follow him through his total shopping experience. We can measure what he looks at, how long he looks, what he selects, and what he rejects. Even more remarkably, we can dynamically modify the store as he walks through it on-line. We can rearrange the virtual aisles and displays to show those items that he is most likely to buy and to move entire departments around at will, to suit the whims of each customer.

In a brick-and-mortar store, the customer is a captive. As illustrated in Figure 2.1, he stays until he walks out the door with or without a purchase, but he always will pass the checkout stand. On the Web, however, a customer exists only in virtual cyberspace. He is one mouse click away from leaving the site or the store, and he may never return to check out his purchases. He can be distracted in a millisecond by another image, a telephone call, or a crying child. Figure 2.2 illustrates a visitor's journey through a dynamic on-line store. The visitor enters

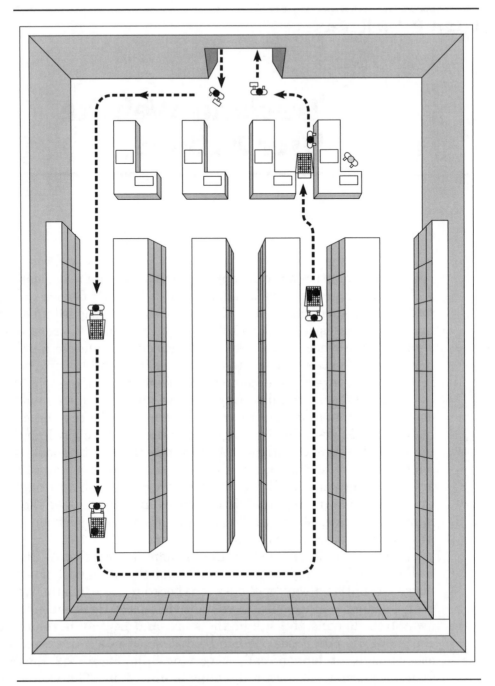

FIGURE 2.1   Shopping in a Brick and Mortar Store

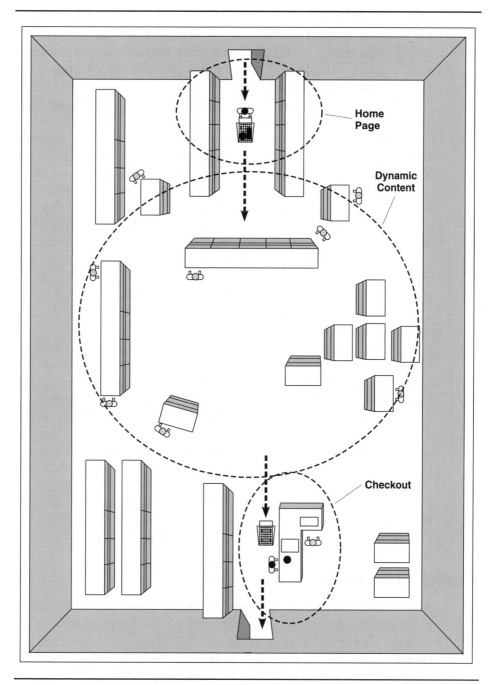

FIGURE 2.2   Shopping in an E-Store

through a static home or portal page, but once identified, he traverses a store that's completely dynamic in content. We can imagine a crew of stagehands arranging an optimum set of displays as the visitor searches and browses. Finally he is directed to a checkout counter where once again, content is relatively static.

Every well-designed Website incorporates tools for tracking visitors and their actions, as a means of measuring the site's effectiveness and impact. This tracking information can then be used to personalize dynamic site content, increasing the content's relevance and interest as the session progresses or the user returns to the site at a later date.

This chapter examines and categorizes the actions of Web users. Regardless of a user's motivation for accessing the Web, the number of actual actions that he can take is limited by the mechanics of browser software and Web protocols. We can capture many of these actions using two data sources: We can collect the information that is inherently contained in the Web's communications protocols (e.g., HTTP), and we can instrument our Web server applications to capture additional information about a user's activities once he reaches our site and we have established a session identity for him.

The first data source, called the clickstream, is recorded by the Web server's log mechanism. The second data source is supplied by a site's application servers and is the data that would be captured by any application such as order entry, text search, or credit reporting. In the Web-enabled data warehouse we will merge these sources of information into a single, coherent form.

This chapter discusses user actions on the Web, and also examines the elusive issue of user identification, of determining who a user is, and correlating his visit with previous visits to your Website. Our goal is to track the user and his actions from the moment he enters the Website, until the moment he exits, assigning a session ID to the record of these actions, and if desirable, identifying the user.

A BRIEF CATALOG OF USER ACTIONS

A Web user's actions can be motivated by a number of different needs, and these needs may change from moment to moment during a browser session. The breadth of motivating influences and responses to these is considerable. Since any on-line system can be provided with a Web browser interface, any application can theoretically be brought to the Web.

Here are some of the more common actions that a user may take during a Web session. It's important to realize that visitors can jump back and forth between these actions at any moment and can easily get lost in a maze of pages and links and not be able to find their way back to where you would like them to focus.

- **Searching.** Finding a specific product, service, or information source.
- **Information gathering.** Comparing products and prices, reading FAQs.
- **Entertainment.** Reading *Dilbert*, "window shopping," cooperative game-playing.
- **Education.** Using manuals, interactive classes, on-line books and papers.
- **Communication.** Joining discussion and news groups, using browser-based e-mail.
- **Status tracking.** Locating express shipments, verifying stock trades.
- **Downloading.** Fetching images, real audio/video, software.
- **Shopping and ordering.** Selecting and purchasing hard or soft goods, often with a credit card.
- **Accidental entry.** Clicking the wrong button or object, URL errors, broken links.

Each of these user actions may have special database architectural needs, both for tracking user's actions and for dynamically delivering content. For example, searching, either at a portal site or within a Website may require a text search engine. Shopping will almost always be supported by relational databases, while downloads and many communication applications may best be supported by object-enabled relational databases.

An active Website can impose ferocious capacity demands on its databases. As an example, Pacific Telephone, which serves most of California and Nevada, completes about 90 million telephone calls per day. An active Web-based portal, retailer, or brokerage can easily approach or exceed this many page hits daily. The database volumes required for log processing at an active Website can be equated to the billing system of a large telephone company, both in volume and in complexity. Chapter 14 of this book discusses optimum architectures for databases that are capable of event tracking and content delivery for high-activity Websites.

STEPS IN PRODUCT PURCHASE

Consider this catalog of user actions while thinking about how a visitor might approach your Website. Imagine that you can look over the shoulder of a customer in an on-line drugstore.

Recognition of Need

The first step in a product purchase is some recognition of need by the customer. She may be initially motivated in dozens of different ways, but for our example let's assume that she begins by noticing that she is running low on a particular vitamin supplement. She remembers seeing a URL on a prescription bottle, and remembers that the URL was "www.rx.pharmco.com." In our catalog of actions, she has made a tentative decision to take a "shopping and ordering" action.

This is our first opportunity to track the user's actions. If the prescription bottle contains a URL that is *unique* to prescription bottle labels, in this case, by using a subdomain of "rx,", we can positively identify page hits to this URL as having originated from a bottle label. If we get a lot of hits to this subdomain we can assume that having a URL on a prescription bottle is an effective way of publicizing our site.

Trying to Find What's Needed

The weather outside is terrible, so our customer turns on her computer, opens a browser, and types in the URL for the drugstore. The home page for the drugstore has a button that says "medications." This looks right, so she clicks it. It takes her to a page that extols the virtues of the store's prescription department and provides a search for information on the side effects of various medications, but alas, no nonprescription vitamins. So she clicks a "back" link on the Web page and finally finds on the home page a link labeled "search for a product." She clicks the link, is presented with a search form, and enters "vitamin C." In our catalog of actions, she has now switched to a *search*. She isn't shopping at the moment; she is trying to find a specific result using a search engine.

It is important to track the miscue that occurred during this step. The customer was already a prescription customer and didn't need to be taken to a page that advertised a product or service she already used.

Searching for Information about Alternatives

The customer's search for vitamin C returns at least a hundred hits, because there are a great many different brands and sizes carried by the store. The customer has a choice of scrolling down through a long list of items returned by the search (perhaps with a "next page" link), or refining her search. She types "natural" and gets three thousand hits. Then finally "natural vitamin C". She finds what she's been looking for—several items that contain vitamin C with rose hips. At this point the customer might make some price comparisons based on the information returned to her by the Website's search engine.

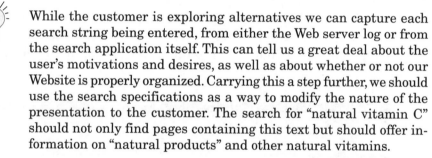

While the customer is exploring alternatives we can capture each search string being entered, from either the Web server log or from the search application itself. This can tell us a great deal about the user's motivations and desires, as well as about whether or not our Website is properly organized. Carrying this a step further, we should use the search specifications as a way to modify the nature of the presentation to the customer. The search for "natural vitamin C" should not only find pages containing this text but should offer information on "natural products" and other natural vitamins.

Selection

Our imaginary customer homes in on a particular brand and size of vitamin C with rose hips and clicks an "add to cart" button. This action effectively places the item on a virtual cash register receipt that hopefully will grow as she continues to peruse the store. By the action of selecting a particular item, she has told us not only what she has chosen, she has also shown us what she rejected.

Cross-Selling and Up-Selling

At this point, even though we haven't specifically identified the customer we already know a good deal about her, and we can begin to offer content that is specific to her interests or needs. We know, for example, that she is probably a customer of our pharmacy, that she prefers "natural" to "nonnatural" products. We can guess from her specific vitamin C selection whether she will pay a premium for branded goods or whether she prefers the economy of a house brand. We also can begin to do some profiling based on her choice of search strings and the length of time she has dwelled on each page she has visited. In short, we are ready to begin to generate dynamic content based on specific things that we know or can guess about the customer.

The bits of information we have gleaned about the customer allow us to cross-sell into other product lines that are similar to selections she has already made. This information also gives us hints for up-selling to higher value or higher margin products that match her buying habits. In Figure 2.3 we show a catalog page for a guitar, with two dynamically inserted up-sell links; first, a link to guitar cases and second, a link to tuning forks. In some cases we may even suggest products that our business does not carry, because we know we can source and link to these products elsewhere, using the Web.

If our store is dynamic in real time, we can begin to deliver customized content at the customer's very next mouse click, for example, by suggesting other "natural" product lines. It may not be feasible or even

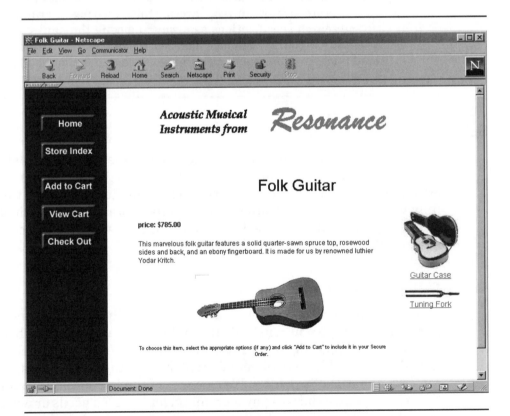

FIGURE 2.3   An Example of an Up-Sell Link from the E-Store

desirable to attempt to compute an optimum approach to the customer in real time. We may choose instead, because of computational constraints, to use a deferred (perhaps overnight) process to develop content customization strategies for the customer's next visit. We can then store the pre-computed responses on our hot response cache for immediate retrieval. The deferred approach also allows us to integrate all of the actions taken in the current session with the actions from previous sessions to develop a more comprehensive profile and marketing strategy. Figure 2.4 illustrates a pre-computed greeting from a hot response cache. We have greeted the user by name, suggested new products that might be of interest to him, and acknowledged his individual interests based on a previous visit.

We can also adopt a middle ground between these two approaches. Computationally intensive deferred processing can produce *hints,* or rules to be used for a particular customer when calculating dynamic content

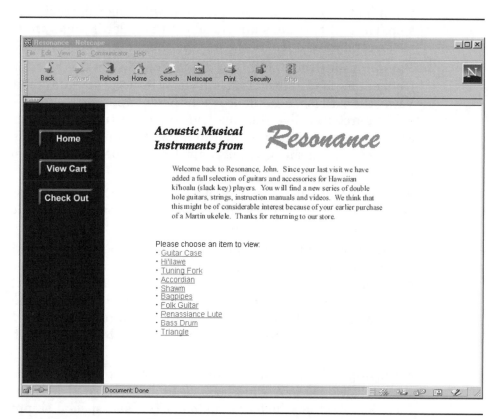

FIGURE 2.4   A Personalized Example from the Hot Response Cache

in real time. These hints can include rules we have developed based on customer behavior and explicit rules that have been requested by the customer about content they want to see every time they visit our on-line establishment.

Checkout

When customers finish selecting their merchandise, they're ready to purchase it using some kind of checkout process. If a particular customer hasn't already been identified, this is the step in which we will determine his or her identity for this and future visits. The checkout process may include the following items:

- **Order review.**   Give customers an opportunity to review the contents of their carts, adjust the quantity of each item, add additional items, or reject items they have chosen. To shorten the checkout process you might want to combine this step with the Contract Signature step. The ability to back up and adjust the order is hugely important to the comfort and feel of the on-line shopping experience.

- **Payment method.**   If it isn't already on file, obtain the customer's payment method information and verify its accuracy and credit limit. Verify the card for fraudulence to the extent appropriate for the value of the purchase. Give the customer the opportunity to use another card if the one he has entered is at its credit limit. Give the customer a chance to park the order, perhaps for days, before completing this step.

- **Addressing.**   Obtain the customer's billing and shipping addresses. Obtain his e-mail address and telephone number, so that order confirmations can be forwarded.

- **Validation.**   Validate as much of the customer-provided information as possible. Many fraud detection checks can be made at this point: Validate the street name relative to city and state. Verify that the street address exists within the specified zip code. Compare the telephone area code and exchange with the address. Do a DNS lookup on the domain portion of his e-mail address to verify that the domain exists.

- **Shipping.**   If this is a tangible goods order, present the customer with a choice of shipping methods, costs, and estimated delivery dates. Include a field in which the customer can add special shipping instructions, if appropriate.

- **Contract signature.**   Give the customer a summary of all his costs, including applicable shipping and handling surcharges and taxes. Include appropriate sales or license agreement boilerplate here, with a notice to the customer that by clicking "submit" or "OK" he agrees to the terms.

- **Order acknowledgment.**   Return an order tracking number for the customer. Include a URL, e-mail, and postal address for order inquiries. Include a final thank-you at this point.

 If the customer is already a prior registered customer and has agreed to let us hold his credit card information, most of the checkout steps can be bypassed with a simple "buy now" button.

Post-Order Processing

Once the order has been submitted and initially processed, send an e-mail copy of the order acknowledgment to the customer if this doesn't present an unencrypted-text security problem. If the order acknowledgment e-mail bounces, you may wish to hold the order pending verification of a correct e-mail address. Other advisories e-mailed to the customer can include an express shipper tracking number, a back-order notification, and a customer survey. Always give the customer a way of declining any further solicitations if state or federal law requires you to do so.

STEPS IN SOFTWARE OR CONTENT PURCHASE

The Web has provided opportunities for selling a huge range of software, content, and services directly to consumers. These already include CD-quality music, newspaper and magazine content, software, games, and books. Soon this will include video. Equally promising is the rental of software via the Web on a per-use basis. This, of course, bypasses intermediaries and channels such as paper-and-ink publishers, record stores, video rental shops, and TV networks. This kind of selling is particularly suitable to the Web because the merchandise can be downloaded for immediate consumption, satisfying the customer's desire for immediate gratification. The steps in selling content and on-line services in a Web-based setting are very much like those for the tangible goods example cited earlier. Two additional steps can be identified: a trial or demo of the product and post-purchase downloading of content.

Trials and Demos

Before a customer pays for downloading an audio track or a computer program he may want to sample what he's getting. For example, a customer who's thinking of downloading an MP3 audio track will want to hear a clip of it first, just as in some record stores he can listen to a CD before purchase. The prospective purchaser of a video game may want to download a trial copy of it first. It's important to track these trials for the marketing information they provide. For instance, if a customer listens to only the first five seconds of a streaming audio sample, you can be pretty sure he doesn't like the music or the performance. If he listens to the entire track without buying, there's probably a different barrier to the purchase.

Software is often available for download as a try-then-buy arrangement, with a purchased access key being used to unlock the software for unabridged use. At the time of this writing (1999) almost all such keys can be cracked with downloads from free pirate "warez" sites.

Downloads

When the customer agrees to the purchase of downloadable goods or services, their browser usually handles the actual download. For many current browser/platform combinations the download can be an asynchronous process that will not block continued use of the browser for other tasks. This can automatically be determined from the user agent information in the HTTP header. However once a download starts, many users will stop using their browsers for fear of affecting the outcome of the download. It's good practice to delay the downloading of soft content to the end of a shopping session in order to encourage the customer to select multiple items.

If a download is unsuccessful, be prepared to reverse any credit card charges that might be pending. Be sure to capture the IP address to which the download is being made. You will probably want to return the customer to a point at which they can purchase additional software or content at the end of each download.

ELEMENTS OF TRACKING

Where did the visitor come from? How did he find your Website? How did he arrive at a particular page or image or order form? The answers to these questions are of singular importance to the marketing department and Webmasters because they determine the effectiveness of site promotion. Attracting visitors can be extremely expensive, and new ways of getting visitors are continuously being invented. There are a number of common ways of getting users to your site.

User Origin

If you are very, very lucky your site is the default home page for the visitor's browser. Every time he opens his browser, your page is the first thing he sees. This is pretty unlikely unless you're the Webmaster for a portal site or an intranet home page, but many sites have buttons that, when clicked, prompt the user to set their URL as the browser's home page. Unfortunately, there is no easy way to determine from a log whether or not your site is set as a browser's home page.

A visitor may be directed to your site from a search at a portal such as Yahoo or Alta Vista. Such referrals can come either from the portal's index or table of contents, for which you may have paid a placement fee or from a word or content search.

If the referral was via a word or content search, the initial referral record may contain the query string that was entered by the visitor while searching. This is valuable marketing information, as it can be used to identfiy specific keywords to be included in metatags inserted into your pages for search engine spiders.

For many Websites, the most common source of visitors is from a browser bookmark. In order for this to happen the user will have to have previously bookmarked your site, and this will occur only after the site's interest and trust levels cross the user's bookmark threshold.

Finally, your site may be reached as a result of a clickthrough—a deliberate click on a text or graphical link from another site. This may be a paid-for referral as via a banner ad or a free referral from an individual or cooperating site. In the case of clickthroughs, the referring site will almost always be identifiable in the Website's referrer log data. Capturing this crucial clickstream data is important in order to verify the efficacy of marketing programs. It also provides data for auditing invoices you may receive from clickthrough advertising charges.

To evaluate the comparative effectiveness of various banner or other ads you might want to use a unique link and dummy entry page for each different ad you're employing. This will let you collect independent statistics for each ad for every referring site.

Session Identification

Most Web-centric data warehouse applications will require every user session (visit) to have its own, unique, identity tag, similar to a supermarket ticket ID. Throughout this book we will call this the *session ID*. The records of every individual user action in a session, whether it is derived from the clickstream or from an application interaction, must contain this tag. This session ID will be carried throughout the data warehouse. In many cases a session ID may not be available immediately, when the events first relating to the session are logged. In such cases, *a temporary session ID* will be needed, and this will later be resolved into an enterprise-acceptable session ID that will follow the log information through the data warehouse.

The basic protocol for the World Wide Web, HTTP (hypertext transfer protocol) is stateless—that is, it lacks the concept of a session. There are no intrinsic login or logout actions built into HTTP, so session identity must be established in some other way. There are several ways to do this:

1. In many cases, the individual hits comprising a session can be consolidated by collating time-contiguous log entries from the same host (IP address). If the log contains a number of entries with the same host ID in a short period of time (e.g., one hour) you can reasonably assume that the entries are for the same session. This method breaks down for Websites with large numbers of visitors because dynamically assigned IP addresses may be reused immediately by different users over a brief time period. Also, different IP addresses may be used within the same session for the same user. This approach also presents problems when dealing with browsers that are behind some firewalls. Notwithstanding these problems, many commercial log analysis products use this method of session tracking, and it requires no cookies or special Web server features.

2. Another, much more satisfactory method is to let the Web server place a session-level cookie into the user's browser. This cookie will

last as long as the browser is open and in general, won't be available in subsequent browser sessions. The cookie value can serve as a temporary session ID not only to the browser, but also to any application that requests the session cookie from the browser. This request must come from the same Web server (actually, the same domain) that placed the cookie in the first place. Using a transient cookie value as a temporary session ID for both the clickstream and for application logging allows a straightforward approach to associating the data from both these sources during post-session log processing. But using a transient cookie has the disadvantage that you can't tell when the user returns to the site at a later time in a new session.

3. HTTP's secure sockets layer (SSL) offers an opportunity to track a user session because it may include a login action by the user and the exchange of encryption keys. The downside to using this method is that to track the session, the entire information exchange needs to be in high-overhead SSL, and the user may be put off by security advisories that can pop up using certain browsers. Also, each host must have its own unique security certificate.

4. If page generation is dynamic you can try to maintain user state by placing a session ID in a hidden field of each page returned to the user. This session ID can be returned to the Web server as a query string appended to subsequent HTTP request in much the same way that a baton is passed during a relay race. This method of session tracking requires a great deal of control over the Website's page generation methods to ensure that the thread of session ID is not broken. If the user clicks on links that don't support session ID baton-passing, a single session will appear to be multiple sessions. This approach also breaks down if multiple vendors are supplying content in a single session.

5. Finally, the Website may establish a *persistent cookie* in the user's machine that is not deleted by the browser when the session ends. Of course it's possible that users will have their browser set to refuse cookies or may manually clean out their cookie file, so there is no absolute guarantee that even a persistent cookie will survive. Although any given cookie can only be read by the Website that caused it to be created, certain groups of Websites can agree to store a common ID tag that would let these sites combine their separate notions of a user session into a "supersession." Microsoft, for example, implements a form of common ID known as a Global User ID (GUID) to identify users across diverse Microsoft-owned Websites.

In summary, the most reliable method of session tracking from Web server log records is obtained by setting a persistent cookie in the user's browser. Less reliable but good results can be obtained by setting a session-level, non-persistent cookie and by associating time-contiguous log entries from the same host. The latter method requires a robust algorithm in the log post-processor to ensure satisfactory results and to decide when not to take the results seriously.

User Identification

Identifying a specific user who logs into your site presents some of the most challenging problems facing a site designer, Webmaster, or manager of data warehousing.

- Web users wish to be anonymous. They may have no reason to trust you, the Internet, or their computer, with personal identification or credit card information.
- If you request a user's identity he is likely to lie about it. It is believed that when asked their name on an Internet form, men will enter a pseudonym 50 percent of the time, and women will use a pseudonym 80 percent of the time.
- You can't be sure which family member is visiting your site. If you obtain an identity by association, for instance, from a persistent cookie left during a previous visit, the identification is only for the computer, not for the specific user. Any family member or company employee may have been using that particular computer at that moment in time. While some operating systems (e.g., Windows 2000) have facilities for customizing a PC for each family member, we don't believe that this added layer of complexity will be used in most families.
- You can't assume that an individual is always at the same computer. Server-provided cookies identify a computer, not an individual. If you access the same Website from your office computer, your home computer, and your laptop computer, a different Website cookie might be put into each machine.

Anonymity

Most Web users want to preserve their anonymity. They want the freedom to use the Web without being concerned that someone is watching them or that their e-mail address is being given to spammers. They want to be sure they can trust the sites that they visit. The element of trust is extremely important. If a user doubts the trustworthiness of a site he will not return. It is important, therefore, to avoid asking users to provide any information about themselves until it is absolutely necessary—for example, for a credit card purchase.

For many purposes you might never need or want to know the actual identity of a user. It may be adequate to retain a persistent user ID throughout your entire Webhouse without specific association to the user's actual identity, e-mail address, or other identifying features. Other applications require you to identify the individual or household. In any case, it is almost *never* a good idea to carry an identity in the data warehouse. Because of the need for privacy and the uncertainty of future privacy legislation, you should keep your warehouse data and your identity data separate. Assign unique but meaningless user and household IDs and keep associated personal, household, and e-mail elsewhere where they can be fully protected.

False Identities

When asked for their identity or e-mail address without a bona fide purpose, at least half of all Web users will supply false information. As we discussed previously, the act of soliciting this information immediately lowers the site's trust level. Because of the prevalence of misrepresentation on the part of the user it is always best to avoid asking for personal information just for the purpose of user tracking. Don't trust identity information that can't be validated in some way. And above all, don't use nonvalidated identity information for e-mail or marketing purposes. Rather than trying, prematurely, to establish user identity, it is much better to simply accept the user's wish for anonymity and track their session and their repeat visits with an anonymous user ID.

Intimacy and the Presumption of Trust

The new technologies of the Web allow us to track every "gesture" made by a visitor to our Website. We see how long they spent on a page, and what the sequence of pages was. If we are an ISP, we have an even more intimate view of the person using the computer. The ISP knows the exact machine identity of every connected user. The ISP sees every click and can account for complete sessions. Obviously, this intimacy creates fear in the mind of the user because most users would rather be anonymous unless they have granted trust to the Website or the ISP.

Householding

Because several members of a household can use the same computer you can't necessarily assume that you know who's sitting at the keyboard, even if you've identified the machine through a cookie. This is especially true if you're depending on an independent profiler to supply the identity of the user—the profiler's view is of a composite of all users of the machine, not of an individual. Depending on your site type, you may be able to identify a particular household member using content-driven profiling—looking at the specific products or news articles being accessed and making an educated guess as to the user's age and gender. It's easy to be misled into thinking you know something about your user, when you only know about a household.

As an example, the *New York Times* Website requires a user login and password in order to view news content. Demographic data (including your age and gender) and your e-mail address are collected by the *Times* site when you initially get a password. There's no charge for this login and you aren't asked for your name, but you can't view the site unless you supply the information, be it real or bogus. If you use the same login from a number of different computers, the *Times* site can track you, as an individual, from computer to computer if you use the same login. However the *Times* also lets you save the login and password as a cookie that lets you bypass the login in subsequent visits. So the information about gender and age becomes suspect. Another family member or co-worker may be using the machine. What started out as an attempt to track an individual has instead devolved into tracking a computer.

Roaming Users

An individual may not always use the same computer to access our Website, but we would like to keep track of the customer regardless of whether they're using their office, home, or portable PC. See Figure 2.5. It's difficult to establish an identity for roaming users unless they use a common login. An individual may log onto the *New York Times* Website as hlmencken from their office, and as marktwain from home. If he provides a different e-mail address for each identity, then there isn't a way to associate his two identities.

Because they have access to multiple PCs, roaming users may often be more computer-comfortable or in a higher-income segment than other users. This makes them particularly attractive candidates for on-line marketing. Identifying and merging roaming users is a significant strength of independent profilers who tie user identifications to user demographics. Because they are placed in the identification loop for

In the Office

In the Field

At Home

In a Hotel

FIGURE 2.5   The Roaming User: the Office, the Field, at Home, in a Hotel

multiple Websites and maintain their own cookie in target computers, profilers can put together logins from diverse machines and associate those machines as belonging to the same individual. This can be done by an individual Website, as long as the individual uses a consistent login from machine to machine for a particular Website.

BEHAVIORAL ANALYSIS

A user's behavior during a Website visit can provide valuable insights into the effectiveness of the site, as well as to the user's browsing habits. There are many aspects of behavior that can be measured and recorded by a properly instrumented Website.

Entry Point

Many users will enter your site via its home page, simply because they have entered the site's URL in their browser. However, users don't always enter a site at its home page. They may enter anonymously, via a page deep in your site that's been linked by another site—a link that you might not even know about. They may have a subsidiary page rather than your home page bookmarked. You can generally determine whether a link is involved because a link will produce a referrer log record. The entry point information is important marketing and design information, because every page commonly used for entry should invite the user to explore your entire site.

Dwell

Dwell is the amount of time that the user actually has a Web page visible on his browser. If we make the assumption that the user remains within the same Website during an entire session, then dwell time is the time between HTTP requests, minus the time required to download the entire contents of the page. Capturing this information for a Website is very much like being able to watch someone reading a magazine and measuring with a stopwatch, the amount of time they spend reading each page!

If dwell time for a Website page is very short, then we can suspect that the page has been reached in error or its content is irrelevant to the user. If dwell time is negative, then the user stopped the download before it completed. If dwell time is extremely long then we can suspect that the user has been distracted or has left our site for some reason. Very long dwell times can also result from a user re-visiting pages that are already in their browser cache. Switching between cached pages leaves no trace at the Web-server level.

If a page contains streaming media—real-time audio or video—you should assume that the dwell time begins as soon as enough streamed data is cached in the user's PC to begin to play the content. The user's attention will be drawn to this content as soon as it begins to play on the PC.

For testing the effectiveness of high-traffic pages, ads, and catalog pages, we might want to establish an *expected dwell time*, and track the difference between the estimated dwell and actual dwell for the user. This will give us an excellent metric for evaluating the effectiveness of the content and provide a basis for tuning the site content to give us the desired user response.

Querying

The search arguments that a user enters on a Web form can tell us a great deal about both the user's mindset and the usability of our site. If a user can drill down to the desired information in one or two query requests, then we have an effective indexing system. If the user enters several queries before finding the results or abandons their search completely, we have a problem. We also need to acknowledge that a large user population is uncomfortable with free-form searches and cannot or will not use them. For this substantial user group a prompted drill-down table of contents is much more appropriate than a free-form search. In either case we want to ensure that the user gets the information or direction that they are asking for—that they aren't left without results and that they aren't presented with so many irrelevant choices that they exit the site in frustration.

For tracking free-form searches we need to capture the user's search keywords and result count, as well as the outcome: Did they end up at a page on which they dwelled the length of time that we had hoped? Most commercial search engines provide excellent statistics for free-form searches and provide feedback for improving or adding keywords to facilitate a higher hit rate.

A Website that supports drill-down table-of-contents searches using database-driven dynamic pages should have user search tracking built into the application from the outset in order to collect query navigation details.

Intra-Site Navigation

The way a user navigates through the Website can provide additional metrics of value to the site designers. At one extreme, a "hit-and-run" user might have a particular page bookmarked, and always go directly to that page within our site, without exploring much beyond that page. This kind of visit can also result from a referring site's "deep link"—a link to a low-level page on another site that bypasses the home page of the linked site. At the other extreme, the user might enter through a home page and then take a nondirected random walk, window-shopping just to see what the site contains. In the middle is the search user, who enters the site and immediately starts to query for specific information. In Figure 2.6 we show paths that a hit-and-run visitor and window shopper might take through a Website. Both qualitative and quantitative information can be collected about navigation behavior from clickstream data, using referrer log records. A user's navigation style derived from

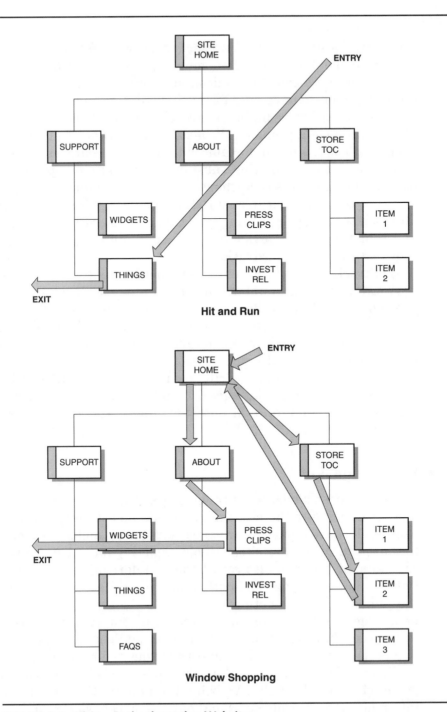

FIGURE 2.6 Visitor Paths through a Website

the clickstream can be used for site tuning and for optimizing future information presentations using dynamic content management.

Exit Point

When the user leaves your site, they will generally leave no trace because they won't in any way be required to log off. Remember that HTTP is a stateless protocol. You will have to assume that if the user hasn't made a content request for perhaps 30 minutes, they are gone. The last page requested before the user became missing in action is their exit point. With the determination of the exit point and the assignment of a session ID, all of the basic user tracking is complete. It now becomes necessary to associate other actions that occurred during the session.

ASSOCIATING DIVERSE ACTIONS

Once we have a handle on the user's session map and have assigned it an ID we can associate the session with other related user actions. This allows us to enrich the session profile and complete all of the information collection needed for future site personalization. These diverse actions might be handled by systems other than the Web-hosting system, in which case association algorithms must be defined.

The actions include:

- **Catalog browsing.** The specific products that a user views during a session should be tied to the session ID. In addition, an attempt should be made to categorize these selections so that the user's interests can be recorded.
- **Purchasing.** Any purchases a user makes during a session or as a result of that session should be associated. If the user has made any selections from a print, rather than an on-line catalog, the catalog edition should be included.
- **Product support.** When product support is requested, the support request should be tied with a specific product category or SKU.
- **Reshelved purchases.** If a customer puts an item into his cart and later removes it before checkout, this fact and the product ID should be added to the session profile.
- **Product delivery.** The common carrier's bill of lading number should be associated with the session ID during which the order was placed.

- **Physical product return.**   If a product is physically returned, the return authorization code should be associated with the Web session ID in which the product was bought.
- **Human contact.**   Any human contact, which resulted from a Web session, should be associated with the session ID. This includes e-mail, Website support calls, product questions, customer service, and technical support. In the case of an electronic purchase this can be greatly assisted by allowing a customer ongoing access to his order ID.

THE REQUIREMENTS OF PERSONALIZATION

The Website tracking techniques discussed in this chapter provide the basis for site personalization—supplying content to a Website visitor tailored specifically to appeal to that individual. In this section we look at some of the requirements of personalization, and which of the tracking techniques provide support.

Personalization has been a major Web-related research topic since the middle 1990s. One of the significant areas of study is automatic collaborative filtering (ACF), where the content presented to a Website visitor is selected based on the content other people like the visitor already have requested. ACF approaches range from complete automatic predictions of desirable content, to "assisted" filtering, where users name their preferences explicitly or supply quality scores to various documents. There are many collaborative filtering systems available for picking Website content. Certainly, the data Webhouse could serve as the analysis foundation for finding the correlations that would lead to content recommendations.

Personalization is generally distinguished from customization, although neither of the terms are used in a highly disciplined way. Customization generally refers to the ability of the Website visitor to explicitly set viewing preferences, much like preferences in a software program. In this case, no attempt is made to guess the customizations, but rather the Website visitor is give a range of feedback and navigation options that make the site more comfortable to use.

Recognition of Re-visits

In order to personalize a Web session it's essential to have access to the prior knowledge about the individual or householder. This prior knowledge is, in part obtained from previous visits to your Website. The first order of business is to correlate the new visit with an already-existing household ID or user ID. Cookies provide the primary basis for this. Unless this correlation is trustworthy, it is futile for the system to attempt to present personalized content. An inaccurate identification can provide negative results—a user will view another user's target material rather than broad-spectrum content designed for a first-time visitor.

User Interface and Content Personalization

The first aspect of personalization is user interface selection. This requires identification of the user's browser type and version, in order to avoid unsupported content features. If we plan to use optional Java, JavaScript, or ActiveX components, it's essential to ensure that the browser supports them.

User interface personalization can take other aspects as well. For example, if a user has previously shown a proclivity to use drill-down tables of content rather than free-form queries, we want to be sure to emphasize this feature. Since we have knowledge of the user's previous visits we can also personalize the content which they see and feature the items which they might be most interested in. A note of caution is appropriate here: Excessive content personalization can shield the customer from viewing parts of your site that the customer might want to see. Their interests might be much broader than you deduce from a limited number of previous visits. Targeted banner and spot ads are also a primary personalization target. Regardless of whether the advertisement is for your product or someone else's, advertising content should be based on prior visits whenever possible.

Collateral and Impulse Sales

Knowing the customer from previous visits will allow you to target sales of collateral items. If a customer puts a cell phone in his shopping cart you may want to recommend the collateral sale of a cell phone carrying case. But you may know from some previous visit that this customer has recently purchased a hand-held PDA. You might, therefore, want to also suggest a carrying case that will hold both the cell phone and a PDA.

Similarly, supporting impulse sales can be guided by a prior knowledge of the customer. In your on-line bookstore you might want to recommend impulse items—"customers that bought this book also bought . . ." If you know that your customer always avoided hardbound editions, you might want to omit these from your impulse suggestions and stick to paperbacks.

Active Collaborative Filtering

As we build up demographic profiles of our customers, we can group similar customers together. Knowledge of these groups can be used to recommend collateral purchases, as described earlier. But simply collecting purchase behavior may be inefficient. Why not ask the customer to help directly with recommendations of other purchases? Perhaps in exchange for a discount or a free gift, our Website can elicit high-quality direct suggestions. The unexpected, creative response is worth a lot in this situation because by its nature it would not have shown up directly just by watching what people bought. This kind of active collaboration has been explored by a number of researchers and Website designers, and is known as "active collaborative filtering."

Calendar and Lifestyle Events

Some sales events can be correlated with certain times of the year, every year. See Figure 2.7. For instance, in early May your store might feature Mother's Day gifts. If, in your on-line pharmacy, you have sold a particular perfume fragrance to a male customer just before a previous Mother's Day you might want to suggest the same fragrance this Mother's Day, but in a different product—soap or bath oil instead of perfume.

Lifestyle events are also important. Although Christmas comes around every year, if an individual is in the parenthood phase of his life the suggestions for Christmas shopping may be considerably different than if he has recently retired. Taking annual and lifetime events together gives us a powerful tool for narrowing down an individual's focus at any time. The tracking of our customers' lifetime calendar events, implies a kind of lifetime relationship to the customer. We will go though life together.

Localization

Prior knowledge of the customer allows us to personalize a site for their nationality and language. The degree of localization can vary widely. For example, you might have a repeat visitor to your site whose profile shows the customer as a native Brazilian with a working knowledge of English. Even though you don't support a fully international site you might want to greet this particular customer with a Portuguese home page before leading them to the primarily English content of your site. A Canadian customer might be offered a choice between English and

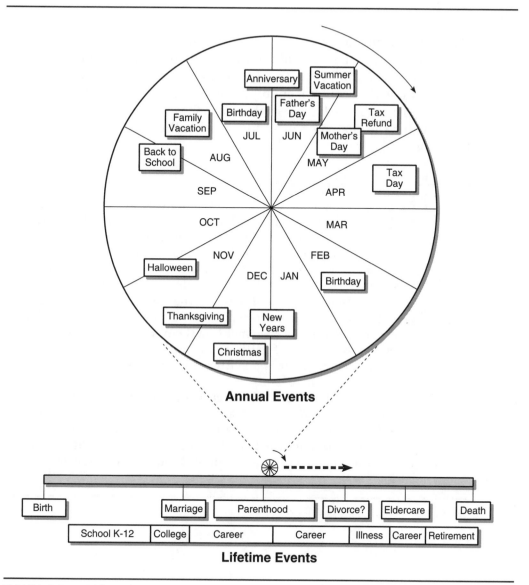

FIGURE 2.7   Yearly and Lifetime Calendar Events

French, and a dropdown box listing the Canadian provinces instead of states. Localization of other items is also possible if you have some prior knowledge of your user. This includes time and date formats, currencies, and shipping alternatives.

SUMMARY

This chapter has described many of the inputs to a CRM environment and is intended to be a list of requirements for information we hope to glean from the actual clickstream. We have created a taxonomy of customer actions that can reasonably be measured from logs of Web behavior. We have suggested a few of the responses we may need to generate as we watch the customer, including cross-selling, up-selling, and order tracking.

We have reminded you that there is more to life than ordering a product, and many of the ancillary activities of information gathering, window shopping, and downloading of samples are part of a pleasing customer experience. And, of course, the implication is that these ancillary activities also shed considerable light on the preferences of the customer.

Since identifying and describing the customer is an all-important step, we have begun to explore the boundaries and limitations of figuring out who the customer is in the Web medium. But in many ways, the experience of getting to know the customer is like real retail environments. It is a matter of progressive disclosure based on the building of trust.

We have shown that the clickstream contains unprecedented detail about the "aisles" walked by the customer before checking out. We can see the entry points, the exit points, the successful purchases, and the abandoned purchases. In many cases, with cookies, we can see when a customer, even an anonymous customer, comes back.

CHAPTER 3

Using the Clickstream to Make Decisions

Now that we understand the range of customer actions that are recorded by Web servers, we pause to talk about the decisions that we want to make if only we had all of this behavioral data. Then in Chapter 4, we dig deeper into the realities of the clickstream data to see how closely we can meet these objectives.

It is very important that we focus at this early point in the book on the final decisions to be made with the clickstream data. The clickstream data is a classic example of fascinating data that can be overwhelming. There is so much data and parts of it are so interesting that we can spend all our energy wrangling the data and never focus on an objective. Although the idea is a little hackneyed, it is still valuable to consider the following progression:

data ➜ information ➜ knowledge ➜ decisions

Data by itself is virtually useless, especially because we are capable of generating so much of it. When the data has been organized coherently and we can see its patterns, then we have something much more useful. We probably can give suggestive names to the patterns, and we usually can describe the patterns far more succinctly than just enumerating the original data. Let us call these patterns *information*.

But even seeing and describing the patterns does not lead to action. When we can identify cause and effect and correlation, then we have further refined the information into useful knowledge. Even knowledge in this sense is not the final step. It does no good to be wise without taking action. The real, final, tangible output from any data warehouse should be decisions made as a result of the knowledge gained. Every data warehouse and every data Webhouse must strive to be a true decision-support system (DSS), in the original sense of the term.

Interestingly, the focus on decisions as the output of a data warehouse makes the calculation of the return on investment (ROI) of the data warehouse much more straightforward. In this book we will dig quite deeply into calculating the profit of various parts of our Web-enabled businesses. We will use the clickstream to identify customers, to segment them, and to organize them into groups to which we can assign revenue and costs. In this way we will develop some sophisticated profit and loss (P&L) views of our customers and the services we provide them.

But at the same time we will be capturing and remembering many of the decisions that we have made as a result of using the data Webhouse. We will take "partial credit" for all of the decisions made using data Webhouse data. Since the financial impact of many business decisions can be measured retrospectively, we wait until the financial impact of the decisions is revealed, and then we claim our partial credit to be balanced against the data Webhouse investment. In this way we calculate an ROI for the data Webhouse. We are careful not to claim too much partial credit for a couple of reasons. First, any business decision comes about as a result of information and knowledge provided by IT as well as the end user's business instincts, creative hunches, and the willingness to lead effectively as a manager. So it would be over-reaching for the data Webhouse to claim all the credit! But secondly, and just as important, many of the financial impacts are so large that it only takes a small percentage of these impacts to be applied against the Webhouse implementation expenses in order to show a profit for the Webhouse itself. As Webhouse builders, we can afford to be modest in what we claim.

Calculating the ROI for a Webhouse is easy if you aggressively capture and quantify the decisions made while using the Webhouse, and if you are content to only look at ROI retrospectively.

In the next few sections we analyze the kinds of decisions that can be made using clickstream data. In some cases, the clickstream data can drive the decisions all by itself. In many other cases, the clickstream data must be combined with other data marts that make up the overall enterprise data warehouse before a decision can be made. We briefly identify these companion data sources within the "tips" (indicated by light bulbs in this chapter). We won't do any detailed database designs at this point or explain in detail what the suggestive data mart names really mean. We will wait until Chapter 7 to actually build the clickstream data marts, since at that point we will have succeeded in capturing the data and are actually trying to present it to our customers.

This chapter is intended to sensitize you to the most valuable possible content in the clickstream data. Then in Chapter 4 we will try to dig this content out of the Web server log files and other clickstream sources.

 Rather than waiting until the end of this chapter to tie the content to the topic of CRM, we must point out at the beginning that this chapter *is* CRM. Everything in this chapter is focused on identifying the customer, understanding the customer, seeing what works with the customer, and driving toward increased profitability.

DECISIONS ABOUT IDENTIFYING AND RECOGNIZING CUSTOMERS

In this section we show some of the decisions that can be made if we simply identify and recognize customers arriving at our Website.

Customizing Marketing Activities by Identifying Your Customers

The goal of identifying and recognizing the customer is to establish a more meaningful relationship than is possible with an anonymous transaction. We can begin to personalize our interaction with the customer when we see that the customer has returned to our site. As our experience with the identified customer grows, we will offer different deals, different opportunities, and different "customer faces" to:

- High-profit customers vs. low-profit customers,
- New customers vs. returning customers, and
- Reliable product keepers vs. frequent product returners.

Identifying the customer entering our Website is the most basic single requirement of the clickstream analysis. Identifying the customer is the foundation for almost all of the decisions discussed in this chapter. There are four levels at which we may be able to recognize the customer, in order of increased knowledge of who the customer really is:

1. A persistent identifier that only tells us that a Web browser on a particular computer is engaging in a session at this moment. This level-1 anonymous tag cannot be used as a reliable guide to identifying a future session from the same computer.

2. A persistent identifier that tells us the same Web browser on a particular computer has returned for a repeat session.

3. A persistent identifier that tells us a particular human being has returned to our Website.

4. A permanent and specific personal identifier that tells us reliably that a known customer has returned to our Website. In this case we know the true name of the customer and some of the customer's demographic information. We may have obtained the demographic information in a cooperative way by asking the customer, or we may have purchased demographic data from a data supplier by linking through the customer's known name and address.

Even level 1 is useful, if that is all we can get. Level 1 at least allows us to track an anonymous session and perhaps to classify the session as successful or unsuccessful. We can make some of the decisions described in later sections about the presentation of our Website.

Levels 2 and 3 are significantly better because we can measure return visits. A return visit is very significant because it means the customer is interested in our site. We are providing something useful or interesting. The customer has made our site part of his or her life.

Of course, level 4 is our goal. When we have some idea who we are dealing with, we can be far more responsive and present far more of a customized interface. In many cases, we have a level-4 understanding of who the customer is because the customer has actually made a purchase or has used our services in a way that reveals their identity.

 It is always worthwhile to specifically identify the visitor to our Website, but at the same time we must be reassuring, gentle, and ethical in our seeking this identity.

Targeting Marketing Activities by Clustering Your Customers

Once we have at least a level-2 identification of the customer, we can measure certain characteristics of the return visits to our Website. A classic, simple way of clustering customer behavior is to accumulate three basic measures: recency, frequency, and intensity.

- *Recency* is how many days it has been since we last saw the customer on our Website.
- *Frequency* is how many times we have ever seen this customer on our Website.
- *Intensity* is the grand total of the customer's purchases or some other quantitative measure of our basic Website objective. Sometimes intensity is called "monetary."

If we create five ranges for each of these measures, perhaps corresponding to our intuitive understanding of High, Medium High, Average, Medium Low, and Low, then any given customer will fall into one of 125 possible cells (five recency ranges times five frequency ranges times five intensity ranges). Placing all possible customers into this three-dimensional cube may show some obvious clusters. See Figure 3.1. The nice thing about this simple clustering methodology is that the identified clusters make sense. Perhaps one of them is High Recency, High

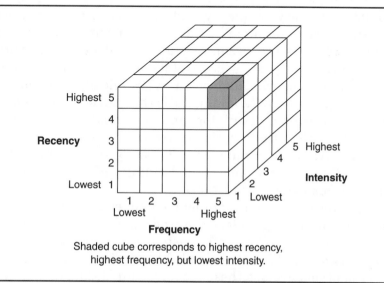

Shaded cube corresponds to highest recency,
highest frequency, but lowest intensity.

FIGURE 3.1 Clustering Customers in the Recency, Frequency, Intensity Cube

Frequency, Low Intensity. These are people who are interested in our site, but we aren't achieving our aim of selling them our services or product or getting them to use our site the way we want them to.

Clustering customers by recency, frequency, and intensity is attractive because we may be able to use the clickstream data by itself to perform the whole analysis. Certainly, the recency and frequency measures can be measured in the clickstream. The intensity measure may or may not be available directly in the clickstream. If the intensity measure is directly related to a page event in the Web server log, then it is in the clickstream. But if the intensity measure is the total volume of purchases as recorded in a companion transaction system fed, but not captured, by the Web server, then we will have to generate the intensity measure by drilling across to the sales transaction data mart. Similarly, we might decide that the intensity measure such as total sales includes sales that didn't happen exclusively through the Web interface. In this case we are absolutely committed to drilling across to the non-Web source to complete the clustering measures.

> Driving marketing activities needs clickstream and sales transaction data marts.

Cluster analysis can be much more sophisticated than simply accumulating recency, frequency, and intensity. If we have a good verbose demographic description of the customer with many textual and numeric attributes, then we have a full-fledged data mining problem. If we have thirty demographic descriptors of the customer, we do not build a thirty-dimension cube and look at it graphically! Fortunately, there are a host of powerful data mining tools that can sort through a large number of demographic descriptors and numerical measures and advise the analyst which of these variables combine to show interesting clusters. Decision-tree data mining tools are very good at sorting through many text and numeric variables and deciding which ones best predict high-revenue customers, for instance.

Clustering and data mining techniques can be used to directly recommend marketing decisions. Rather than simply clustering customers relative to revenue or profit, customers can be clustered according to their history, and hence their likelihood, of responding to certain kinds of promotions. We use these techniques to decide how to cross-sell, up-sell, and create promotions for each specific customer.

Deciding Whether to Encourage or Support a Referring Cross-Link

Building on the previous two sections, we identify the customers coming to us from a particular cross-link. Every arriving page request from the Web will normally identify the referring site from which the page request was launched. We assign the newly arrived prospective customers to known clusters of customers whose behavior we understand. The customers coming to us from the link in question perhaps can be rated by likelihood to buy, by revenue, by profit, by lifetime value, by propensity to return the product, or by propensity to invoke costly support. All of these factors would allow us to make an informed decision whether to encourage or support a referring cross link. See Figure 3.2. In many cases, of course, we are paying the referrer for each arriving Website hit.

Paid Website referrals can be abused. Without careful monitoring, we can't be sure just what the context of the referral might have been. We do know we have to pay the referrer when they dump a "customer" in our lap. So let's try to develop an informed opinion about the worth of these new customers.

Deciding whether to encourage or support a referring cross-link needs the clickstream data mart.

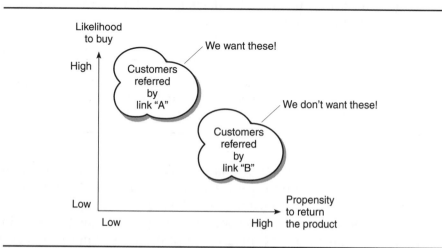

FIGURE 3.2 Productive vs. Unproductive Origins

Later in this book we will analyze the referrer information in the Website logs more deeply. Usually if the page request arriving at our site has come from a search engine, the search string used by that engine is also available. This scenario is even more compelling if we have our own intra-site search facility because then we will know much more about the context of the search. In either case, if we can parse the search string, then the context of the search may be understandable. We may be able to add metatags and verbiage to parts of our Website to draw in more productive hits, and we may be able to remove items that are causing nonproductive hits.

Deciding Whether a Customer Is About to Leave Us

There are several situations where we would like to know if a customer is about to leave us. During an actual session, we may be able to tell that someone can't find what they want, and that they may be frustrated. If we detect this in real time, we may be able to present a custom Web page and ask them directly what is wrong. The diagnosis of a frustrated on-line customer can be based on how they arrived at our site, especially if the search criteria from a search engine is available. The speed and breadth of the customer's page requests may be another good indicator. If the customer is clicking very quickly, they aren't reading the page. Of course it helps to know if this is a repeat customer. A repeat customer may know exactly where to click to get to a destination. But a new customer is probably jumping from place to place because they aren't finding anything useful. The decision that we are trying to make is whether to intervene.

Deciding whether a customer is about to leave us requires the clickstream, sales transaction, and customer communication data marts.

A more serious form of abandonment is the established customer whose trust or whose interest we are about to lose. In this case, a more complex pattern must be analyzed. We might look in the clickstream for recency, as well as frequency and intensity in the most recent time periods. We might also look for unsuccessful visits, where the established customer came to our site but left without completing a transaction.

Again, the decision that we are trying to make is whether to intervene and ask the customer if there is anything we can do to help. Depending on the business and the depth of our relationship with the customer, we may also want to reach the customer personally through another channel, such as e-mail, a letter, or a phone call.

DECISIONS ABOUT COMMUNICATING

Our Website is, first and foremost, a place where we communicate. The communications go in both directions. The customer sees, and maybe listens to our Web pages. The customer communicates with us through the Web page gestures (clicks) and through information filled into forms. Although many serious commercial Websites are offering a dynamic, tailored experience for each Website visitor, even a site with static pages can constantly decide whether their content communicates and whether the message should be changed. There are many, many communications decisions to make, and the clickstream data is the foundation for most of these decisions.

Deciding Whether a Particular Web Ad Is Working

We would like to measure whether an ad on our Website or on a remote Website leads to increased sales, increased profits, and better customers. In this case, we assume the customer does not explicitly interact with the ad by clicking on it or treating it as a link. Explicit interactions are easy to measure and make decisions about. The more subtle problem we are trying to measure here is a *soft causal* effect. This is similar to measuring advertising effectiveness in conventional media such as radio, television, or newspaper. In these cases, we don't know whether our ad registered on the consciousness of the customer or whether the ad led to the customer seeking our products. Causal effects and causal dimensions are explained in detail in Chapter 6.

In the world of conventional media, ad campaigns can often be measured only by an indirect increase in sales that "seems" to be in response to the ad. In a complex marketplace where we and our competitors are bombarding the customers with overlapping and conflicting stimuli, it is often a guess or an article of faith that an ad campaign has done very much. The most direct measures of ad effectiveness are surveys of brand awareness created by the ads. But it is still a leap of faith that brand awareness is the reason for increased sales.

Deciding whether a particular Web ad is working needs the clickstream data mart with the causal dimension describing ad placements.

In the world of Website advertising, we have some advantages over the conventional media. We can be pretty sure the customer was looking at the screen when our ad was visible. We also can measure how long it took after the ad exposure for the customer to visit our Website. If the ad is quite product specific, then we can be even more confident that the ad worked if the user visits the specific part of our Website describing that product. Both of these measures can make us more confident that the ad had something to do with the customer coming to our Website.

Although we will discuss this later, notice that we would like to merge the Website logs of the referring site with our own Website logs so we can see who saw our ad and when.

 Deciding who saw our ad and when needs our own clickstream and referrer's clickstream data marts.

Realistically, this raises significant issues of privacy as well as issues of sharing customers with the referring site, but since the referring site has already agreed to advertise us, some of this data sharing may be possible.

Deciding If Custom Greetings Are Working

The generation of custom greetings is a significant decision in an e-commerce environment because it requires a lot of infrastructure to do well. In Chapter 1 we described the architecture for a complete data Webhouse, which included a hot response cache. See Figure 1.1. A major responsibility of the hot response cache is to store and perhaps create custom greetings for customers arriving on the Website. The hot response cache is probably not the same physical server as the main relational database server because the hot response cache must be able to respond instantaneously to the arrival of a customer.

A custom greeting may be a completely precalculated marketing message or there may be a simple cache of summary information that can generate a few predictable messages about the customer's account, the customer's last order, any backorders, and other opportunities, or special deals we think would appeal to the customer. A very important kind of custom greeting is a cross-selling or up-selling proposal. Cross-selling is selling a product or service belonging to a family of comparable products. For instance, a bank may propose that a customer open a savings account to accompany a checking account. Up-selling is selling a product or service of significantly more value than the ones already used. The bank may propose a home mortgage or a small business loan to customers with the right profile and history.

In any case, the cache of custom greetings needs to be updated frequently because it needs to reflect the most current reality. The main business transaction server needs to update the cache whenever a meaningful transaction takes place. The customer may want to see the status of a transaction seconds after it was posted. Also, the main relational database stores of historical data will periodically create custom greeting such as the cross-sell and up-sell proposals based on large groups of customers and based on more significant time histories than are available on the hot response cache server.

The decision whether custom greetings are working is similar to the decision whether ads are working. If the custom greeting is interactive, then we can directly measure a kind of impulsive response. But for the noninteractive greeting and for the delayed response, we have the same soft causal issues described in the previous section. We look at sales to those people exposed to the greeting, and we look at timing of such sales relative to the greeting.

Deciding if custom greetings are working needs the clickstream and sales transaction data marts. Cross-selling and up-selling needs a "core" revenue data mart spanning multiple lines of business.

Custom greetings are more powerful than many other forms of ads because we control who sees the greeting. We can easily create control groups of those customers who see a greeting and those who don't. We can be much more confident that small differences in behavior are due to the greeting or the lack of the greeting.

Deciding If a Promotion Is Profitable

In the previous sections we dealt with the front-line marketing issues of ad effectiveness and custom greeting effectiveness. Our main judgment metric was increased sales, and the main issue in the analysis was whether we could attribute an increase in sales to the ad or the custom greeting.

A deeper issue in marketing is to decide whether a "promotion is profitable." In this case, a promotion is an entire marketing campaign, including development costs, media costs, and all the financial incentives, including temporary price reductions that we pass on to the customer as part of the promotion. It is also very important to realize that when the boss walks into the marketing department and asks whether the "promotion is profitable," the boss isn't really asking whether the incremental transactions recorded as part of the promotion were individually profitable, but several much harder questions:

- Was running the promotion better than not running the promotion? In other words, was the overall profit of the company higher as a result of running the promotion than if we had not run the promotion? Answering this question requires guessing a "baseline" level of sales that would have taken place if only we had not run the promotion. See Figure 3.3.

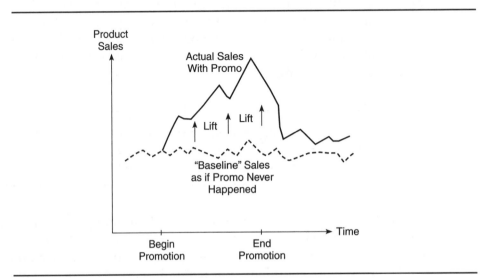

FIGURE 3.3   The Lift of a Promotion

- Did the promotion cannibalize other products that we sell? In other words, did we simply transfer sales from regularly priced products to temporarily low-priced products?
- Did regular sales drop noticeably either before or after the promotion?
- Did we increase the size of our market, even if we did not show an obvious increase in profit?

This book is not the place for a full tutorial on promotions profitability. But we discuss this example here to serve as a warning that the simple question "is the promotion profitable?" is an interesting and complex investigation. If we have the right supporting data, we can answer all of the tough questions posed by the boss. In Chapter 8 we will propose a detailed design for answering the promotions profitability question, but we rest our case at this point by noting the data marts needed for promotions analysis.

 Deciding if a promotion is profitable needs the clickstream, sales transaction, promotions management, and competitive intelligence data marts.

Responding to a Customer's Life Change

In many businesses, major changes in the customer's life create the opportunity to deepen the relationship with the customer and to extend the range of products and services sold to that customer. Significant life changes include

- Marriage or divorce
- Having a child
- Going to college; sending a child to college
- Buying or selling a house
- Moving to a new city
- Becoming a care taker for an elderly relative
- Retirement
- Major health changes

Responding to a customer's life change needs the clickstream, revenue transaction, and third-party demographics data marts.

Just looking at this list and thinking about your company's services and products is a creative exercise. So why not take advantage of your knowledge of the customer and propose new services and products when these life changes happen? Clearly the challenge is detecting the changes. If your business is a financial services business, you may be able to directly detect the customer's life changes. If you are a retailer, and if you know the customer's age, you may be able to guess that a life change has occurred by watching the pattern of purchases. Lacking these direct hints, you may be able to purchase demographic information about your customers from a third party.

Improving the Effectiveness of Your Website

Presumably the style and content of your Website is driven by a few simple goals. You want to communicate effectively with your intended customers. You want to present a good image. You want the customers to return to your site repeatedly. You want them to complete transactions. Specific decisions about your Website include:

- Choosing layout styles (lots of ads, busy intricate pages, clean corporate formal look, very simple pages)
- Whether common choices made by customers (or business partners or employees) are obvious and quickly found
- What characteristics of a page or a site make it a return target
- What characteristics of a page or a site make it a session killer
- Whether the site's text content and metatags are providing the right input to remote search engines to get people to visit your site for the right reasons
- Whether your site has roadblocks that make it awkward for the customer to find what they want, to complete a transaction, or just requires too many clicks
- Identify the places on your site where you hand off the customer to another division or another line of business and thereby either confuse the customer, delay the customer, or increase costs of doing business

Improving the effectiveness of your Website needs the clickstream and sales transaction data marts.

Most of these decisions can be made by performing a detailed behavioral analysis of the clickstream. In Chapter 6 we will revisit all of these questions to show applications can be built to answer these questions using the specific structures of the clickstream dimensional model.

Fostering a Sense of Community

In her book *Customers.com* (Random House, 1998), Patricia Seybold talks about businesses fostering a sense of community. At first this seems like an odd perspective for a commercial entity trying to do business on the Web, but Seybold shows how your Website visitors often have a set of shared interests. Often it is very good business for your Website to be the focus that brings this community together. For example, if you sell products oriented around graphics arts production, it can be very rewarding for everyone to have a forum for sharing their experiences. A moderated forum can be a place where creative contributions can be shared and where technical support issues can be revealed and explained.

 Fostering a sense of community needs the clickstream and customer communications data marts.

A moderated forum can eventually turn into a database that can be searched. Access to this database through your own search engine can be a significant part of your Website. The forum can be augmented by technical support personnel within your company responding to the most common technical support questions. Certainly, if you are generating custom greetings, as discussed in a previous section, the custom greeting should take into account the customer's use of a technical support forum, as in "did you find the answer to your question?"

FUNDAMENTAL DECISIONS ABOUT YOUR WEB BUSINESS

A basic goal of this book is to give you the tools for not only understanding your customers but understanding your overall Web business. In this section, we step back as far as we can and ask the most difficult questions that can be addressed with all the data drawn from various sources into the data Webhouse.

Deciding which Products and Services We Provide over the Web

The answer to this question is ultimately provided by the Web medium itself. Almost every conceivable product and service can be described on a Website. Much of the appeal of the Web shopping experience is the extra information the customer can get compared to standing in a store looking at a product or talking to a less-than-knowledgeable salesperson. Another huge appeal is the convenience of the shopping experience. Many products can be ordered just by clicking a button. The Web medium also invites the customer to track the status of the product or service, whether it is a package being delivered or an investment being tracked. The customer's computer screen is the message.

Taking this perspective, we suspect that any product or service that can be

- described
- ordered in a transaction
- tracked

is a strong candidate for being provided over the Web. It's hard to think of products or services that don't meet at least one of these criteria! How, then, do we understand how successfully our products and services are being described, ordered, and tracked through the Web medium? Once again, we use the clickstream to judge the following:

- Which product descriptions are being read?
- How long are the descriptions being studied during a session?
- What is the correlation between a product description being read and the product being purchased?
- How many button clicks from the start of the session does it typically take for a new customer to order something?
- How many button clicks from the start of the session does it typically take for an existing customer to order something?
- How many product ordering sessions are terminated without completion?

- How quickly can a back order be tracked by the customer?
- How quickly can a financial portfolio be tracked by a customer?
- How often does the customer visit the site to track a financial portfolio?

 Understanding how successfully our products and services are being described, ordered, and tracked through the Web medium needs the clickstream data mart.

Each of these questions can be answered solely from the clickstream. To fully understand the content of a customer's request we would need additional data sources, supplied elsewhere in the Webhouse. But even with just the clickstream data, we should be able to understand the differences between customer group usage patterns and the difference between products. This understanding should lead to direct decisions about which products to offer through the Web and which interfaces or procedures should be improved.

Providing Real Time Status Tracking of Our Operations

In the previous paragraphs we described the attractiveness of providing real-time status tracking for the customer, whether it is tracking a back order or tracking a financial portfolio. The ability to provide real-time status tracking also may be hugely interesting to cooperating business partners in your supply chain, as well as employees. There are an endless number of interesting real-time queries, including order status, payment status, inventory levels, account balances, current credit status, summary of the most recent orders, summary of the most recent payments, and many others.

Many of the system issues of providing status tracking for customers may be very similar for providing status tracking for business partners and employees. An analogous set of questions can be asked on behalf of either business partners or employees to judge how effectively we are delivering the real-time services:

- Which real time services are actually being used?
- What measures are requested?
- Which users access the real-time services?

- What is the average urgency of a real-time request? In other words, how old is the data that is delivered in answer to the user's question? The answer to this question has a big impact on the real-time system design.

- How quickly is the answer to the real-time request delivered to the user?

- How many clicks does it take to make a real-time request? Hopefully we don't need to remind you that business partners and employees are end users, just like customers, and they have the same needs for good user interfaces!

- How many real-time request sessions are terminated without completion?

Real-time status tracking for business partners up and down the supply chain, as well as internal employees, needs the clickstream data mart as well as each operational data mart whose status is being tracked in real time.

The answers to these questions will give us guidance as to which real-time services are being used, which are not being used, which services should be improved, and whether the requests are actually "real time." It is likely that the real-time service is not strictly a read only system like the rest of the data Webhouse, since in many cases, the requesting business partner or employee may wish to change a priority or enter new information. This mixture of query and update is typical of an operational data store (ODS), a familiar construct in the client/server world. The difference here is that these real-time services are provided over the Web.

The final decision of whether it is worth the expense to provide real-time services is a complex one that will have to be answered by senior management. The cost of such a facility will vary significantly depending on the scope and flexibility of the questions that can be answered, and the speed with which operational transactions are made visible in the real-time query system. In many cases, such as package delivery tracking, providing real-time tracking over the Web is a necessary ingredient to stay competitive. The issue may not be whether to provide the service, but simply how.

Determining If Our Web Business Is Profitable

We have saved the hardest decision for last. At some point, every Web business needs to step back and ask the basic profit question. If your entire enterprise is a Web business, then answering this question is easier than if only a small part of your enterprise is a Web business. The company that is totally committed to the Web doesn't have to apportion revenues and costs between Web and non-Web activities. In this case, the annual report itself will show whether the Web business is profitable.

However, in all businesses that are trying to see if their Web activities are profitable, one must break the analysis of profitability down to a very low granularity so that many different views of profit can be constructed. Since so many Web-enabled businesses have a strong customer focus, it is very desirable to ask:

- Which groups of customers are profitable?
- Which groups of products or services are profitable?
- In which time periods are we profitable?
- Which promotions are profitable?
- Are we profitable on an incremental basis? On a fully burdened basis?
- And finally, is the Web business profitable overall?

The secret to answering all these variations of the profit question is to build a complete activity-based profit and loss statement at an extremely low, granular level of the business. For a Web-enabled business, we recommend building this P&L statement at the grain of the individual customer session. We will allocate as much of the costs of the business as we can down to this very low level. In some cases, this allocation process will be painful or controversial, but our efforts will be repaid by being able to answer all of the questions in the preceding list.

We will develop this profitability model in detail in Chapter 7, but as a hint of what is to come, we finish this chapter with a sample P&L statement for a business taking orders over the Web and shipping tangible products from a warehouse.

For each individual customer session on the Web, regardless of the type, duration, and purpose of the session, we build a P&L statement with the following elements:

```
Gross revenue
    Promotional allowances
    Financial terms discounts
```

```
Net revenue
    Product manufacturing or acquisition cost
    Product storage cost
    Product delivery cost
Gross profit
    Product return, restocking, refurbishment, writeoff costs
    Payment fraud costs
    Website system costs
        Hardware, software, labor, ISP, communications, backup
        System downtime costs
        Hacking and security costs
    Marketing costs
    Advertising costs
    PR costs
    Special promotion costs
    Referral costs, commissions
Net Profit
```

The P&L statement for a financial services business would look somewhat different, and we will wait until Chapter 7 to discuss that case.

The P&L perspective shown here is enormously powerful, but this approach is a mixture of good news and bad news. The good news is that once the database containing this information is built, the management of the company has a tool that will allow them to make many of the most important decisions about the Web business in a very well-informed, effective way. The bad news is that the challenge of creating this database is almost entirely in sourcing and allocating all the costs. Most businesses simply can't start out building a "profitability data mart" at this level. This data mart in reality must stand on top of a separate data mart for each one of the cost components. This dilemma is reflected in the following tip.

 These profitability decisions ultimately need the clickstream data mart as well as data marts representing each source of cost.

In Chapter 6, we will address this data mart dependency problem and show how you can build a profitability data mart right from the start to run your Web business, but you must improve it incrementally. As you provide each of the required pieces, your view of profitability becomes more detailed and more accurate.

SUMMARY

In Chapter 2 we described the range of Website visitor actions that are captured by the Web server. In this chapter we then showed what decisions could be made if we had a perfect representation of Web server clickstream data. In some important cases, we need to tie the clickstream data to other data sources, such as operational business processes or third-party demographic data.

Now that we have established the motivation for what the benefit of this data is, we need to dig deeper to understand how to get the data into our Webhouse, as a practical reality. Chapter 4 describes the clickstream data source in detail, and Chapter 5 shows how to engineer your Website to make this whole job much easier. Then finally, Chapters 6 and 7 deliver the detailed designs for the final Webhouse data.

CHAPTER 4

Understanding the Clickstream as a Data Source

One of the sources of data that will feed our data Webhouse is the HTTP clickstream itself—the log records produced by the Web server each time a request is satisfied. In this chapter we'll discuss the content of the clickstream and ways of handling the enormous volume of data that will be generated by a busy Website. We will introduce *a clickstream post-processor* that receives raw log data from a Web server and normalizes it into a format in which it can be combined with application-derived data and piped into the data Webhouse. The database volumes required for log processing at an active Website can be equated to the billing system of a large telephone company, both in volume and in complexity. Part Two of this book presents detailed architectures for databases that are capable of event tracking and content delivery for high-activity Websites.

 In this chapter we describe how customers and Websites communicate with each other. We also show you how some important third parties like banner ad providers and customer profilers, attach to your session and become part of the available data.

We study in some detail how much information can be derived from a cookie and what the limitations of even a "good" cookie may be.

We describe what is known as "referral" information, which is a potentially amazing source of insight into why the user arrived at your Website. From the referral information we should be able to sort out the customers who arrived for the right reasons, customers who arrived for the wrong reasons, and perhaps what all of these customers were thinking about when they entered your site.

We conclude the chapter by proposing an architecture for processing all of this data in the back room before it can become available in our databases for analysis.

Before we describe the specific data elements in the clickstream, it might be useful to review how a Web browser and Website interact.

WEB CLIENT/SERVER INTERACTIONS—A BRIEF TUTORIAL

Understanding the interactions between a Web client (browser) and a Web server (Website) is essential for understanding the source and meaning of the data in the clickstream. Please refer to Figure 4.1 in this discussion. In the illustration we have shown a browser, designated My Browser. We'll look at what happens in a typical interaction from the perspective of myself as a browser user. The browser and Website interact with each other across the Internet using the Web's communication protocol—HyperText Transfer Protocol (HTTP).

Basic Client/Server Interaction

First, I click a button or hypertext link (URL) to a particular Website, shown as action (1) in Figure 4.1. When this HTTP request reaches the Website the server returns the requested item (2). In our illustration, this is a document in hypertext markup language format (HTML)—*your-page.html*. Once the document is entirely retrieved, my browser scans your-page.html and notices several *references* to other Web documents that it must fulfill before its work is completed; the browser must retrieve other components of this document in separate requests. Note that the only human action taken here is to click on the original link. All of the rest of the actions that follow in this example are computer-to-computer interactions triggered by the click and managed, for the most part, by instructions carried in the initially downloaded HTML document, your-page.html. In order to speed up Web page responsiveness most browsers will execute these consequential actions in parallel, typically with up to ten or more HTTP requests being serviced concurrently.

The browser finds a reference to an image—a logo perhaps—which, from its URL, is located at your-site.com, the same place it retrieved the initial html document. The browser issues another request to the server (3) and the server responds by returning the specified image.

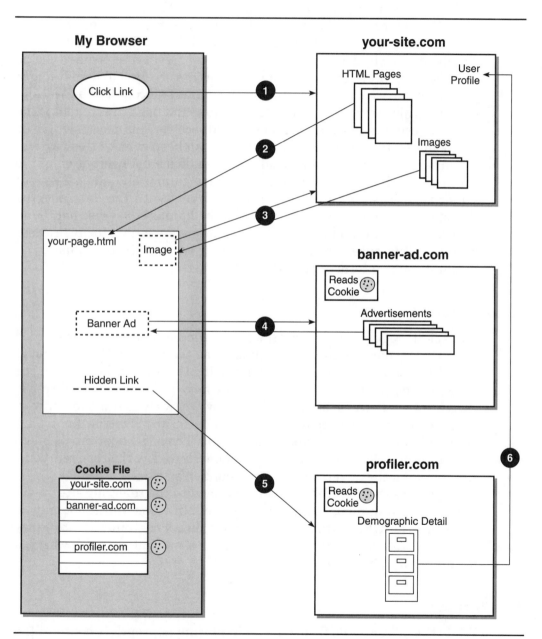

FIGURE 4.1 Web Client/Server Interactions

Advertisements

The browser continues to the next reference in your-page.html and finds an instruction to retrieve another image from Website banner-ad.com. The browser makes this request (4), and the server at banner-ad.com interprets a request for the image in a special way. Rather than immediately sending back an image, the banner-ad server first issues a cookie request to my browser, requesting the contents of any cookie that might previously have been placed in my PC by banner-ad.com. The ad Website retrieves this cookie, examines its contents, and uses the contents as a key to determine which banner ad I should receive. This decision is based on my interests or on previous ads that I had been sent by this particular ad server. Once the banner-ad server makes a determination of the optimum ad, it returns the selected image to me. The advertisement server then logs which ad it has placed along with the date and the clickstream data from my request. Had the banner-ad server not found its own cookie, it would have sent a new persistent cookie to my browser for future reference, sent a random banner ad, and started a history in its database of interactions with my browser.

The Referrer

The HTTP request from my browser to the banner-ad server carried with it a key piece of information known as the *referrer*. The referrer is the URL of the agent responsible for placing the link on the page. In our example, the referrer is "your-site.com/yourpage.html". The referrer is *not* a browser. Because banner-ad.com now knows who the referrer was, it can credit your-site.com for having placed an advertisement on a browser window. This is a single impression. The advertiser can be billed for this impression, with the revenue being shared by the referrer (your-site.com) and the advertising server (banner-ad.com).

If you are sharing Web log information with the referring site, it will be valuable to share page attributes as well. In other words, not only do you want the URL of the referring page, but you would like to know what the purpose of the page was. Was it a navigation page, was it a partner's page, or was it a general search page?

The Profiler

While the ad server deals primarily in placing appropriate content, the *profiler* deals in supplying demographic information about Website visitors. In our example, the original HTML document, your-page.html had a hidden field that contained a request to retrieve a specific document from Website profiler.com (5). When this request reached the profiler server, the profile.com server immediately tried to find its cookie in my browser. This cookie contained a userID that had been placed previously by the profiler, which is used to identify me, and serves as a key to personal information contained in the profiler's database. The profiler might either return its profile data to my browser to be sent back to the initial Website, or send a real-time notification to the referrer, your-site.com via an alternative path advising the referrer that I am currently logged onto his site and viewing a specific page (6). This information could also be returned to the HTML document to be returned to the referrer as part of a query string the next time an HTTP request was sent to your-site.com.

Composite Sites

Although Figure 4.1 shows three different sites involved in serving the contents of one document, it is possible, indeed likely, that these functions will be combined into fewer servers. It is likely that advertising and profiling be done within the same enterprise, so a single request (and cookie) would suffice to retrieve personal information that would more precisely target the ads that are returned. It is equally possible that a Web page contains references to different ad/profile services, providing revenue to the referrer from multiple sources.

PROXY SERVERS AND BROWSER CACHES

When a browser makes an HTTP request, that request is not always served from the server specified in a URL. Many Internet Service Providers (ISPs) make use of proxy servers to reduce Internet traffic. Proxy servers are used to cache frequently requested content at a location between its intended source and an end user. Such proxies are commonly employed by large ISPs like America Online and Earthlink. In some cases, an HTTP request may not even leave the user's PC. It may be satisfied from the browser's local cache of recently accessed objects.

Figure 4.2 illustrates several aspects of the proxy problem. Proxy servers can introduce three problems: First, a proxy may deliver outdated content. Although Web pages can include tags that tell proxy servers whether or not the content may be cached and when content expires, these tags are often omitted by Webmasters or ignored by proxy servers. Second, proxies may satisfy a content request without properly notifying the

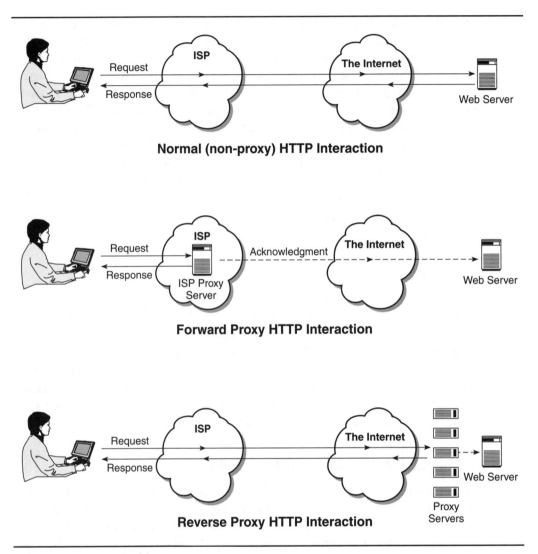

FIGURE 4.2 Proxy Architectures

originating server that the request has been served by the proxy. When a proxy handles a request, convention dictates that it should forward to the intended server, a message that indicates that a proxy response has been made. This is not reliable. As a consequence your Webhouse may miss key events that are otherwise required to make sense of the events that comprise a browser/Website session. Third, if the user has come though a proxy, the Website will not know who made the page request unless a cookie is present.

It is important to make liberal use of expiration dates and no-proxy tags in the HTML content of your Website. This will help ensure that you are getting as much data as possible for your warehouse.

The type of proxy we are referring to in this discussion is called a *forward proxy*. It is outside of your control because it belongs to a networking company or to an ISP. Another type of proxy server called a *reverse proxy* can be placed in front of your enterprise's Web servers to help them off-load requests for frequently accessed content. This kind of proxy is entirely within your control and usually presents no impediment to Webhouse data collection. It should be able to supply the same kind of log information as that produced by a Web server and discussed in the following section.

Browser Caches

Browser caches also introduce uncertainties in our attempts to track all of the events that occur during a user session. Most browsers store a copy of recently retrieved objects such as HTML pages and images in a local object cache in the PC's file system. If the user returns to a page already in his local browser cache (for example, by clicking the "back" button), no record of this event will be sent to the server, and the event not recorded. This means that we can never be certain that we have a full map of the user's actions. At best we can strive to obtain a tree representation of a session, with each leaf an object fetched from a Website and stamped with the time that the object was first requested by the browser.

As with proxies, we can attempt to force the browser to always obtain objects from a server rather than from cache by including appropriate "no cache" HTML tags, but we may not choose to do this because of performance- or other content-related reasons.

A similar uncertainty can be introduced when a user opens multiple browser windows to the same Website. The user may have multiple views of different pages of the site available on his PC screen, but there isn't any way for the Web server to know this.

WEB SERVER LOGS

All Web servers have the ability to log client interactions into one or more log files or databases or to pipe the log information to other applications in real time. These data elements are also available to be passed to real time applications using the Web server's Common Gateway Interface (CGI). Table 4.1 lists some of the typical data elements available from most Web servers.

The original standard for Web server logs was the Common Log Format (CLF), sometimes called the CLOG. This standard included the seven data elements checked in the CLF column in Table 4.1. Two additional elements were added in the Extended Common Log Format Standard (ECLF), and these are checked in the ECLF column of Table 4.1. Various Web servers add additional loggable parameters, but these are inevitably limited by the information contained in the basic HTTP protocol. The log data elements are discussed in more detail in the following paragraphs.

Data Element	*CLF**	*ECLF**	*Description*
Host	✓	✓	Fully qualified domain name of the client or its IP address if the name is unavailable.
Ident	✓	✓	Identity information supplied by the client, if it has identd activated.
Authuser	✓	✓	If the request was for a password-protected document, then this is the userID used in the request.
Time	✓	✓	Time the request reached the server in CLF time format {dd/Mmm/yyyy:hh:mm:ss zone}.
Request	✓	✓	The first request line from the client (usually in quotes).
Status	✓	✓	Three-digit status code returned to the client.
Bytes	✓	✓	Number of bytes returned to the client excluding HTTP headers.
Referrer		✓	URL of the referring server.
User-agent		✓	Name and version of the client (browser).
Filename			filename.
Time-to-serve			Time to serve the request (seconds).
IP-address			IP address of the remote host (see "host" above).
Server-port			Canonical Port of the server serving the request.
Process-ID			Process ID of the child that serviced the request.
Formatted-time			The time, in the specified strftime(3) format.
URL-requested			The URL path requested.
Server-name			The canonical name of the server serving the request.
Cookie			The value of the cookie retrieved from the client's cookie file.

* Common Log Format (CLF) and the Extended Common Log Format Standard (ECLF).

TABLE 4.1 Web Server Log Data Elements

The Web server's log data is the primary source of the clickstream. Each time the Web server responds to an HTTP request, an entry is made in the Web server's log file. The log file presents a particularly difficult analytical challenge. Although an entry is made for each service response, the server may be servicing hundreds or even thousands of user sessions concurrently. Because of this, the entries for a particular session are not contiguous. Individual records that comprise the session's footprints are scattered throughout the log and must be gathered together before a complete session analysis can be completed. Figure 4.3 shows a fragment of a log file. The log records have been truncated to 80 characters in order to fit onto a page in this book. Note that of all the records in the sample log, three belong to a single session from IP address 162.119.232.100.

Host

The host is the Internet address of the browser or other agent making the HTTP request. This is the address to which the server's response will be sent. In our example this would be the IP address of the customer's PC; the host is initially acquired by the Web server as a numeric IP address, like "209.45.122.19." Most Web servers have the ability to resolve this address into a text domain name using an Internet query protocol called *reverse address lookup*. The IP address is sent back through the Internet to a router that can authoritatively resolve the domain name, which is then returned to the requestor. This makes logs much more readable, but doing reverse address lookup in real time can increase the load on the server by as much as 40 percent, an unacceptable overhead in high-volume systems.

IP address resolution can be done downstream from the Web server in the clickstream post-processor, and this is the method we will recommend for high-volume Websites.

Most networked PCs don't have fixed IP addresses. Rather, the IP address is assigned dynamically to the PC at the time that the user makes a connection to his ISP through a dial-up or cable modem. Even though the IP address is dynamic, it remains fixed during a browser session and can be used to tie the session events together.

```
204.184.107.249 - - [26/Jul/1999:10:30:40 -0800] "GET ~lpease HTTP/1.0" 302
202.231.204.76 - - [26/Jul/1999:10:31:44 -0800] "GET /~webcom/html/publiciz
198.253.36.22 - - [26/Jul/1999:10:31:44 -0800] "GET /~teapot/vr9.html HTTP/
209.185.188.232 - - [26/Jul/1999:10:31:44 -0800] "GET ~progsys HTTP/1.0" 30
208.255.225.254 - - [26/Jul/1999:10:32:48 -0800] "GET / HTTP/1.0" 200 9345
199.206.254.61 - - [26/Jul/1999:10:34:56 -0800] "GET / HTTP/1.0" 400 848 ""
216.81.26.224 - - [26/Jul/1999:10:34:56 -0800] "GET /index.html HTTP/1.0" 2
162.119.232.100 - - [26/Jul/1999:10:34:56 -0800] "GET /info/raves/ HTTP/1.0
207.34.100.198 - - [26/Jul/1999:10:37:04 -0800] "GET /duplex/sk8_1184.html
206.154.159.40 - - [26/Jul/1999:10:38:08 -0800] "GET /~ctt/insects.html HTT
195.122.15.31 - - [26/Jul/1999:10:38:08 -0800] "GET /jyda HTTP/1.0" 302 390
166.70.45.193 - - [26/Jul/1999:10:28:32 -0800] "POST /cgi-bin/dns_check HTT
205.142.31.16 - - [26/Jul/1999:10:34:56 -0800] "POST /cgi-bin/dns_check HTT
205.142.31.16 - - [26/Jul/1999:10:36:00 -0800] "POST /cgi-bin/dns_check HTT
199.8.80.189 - - [26/Jul/1999:10:33:52 -0800] "POST /cgi-bin/dns_check HTTP
204.184.107.249 - - [26/Jul/1999:10:30:40 -0800] "GET ~lpease HTTP/1.0" 302
202.231.204.76 - - [26/Jul/1999:10:31:44 -0800] "GET /~webcom/html/publiciz
198.253.36.22 - - [26/Jul/1999:10:31:44 -0800] "GET /~teapot/vr9.html HTTP/
209.185.188.232 - - [26/Jul/1999:10:31:44 -0800] "GET ~progsys HTTP/1.0" 30
208.255.225.254 - - [26/Jul/1999:10:32:48 -0800] "GET / HTTP/1.0" 200 9345
199.206.254.61 - - [26/Jul/1999:10:34:56 -0800] "GET / HTTP/1.0" 400 848 ""
216.81.26.224 - - [26/Jul/1999:10:34:56 -0800] "GET /index.html HTTP/1.0" 2
162.119.232.100 - - [26/Jul/1999:10:35:58 -0800] "GET /help/webcommerce/bui
207.34.100.198 - - [26/Jul/1999:10:37:04 -0800] "GET /duplex/sk8_1184.html
206.154.159.40 - - [26/Jul/1999:10:38:08 -0800] "GET /~ctt/insects.html HTT
195.122.15.31 - - [26/Jul/1999:10:38:08 -0800] "GET /joda HTTP/1.0" 302 390
205.188.208.70 - - [26/Jul/1999:10:36:00 -0800] "GET /~pinknoiz/covert/wilc
198.253.36.22 - - [26/Jul/1999:10:33:52 -0800] "GET /~amraam/es3a.html HTTP
207.34.100.198 - - [26/Jul/1999:10:39:12 -0800] "GET /duplex/sk8_1188a.htm
142.165.107.52 - - [26/Jul/1999:10:39:12 -0800] "GET ~dynamic HTTP/1.0" 302
207.34.100.198 - - [26/Jul/1999:10:34:56 -0800] "GET /duplex/sk8_1058.html
162.119.232.100 - - [26/Jul/1999:10:38:08 -0800] "GET /help/webcommerce/sho
207.138.42.10 - - [26/Jul/1999:10:39:12 -0800] "GET ~wrsl HTTP/1.0" 302 178
129.74.235.127 - - [26/Jul/1999:10:40:16 -0800] "GET /oldgolf/feathery.html
161.142.78.82 - - [26/Jul/1999:10:37:04 -0800] "GET / HTTP/1.0" 200 9345 [2
209.197.236.4 - - [26/Jul/1999:10:42:24 -0800] "GET / HTTP/1.0" 200 9345 ""
208.250.29.19 - - [26/Jul/1999:10:44:32 -0800] "GET /tedsite/drillcompfluid
205.142.31.16 - - [26/Jul/1999:10:36:00 -0800] "POST /cgi-bin/dns_check HTT
208.255.225.254 - - [26/Jul/1999:10:39:12 -0800] "POST /cgi-bin/dns_check H
24.4.254.39 - - [26/Jul/1999:10:34:56 -0800] "POST /cgi-bin/contract HTTP/1
24.4.254.39 - - [26/Jul/1999:10:34:56 -0800] "POST /cgi-bin/contract HTTP/1
205.142.31.16 - - [26/Jul/1999:10:37:04 -0800] "POST /cgi-bin/dns_check HTT
208.255.225.254 - - [26/Jul/1999:10:40:16 -0800] "GET /cgi-bin/application
129.188.33.221 - - [26/Jul/1999:10:32:48 -0800] "GET /help/start.shtml HTTP
216.77.241.11 - - [26/Jul/1999:10:31:44 -0800] "GET /help/webcommerce/build
192.31.7.244 - - [26/Jul/1999:10:38:08 -0800] "GET /help/form_proc/ HTTP/1.
192.31.7.244 - - [26/Jul/1999:10:37:04 -0800] "GET /html/tutor/forms/intro.
209.203.119.62 - - [26/Jul/1999:10:37:04 -0800] "GET /html/tutor/forms/intr
209.30.244.168 - - [26/Jul/1999:10:39:12 -0800] "GET /info/raves/ HTTP/1.0"
208.255.225.254 - - [26/Jul/1999:10:38:08 -0800] "GET /info/options.shtml H
12.10.41.244 - - [26/Jul/1999:10:32:48 -0800] "POST /cgi-bin/dns_check HTTP
203.134.2.91 - - [26/Jul/1999:10:34:56 -0800] "POST /cgi-bin/dns_check HTTP
```

FIGURE 4.3   Web Server Log Example

Because of the prevalence of dynamic IP assignments, many host names, by themselves, provide little information of value. They do, however, provide a key for tying together diverse user session events in the absence of a more reliable mechanism like cookies or server-generated session IDs. Even though many host names are of little meaning, some can provide important information. For example, the country in which the domain is registered may be indicated by a country code such as .uk or .au for the United Kingdom or Australia, respectively. Also, a canonical host name such as ".aol." can be of use in identifying users from large well-known ISPs like America Online or Web TV. A subset of host names will be important to various organizations within your enterprise. For example, a logged host name of "test-scooter.av.pa-x.dec.com" will tell a Webmaster that the Alta Vista indexing spider has visited his site. The need for this information will probably require you to retain the hostname or a portion of it as a dimension in your warehouse schema.

Ident

The ident data element is an arbitrary identifier supplied by client applications that support a protocol called identd (identification daemon). This authentication scheme is seldom, if ever, used by Web browsers.

Authuser

The authenticated user data element is a user ID passed in a request made via the HTTP secure sockets layer (SSL). This field will be filled in if a user has correctly passed a secure server logon, and can be used to associate user log records when operating under the SSL protocol.

Time

This is usually the time when the Web server completed responding to the HTTP request. See specific Web server specifications to determine exactly what time is logged.

Request

Request is the actual request line from the browser. It might typically look like the following:

```
"GET /images/under-c.gif HTTP/1.0"
```

In this example, "GET" is the HTTP method—the action being requested by the browser. The next segment, "/images/under-c.gif" is the URI (Uniform Resource Identifier) of the object being requested. The final segment, "HTTP/1.0" is the protocol version that the client is requesting be used to complete the action. The two most common HTTP methods are GET and POST. GET requests an object from a Web server, while POST sends information from the browser to the Web server, usually resulting in the server forwarding a request for action to a program interfaced to the Web server via the server's Common Gateway Interace (CGI).

Most Web servers have facilities that permit CGI applications to add records to the server's common log files. This can provide an excellent mechanism for enriching clickstream data without the necessity of merging application and log data later in the analytical processes.

Status

Status is the three-digit status code, which the server returns to the browser, such as 200 (OK) or 404 (Not Found). See Table 4.2.

Bytes

Bytes is the count of bytes returned by the server to the client

Referrer

The referrer is a text string that can be sent by the client to indicate the original source of a request or a link. This data element was added to the HTTP 1.0 protocol to allow a Website to backtrack references to their origins. This allows credits for advertisement clickthroughs as well as other types of referral credits. A referrer log entry can take the form of the URL of origin, followed by the resource to which the reference points:

```
http://www.webcom.com/megasite/ -> /index.html
```

User-Agent

The user agent is the name and version of the client software making the request and the operating system under which the client is operating.

100	Continue
101	Switching Protocols
200	OK
201	Created
202	Accepted
203	Non-Authoritative Information
204	No Content
205	Reset Content
206	Partial Content
300	Multiple Choices
301	Moved Permanently
302	Moved Temporarily
303	See Other
304	Not Modified
305	Use Proxy
400	Bad Request
401	Unauthorized
402	Payment Required
403	Forbidden
404	Not Found
405	Method Not Allowed
406	Not Acceptable
407	Proxy Authentication Required
408	Request Time-out
408	Conflict
410	Gone
411	Length Required
412	Precondition Failed
413	Request Entity Too Large
414	Request-URI Too Large
425	Unsupported Media Type
500	Internal Server Error
501	Not Implemented
502	Bad Gateway
503	Service Unavailable
504	Gateway Time-out
505	HTTP Version not supported

These return code examples are taken from the Apache Web server.
Other servers will have similar codes but meanings may vary somewhat.

TABLE 4.2   HTTP Status Codes

This information is used by the Web server to determine the feature set supported by the client browser and to ensure that the response contains only items that can properly be interpreted and displayed by the browser. For example, if a browser doesn't support ActiveX objects, then you don't want to include such objects in your response. User agents need not be confined to browsers, as shown by the second of these two entries:

```
"Mozilla/4.0 (compatible; MSIE 4.01;Windows98)"

"Scooter/2.0 G.R.A.B. V1.1.0"
```

The first of the two user-agent log entries comes from a conventional Microsoft Internet Explorer browser running under Windows 98. The second comes from an Alta Vista search engine spider running on an unspecified operating system. You may want to exclude page requests from spiders and robots in your clickstream analysis.

Filename

The filename is the portion of a URL that specifies the path and name of a file being accessed. It is sometimes expressed as a *fully qualified* (complete) path and sometimes as a path *relative* to the home page in a Website directory structure.

Time-to-Serve

This is time it takes a Web server to send the response to an HTTP request. This metric is useful in computing user dwell time and server performance, but it may not be available from some Web servers.

IP Address

The numeric IP address of a Website. This can be expressed as four binary octets (125.32.221.26) or as a decimal, octal, or hexadecimal number. Note that a forthcoming IP6 standard greatly extends this address length.

Server Port

This is the number of the TCP/IP port on a host, which has served the logged activity. It's standard Web practice to reserve port 80 for an HTTP server and port 443 to a secure HTTP server (using SSL).

Process ID

The number of the Web server child process that has served the request.

URL

A full URL (Uniform Resource Locator) contains several segments as shown in the example below. The scheme specifies a communication protocol such as HTTP or FTP. The hostname is the fully qualified Internet address of the host containing the information and can be a name or IP address. The (optional) port number is the port on the host to address the message. The document path is an absolute or relative pathname to the requested document. The query string is a text string following the path that will be delivered to an application at the host. In common practice the query string is used for myriad application-specific purposes beyond simply carrying queries. Here's an example:

```
http://ralphkimball.com:433/seminars/schedule.html?tokyo+fall+2001
```

scheme	=	`http://`
hostname	=	`ralphkimball.com`
port	=	`:443`
document path	=	`/seminars/schedule.html`
query string	=	`?tokyo+fall+2001` (everything after the question mark)

To add to an already confusing definition, you may occasionally come across the term URI, which is an abbreviation for Uniform Resource Indicator. URI is a generic category that includes both URLs and Uniform Resource Names. A Uniform Resource Name is a loosely specified term for a name that uniquely identifies a resource, such as a document, on the Internet.

COOKIES

In an effort to compensate for HTTP's lack of session state, a mechanism called a cookie exchange was added to Web servers and clients. This mechanism has been universally adopted by Web server and browser vendors, but it isn't officially a part of the standard HTTP 1.1 protocol. The cookie mechanism provides a Web server with the ability to store a text string on a client computer that can later be read by the server. Cookies can be *persistent* or *session level*. A session-level cookie is stored in the client computer's memory but isn't retained once the browser application is closed. A persistent cookie is stored on disk, and can be read at a later date. Cookies are somewhat secure in that they can only be read by an HTTP client at (or purporting to be at) the domain name stored in the cookie file. This, of course, means that a client at domain X can set a cookie to be read later by a server at domain Y, as long as domain Y was specified by the original Set-Cookie script.

Cookies provide the primary means used today to identify users returning to a Website, and the primary mechanism used by profilers to track users from Website to Website. Because the *de facto* cookie standard exists and cookie mechanisms are included (and activated) in all commercial browsers, the cookie mechanism is likely to persist as the primary state object in Web applications for some time, even though more capable and secure alternatives are frequently put forth.

FINDING AND INTERPRETING YOUR COOKIE FILES

Use one of the next two sets of instructions, depending on whether your browser is Microsoft Internet Explorer or Netscape Navigator.

Microsoft Internet Explorer

If you use Microsoft's Internet Explorer, each of your cookies will reside in its own file in the directory `C:\Windows\Cookies\` or, in the Windows NT system, `C:\Windows\Profiles\Administrator\Cookies\`.

Each cookie has its own .txt file. Double-clicking a file name will open the cookie file in the NotePad application. Each IE cookie will have the following format with fields delimited by a new-line character:

```
name
value
domain+path
secure (0 or 1)
expiration date
expiration time
last_used date
last_used time
*
```

Example:

```
CNNid|cf194799|cnn.com/|0|2189574144|32107986|2410210720|29271805|*
```

Cookie Contents

The contents of a cookie are very simple. The uses to which they can be put are not. The standard Set-Cookie script allows the Web server to specify the following:

`Name`	=	Arbitrary string naming the cookie
`Value`	=	String value to be stored in the cookie
`Expires`	=	Cookie expiration datetime (GMT)
`Domain`	=	Domain name of server(s) which can read the cookie
`Path`	=	Pathname in the domain for which the cookie is valid
`Secure`	=	Must be transmitted back to the host via SSL (HTTPS)

Netscape Communicator or Navigator

If you use one of Netscape's browsers, your cookies will all reside in the same file, probably in:

```
C:\ProgramFiles\Netscape\Users\Default\cookies.txt
```

All of your cookies will be in this file, each on its own line. Double-click the file to open it with NotePad. To make the lines easier to read, turn off the Word Wrap option NotePad's File menu.

Each line of the Netscape cookie file will have the following format with fields delimited by a Tab character:

```
domain
secure (TRUE or FALSE)
path
readable by anyone (always FALSE in current versions)
expiration datetime
name
value
```

Example:

```
.cnn.com  TRUE  /  FALSE  2145801632  CNNid  cf194728
```

Cookie Tutorial—Examining Your Own Cookie File

Perhaps the best way to become familiar with the scope of cookies is to examine the contents of your own cookie file(s). If you haven't explicitly turned cookies off in your browser, then you have cookies to examine. If you've used your browser extensively, then you have lots of cookies since almost every major Website will attempt to "cookie" you at some time. Your cookie container varies depending on the specific browser you use.

Cookie Example 1—Portal Site (Yahoo)

If your browser is set to accept cookies, chances are good that you will find one or more cookies in your cookie repository from Yahoo visits. In Netscape format, your Yahoo cookie looks like this:

```
yahoo.com/ TRUE / FALSE 1271362380 B adpddjv3hmqhr
```

The domain and path ".yahoo.com/" instruct the browser to let any server at yahoo.com access this cookie. The leading period enables any subdomain of yahoo.com, and the trailing slash indicates that any document or application within the domain has similar access permissions. The content of the cookie is simple: The name of the cookie is "B"—probably for browser—and the value assigned to this particular browser by Yahoo is "adpddjv3hmqhr." This value seems to be a fixed ID and doesn't change over time.

Cookie Example 2—Ad Server (DoubleClick)

Even if you don't recall ever visiting DoubleClick's Website, when you review your cookie file chances are very high that you'll find a DoubleClick cookie with the following format:

```
doubleclick.net TRUE   / FALSE 1920500111 id 7c56e94f
```

Your DoubleClick ID, "7c56e94f" is a hexadecimal integer assigned to you (actually, to your browser) the first time you were "cookied" by DoubleClick. When a Website wants to retrieve an ad from DoubleClick, it obtains it from DoubleClick either directly or via a redirect. For example, a page from the *Milwaukee Journal-Sentinel*'s Website contains the following embedded reference to DoubleClick:

```
IMG SRC="http://ad.doubleclick.net/ad/adauction.milwalkee.com/
```

This reference appears to request a banner ad from DoubleClick, selected from a pool of ads judged to be appropriate for Milwaukee-area Websites.

Cookie Example 3—Profiler (MatchLogic)

As you look through your cookie file(s) you may well find an unrecognized cookie with the somewhat ambiguous domain of ".preferences.com." This domain actually belongs to MatchLogic, Inc., a division of @Home Corp. A MatchLogic cookie looks like this:

```
preferences.com  TRUE / FALSE 1182141267 ID t5kYzrcEocZfeRpQMBkqUq
```

The MatchLogic PreferencesID is a unique identifier into MatchLogic's demographic detail database. This ID appears to be long enough to contain error-correcting codes that can detect and correct IDs, that have been modified.

Cookie Example 4—Microsoft GUID

If you've ever visited a Microsoft Website your browser has probably been cookied in a kind of two-for-one deal. Microsoft places multiple cookies with the same ID into your cookie file when you first visit. In this example one cookie is for microsoft.com (the Microsoft Corporation) and the other is for msn.com (the Microsoft Network). This permits diverse Microsoft business enterprises like Microsoft Corp., MSN, and MSNBC to track you under a single ID across Microsoft entities:

```
microsoft.com TRUE / FALSE MC1 GUID=0aa40842122411d3a28a00805fd7cd96
msn.com        TRUE / FALSE MC1 GUID=0aa40842122411d3a28a00805fd7cd96
```

Cookie Example 5—Local Applications

Some browser-based applications in Java and other "sandboxed" languages find the local cookie file is a good place to store state data between invocations of the application. For example, one of the authors' cookie files contains a number of entries like the following, which were placed by a NASA Java satellite tracking program. These are intended for local use for reinitializing the Java application's state, and not for sending back to NASA's Website.

```
liftoff.msfc.nasa.gov TRUE /RealTime/ 948082706 sky 0%2C0%2C300%2C350
liftoff.msfc.nasa.gov TRUE /RealTime/ 948082706 category All
```

UNIVERSAL SYSTEM IDENTIFIERS

When first conceived, cookies could optionally be set to be readable by anyone, so it was possible to write a cookie with a universal ID that would identify your computer to any Web application that queried it. This feature was eliminated because of privacy and security concerns. The idea of universal identifiers has not, however, been abandoned, and we expect that some hardware identification mechanism may eventually become commonly used if current debates on privacy don't result in a legislative prohibition of such uses. A number of candidates are being proposed as seeds for a universal system identifier.

First, every Ethernet network card has its own unique hardware Ethernet address. This addressing scheme was incorporated into the earliest Ethernet specifications drawn up at Xerox's Palo Alto Research Center (PARC) 20 years ago by Messrs. Dalal, Metcalfe, and Shoch. All Ethernet card makers have followed it ever since. In modern network cards this address can be read by the operating system software and is therefore accessible to browser applications. If your computer doesn't have a network card, then it doesn't have an Ethernet address.

The second candidate is a system-readable unique serial number in CPU chips. In PCs this feature has only been seen recently, initially in Intel Pentium III chips. Again, privacy advocates have objected to making this available as a universal identifier and the Pentium III microprocessor serial number can be blocked at a BIOS level if desired.

QUERY STRINGS

In an HTTP request everything to the right of the question mark is considered to be a "query string." The query string needn't contain a query. In fact, it's usually used for any content being returned from a form in the browser to a Website. The HTTP protocol specifies that the query string can't contain spaces. By convention, plus signs (+) are used to represent spaces. Query string contents are expressed as *label=value* pairs, separated by ampersands (&). The following example shows an HTTP request sent from a browser to the cgi-bin/query application at the AltaVista search portal. In the actual HTTP, there wasn't a line separator or space between the end of the URL and the question mark. It's included here for clarity.

```
http://www.altavista.com/cgi-bin/query
?pg=q&kl=XX&q=cd+changer+mechanic+control+software&search=Search
```

This query string has four label=value pairs:

```
pg=q
kl=XX
q=cd+changer+mechanic+control+software
search=Search
```

The third of these pairs (q=) contains the string that was actually entered in the Alta Vista search text field. The value of the query string becomes greatly enhanced when the search engine makes the effort to return the query string to your Website as part of a referrer record. The following entry from the clickstream log of the author's Website shows the value of this information. The Website received this hit from a Czech host, ns.felk.cvut.cz, on May 25, 1999. The referrer string contains not only the information that the clickthough came from Alta Vista, it also contains the actual keywords that the user entered to find this site: "CD changer mechanic control software."

```
ns.felk.cvut.cz.17247927664073820 - - [25/May/1999:15:27:53 -0500]
"GET /moodmake/moodmake.html HTTP/1.0" 200 2197 "http://
www.altavista.com/cgi-bin/query
?pg=q&kl=XX&q=cd+changer+mechanic+control+software"
"Mozilla/4.0 (compatible; MSIE 5.0; Windows NT)"
```

As an aside, the number "17247927664073820" is the value of the cookie set by the author's Web server during this session. Should the visitor return at a later time, this number will help to identify him as a previous visitor.

A Webmaster or site marketing analyst will find referrer information invaluable when evaluating the effectiveness of keywords, metatags, and site advertising. It is essential to retain this information for downstream analysis in the schema of our Webhouse.

Templates

Most Web applications that generate dynamic content place much of this content within the context of a fixed page format or *template*. A news organization, for example, might serve all sports stories embedded into a sports-page template. An on-line movie retailer might put movie reviews into a common template in which only the review content changes, while the page format remains fixed. For page-event tracking, we might want to retain both template and content IDs in our data warehouse. This is particularly true if our site serves identical content into diverse templates, with the template being selected dynamically depending on the visitor profile.

Although the ID numbers for templates and specific content can come from an application server, it is desirable to encode both the template and content IDs in the URI of your pages as they are served. Using this technique ensures that this important data can be carried in the Web server's log records and not detached in some way from the actual content. As an example, here are two URIs for two articles from Yahoo's Reuters news service. Both of these URIs refer to stories from the "tx" news service on 06/01/99. The first is from the health subcategory (hl) and the content is identified as "sm2_1." The second is from the technical category (tc), and the content is identified as "microsoft_23.html." By parsing these URIs, we can retrieve the embedded unique template and content identifiers.

```
http://dailynews.yahoo.com/tx/19990601/hl/sm2_1.html
http://dailynews.yahoo.com/tx/19990601/tc/microsoft_23.html
```

SUMMARY

In this chapter we have examined the clickstream from Web server and Web application logs as the primary data source for our Web-enabled data warehouse. In Chapter 8 we will continue this thread by following the data through the extract/transform/load process we call the clickstream post-processor.

We have not discussed the advisability of making versus buying software to do clickstream post-processing. We know that this is a field that is evolving rapidly and that several commercial products are being developed to serve these needs. In some cases it will be appropriate to purchase these products. In other cases, particularly when dealing with a diverse population of Web servers within the enterprise, it won't be possible to find a commercial solution to the post-processor, and this portion of the system will need to be developed internally.

In the following chapter we will focus on designing the corporate Websites to support data warehouseing, and concentrate on setting standards within the enterprise that will ensure that clickstream data is as accurate and meaningful as possible.

CHAPTER 5

Designing the Website to Support Warehousing

This chapter deals with the special requirements that data warehousing imposes on the design of the systems that provide information to the warehouse. We have seen in virtually all data warehouse applications that the need for conformed, "clean" data inevitably places certain requirements on the upstream systems that collect, process, and deliver this data to the warehouse. In a traditional data warehouse, it is often an arduous and sometimes impossible task to get necessary information from legacy information systems into the warehouse because of organizational inertia, legacy system fragility, and inadequate management support. Though it might not appear that clickstream analysis is handicapped by the constraints of legacy systems, in this chapter we will show that even at this early point in the art there are many issues that, if not addressed from the outset, will make clickstream analysis difficult or even meaningless for data warehouse applications.

This chapter describes the proactive steps that you should take to make your Website most effectively support data Webhousing. The two most important steps are (1) provide an elaborate attribution of each Web page so that the clickstream data mart can understand what the visitor was touching, and (2) set up a cookie program that consistently identifies visitors over time and across the servers that belong to your enterprise.

MONOLITHIC VS. DISTRIBUTED WEB SERVERS

In the previous chapter we discussed the possibility that a Web page's content isn't necessarily obtained from just one Web server, but may be provided by servers outside the enterprise like banner ad servers. We need also to take seriously the likelihood that, over time, your enterprise will be serving the Web from multiple servers. See Figure 5.1. Each

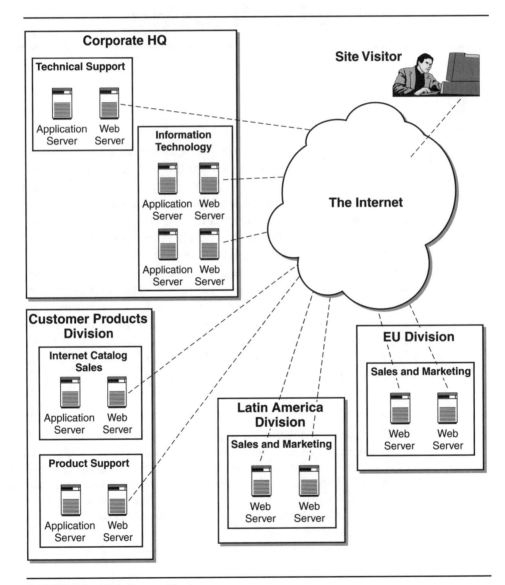

FIGURE 5.1   Web Server Clusters

department will want its own Web server just as it wants its own computers and data marts. In fact, Web services are likely to be developed departmentally at first, and eventually be given company-wide uniform look and feel and navigation standards by a corporate Webmaster.

The corporate Webmaster provides navigation tools that span departmental servers and provides integrated corporate search engines and tables of contents. But the corporate Webmaster probably won't be the final arbiter of content. In most instances, individual departments will control their own content: product catalogs will be maintained by marketing or sales, product help pages by customer service, and press releases by corporate communications. Various divisions and departments may elect to host their content on different Web servers, with the collections of servers appearing to the outside world as a "corporate site."

The corporate Webmaster is your friend, but his or her responsibilities and duties may not include the incentive or authority to ensure the capture of fully conformed data for your marts and warehouses. As a company data Webhouse manager your job will be first to establish data marts for individual divisions and departments, then to ensure that data can be conformed into a central data warehouse with the agreement and assistance of the corporate Webmaster and other key players within your organization. We discuss this further in Chapter 15.

SYNCHRONIZE YOUR SERVERS

The Web-enabled data warehouse collects timestamped event information from many different sources both within and outside the enterprise. Web responses are likely to be delivered by a loosely coupled network of servers and proxies. Analyzing user behavior depends on knowing exactly when an event occurred relative to other events. This requires maintaining a precise time standard across all data sources. Each computer and program involved needs to know what time it is, not to the nearest minute or even to the nearest second, but to subsecond accuracy. This accuracy level is essential in order to properly merge the sequence of user events within a session. For analytical purposes we need to assume that timestamps are accurate to a tenth of a second. We should strive for 100-millisecond accuracy, relative to an absolute standard time. Without setting a goal of this precision, it's likely that the various log records we collect will be at least several seconds out of synchronicity, making the required timing analyses impossible.

Maintaining such clock accuracy across diverse systems is a problem that is well understood in military and aviation systems, and even in some financial applications like securities trading systems (which require 3-second accuracy). Subsecond time precision has not, until now, been a normal concern of commercial IT departments. As the implementer of a Web-enabled data warehouse, you may well meet with skepticism when trying to convince an operations manager that such accuracy is not only necessary but is possible.

The accuracy we need isn't obtainable by manually setting a clock, as we might be tempted to do in our PC. It requires sophisticated synchronization tools.

Time Synchronization Tools and Techniques

Most computers contain a hardware clock to maintain system time. At their heart, computer clocks rely on a quartz crystal exactly like those used in quartz watches. And like quartz watches, computer clocks vary widely in accuracy and their ability to provide consistently accurate time. There aren't any standards for computer clock accuracy, so there's no way of knowing how accurate any given computer clock is likely to be. In our experience there's little correlation between computer price and clock accuracy. Quartz clock crystals are quite sensitive to temperature variations. Very high-quality quartz clocks enclose their crystal in a constant-temperature oven to avoid temperature-induced drift. Wristwatch quartz crystals are calibrated to an "oven" temperature of 98.6 degrees. Unfortunately, you are unlikely to encounter this technology in a computer clock, which can drift several seconds or more every day. We need to come up with methods for compensating for the inevitable inaccuracies of computer clocks.

There are three steps in achieving time synchronization across the enterprise. See Figure 5.2.

1. Reduce the drift of each individual clock, relative to standard time.
2. Synchronize all of the clocks in a system to a single system master clock.
3. Synchronize the system master clock to a primary reference source.

The first and second steps can be achieved with a software solution. There are both commercial and shareware packages available to synchronize the clocks of computers within a network to primary reference

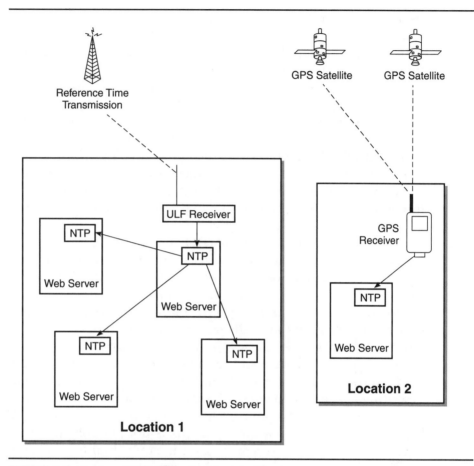

FIGURE 5.2 System-Wide Time Synchronization

source. An excellent source of technical information is the documentation for the Internet Network Time Protocol (NTP), which can be found at http://ftp.std.com/obi/Networking/rfc/rfc1305.txt. The best time synchronization software computes the drift of each dependent machine relative to a primary reference source, and then establishes a correction factor that is applied frequently to each individual computer to keep its clock "nudged" into synchronism with the system selected as the master. Frequent small nudges are greatly preferable to larger ones since they minimize cumulative drift and compensate for different drift rates among different machines.

The final task is to keep the master CPU synchronized with a primary reference source like the National Bureau of Standards. This has become quite easy in the last few years. There are several sources of accurate standard time. First, the National Bureau of Standards and other standards bodies broadcast coded time over ultra-low-frequency (ULF) radio signals. These can be picked up by special receivers designed for the purpose and can be queried by the master computer in a network. These receivers are very accurate and quite expensive. Second, time can be obtained from the Internet itself by querying a standards organization like the U.S. Naval Observatory or the Bureau of Standards. However because the network latency time varies and is unpredictable, this method isn't recommended. The third, and most satisfactory way to obtain accurate time is from the satellites of the Global Positioning System (GPS). GPS time signals accurate to within a microsecond are now obtainable from inexpensive GPS clocks that have standard RS-232 serial ports for direct computer connection. We recommend this method of obtaining the master, benchmark time for your computer system. It is inexpensive and precise. GPS clocks are also useful for systems that, because of location or platform peculiarities, can't be serviced by standard time synchronization software.

Some of your clickstream data or related events will come from sources like profilers and advertising servers that are outside of the control of your IT organization. Make sure that the timestamps on such externally derived data meet the same stringent accuracy requirements that you require for internal data. It is advisable to obtain a guarantee in writing of such when subscribing to these services, and to verify that the service has the technology in place to actually deliver data with fractional-second time accuracy. If this is not possible, make sure that in using this data, you recognize that it can be highly misleading.

Finally, beware of time-zone differences and daylight savings time. Try to establish an enterprise-wide standard for clock time. In the best of cases this will be Coordinated Universal Time (UTC), also known as Greenwich Mean Time (GMT). It won't be possible to use UTC in many instances because of IT department tradition or standards, so you will have to ensure that data from diverse sources is conformed to whatever standard your IT department has previously embraced. Hopefully this will be standard time in a specific time zone. In any case, don't accept data that switches back and forth from standard to daylight time. Most session identification algorithms won't understand these arbitrary time swings.

 All time stamps must be converted to UTC before they reach the Webhouse. Later in this book, we will augment these UTC times with end user wall clock times.

CONTENT LABELS FOR PAGES

If your enterprise Websites are typical, there won't be any standards for labeling Web content or for assigning descriptive attributes to this content. The need for supplying such labels will be low priority to the content providers in your enterprise; their highest priority will be to ensure that their Websites hang together and that there aren't any navigational dead ends or broken links.

Nonetheless it is essential that content labels be developed that will permit page events to be classified and coded for later analysis. These labels must be maintained at a division and/or departmental level because the source of the information is there. However, in a highly dynamic Website these labels may be generated from application files or directory structures without human intervention. The labels described here will directly affect the design of the page dimension in the clickstream data mart developed in Chapter 6. Although conceptually the assignment of descriptive labels to Web pages is simple, this is one of the most important and problematic steps in the entire development of the data Webhouse. Over the long run, the multiple attributes of a page cannot be deduced from the page's location in the Web server's filing system. In other words, don't expect the page's URL to describe the page. Attributes for a page need to be assigned by a joint team of Website and data Webhouse developers, and then made available to the Web log extract system so that pages can always be described accurately and fully. As large Websites morph in their structure and content, the Webhouse team must responsively track the attributes of these pages.

Bearing in mind that every business has its own unique information needs, here are a few examples of content labels and what they might be used for:

- Page source (How was the page event generated?)
  - Static
  - Dynamic order entry
  - Dynamic customer support
  - Open-ended number of dynamic page labels
  - Unknown
- Page template (What template set was used for delivery, e.g., frames vs. nonframes ?)
  - Catalog page—left navigation bar with banner ad and desert color scheme

- Index page—Top navigation buttons, no banner ad
- News frame type 1
- News frame type 2
- Page function (What kind of information does this page supply?)
  - Portal (welcome or splash page)
  - Site index
  - Product index
  - Catalog page
  - Product spec sheet
  - FAQ
  - Press release
  - News story
- Item code (What does a particular item number mean?)
  - Product code (manufacturer)
  - UPC (retailer)
  - ISBN (bookseller)
  - Story ID (news provider)
  - Lot ID (auction site)

Content Indexes for Static HTML

For Websites whose content is mostly in the form of static pages and ancillary object files, the primary source of page events is likely to be Web server log records. These records contain the URL of the requested object. Content indexes for this type of site will consist of separately maintained tables that cross-reference specific URLs to code values. For instance, an index entry might indicate that URL http://www.mysite/specs/sku_1407 refers to a product specification sheet, and that it refers to SKU 1407. This cross-reference table is a crucial table in the extract-transform-load (ETL) pipeline we set up to describe user sessions.

Content indexes for static HTML will need to be coded manually. The initial coding of a Website can be a painful process since it involves both the data warehouse group and the departmental or divisional content managers. Once it is done, however, it is easily maintained if the site doesn't undergo frequent radical changes.

Content Indexes for Dynamic HTML

If your page-event transactions are derived from a dynamic HTTP applications it is likely that the application servers can be asked to generate appropriate page event log entries, and that for the most part, the Web server log will provide mostly ancillary information. For this type of site the page content indexes can be derived directly from the content-providing application. In order to maintain consistency across the enterprise, the data warehouse group will have to supply code standards and values, and perhaps build or supply some kind of translation table if codes can't be coaxed directly from the content-supplying application.

A Simple Content Index Application

It may be necessary for the data warehouse group to provide a simple application that will enable the department content manager to quickly and easily construct and maintain the code tables needed by the data mart. For static Web pages, this simple client/server application will allow the local Webmaster to assign codes for each page using the URL (which automatically appears in the server logs) as a key. For dynamic page application servers, the content code tables serve key values and definitions that will be used in adding content codes to the dynamic content driver tables. Figure 5.3 shows what such an application might look like.

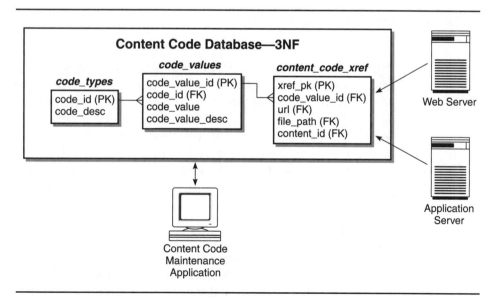

FIGURE 5.3   Code Table Maintenance Application

Table	Column	Description	Source	Example
code_types	code_id	Unique serial primary key	APP	3
	code_desc	Description of the code	DW	"Page Function'"
code_values	code_value_id	Unique serial primary key	APP	45
	code_id	FK to code_types table	APP	3
	code_value	Assigned code value	DW	5
	code_value_desc	Text definition of code value	DW	"Product Spec Sheet"
content_xref	xref_pk	Unique serial primary key	APP	5407
	code_value_id	FK to code_values table	APP	45
	url	Content URL (static content only)	DEPT	"www.mysite/specs/ sku_1407"
	file_path	Location of content (static or dynamic)	DEPT	"/specs/sku_1407.004"
	content_id	Unique content ID (dynamic content)	DEPT	93007621

APP = supplied by the application DW = entered by data warehouse group DEPT = entered by department-level personnel

TABLE 5.1   Content Code Database Schema

The code table maintenance implementation shown in Figure 5.3 consists of a simple third normal form database with a client/server or browser-based data entry application and connectivity to departmental or divisional Web and Web-application servers. The purpose of the application is to maintain content code indexes. Table 5.1 is a schema for this application. Note that most of the data is supplied by the Data Warehouse group or by the application itself. The departmental role is simply to code each new content element as it's added to the warehouse.

CONSISTENT COOKIES

We have already discussed the benefits—even the necessity—of cookieing visitors so that we can track their return visits to our Website. We've also discussed the distribution of departmental and divisional Websites within the corporation, and the imperative for local content control by diverse organizational elements. Over time it will be in the enterprise's best interest to maintain one cookie on a visitor's computer that can serve all organizations within the enterprise even if the enterprise's Websites are departmentally or divisionally distributed. Keeping in mind that a cookie can only be read by the host that placed it there, it becomes essential that cookie placement and acquisition be centralized. This is the role of a cookie server.

An enterprise-level cookie server is probably maintained by the corporate Webmaster. The purpose of the cookie server is to maintain an identity for each visitor regardless of his entry point into the enterprise Website complex. The user may have entered through a main corporate portal or may have entered a departmental server using a previously bookmarked URL. With an enterprise-level cookie server you will be able to tie together the user's visits regardless of his entry point. We suggest the use of a single cookie with the ID encoded into the cookie value and containing checksums or perhaps even error correcting codes so that you can detect and discard cookies that have been altered by the user or by cookie protection software. To avoid later privacy conflicts, don't put any human-readable information into cookies.

There are many different ways of using the cookie server. One method of obtaining a cookie-encapsulated user ID is to place on every potential departmental or divisional entry page a tag that calls the cookie server to read the corporate-level cookie. If the distributed server needs this value for site personalization the user ID can be returned to a hidden field in the page's HTML for later use—perhaps to be returned in the query string of the next HTTP request. If the user ID is only needed for post-analytical purposes, the cookie server can generate a server log entry to be merged with other log entries for post-session clickstream analysis.

NULL LOGGING SERVER

Throughout this discussion of data-warehouse enabled Websites we have made the assumption that page content information for the Webhouse database is extracted from Web server and application server logs. For various design, performance, or even political reasons it may not be possible to tap existing Web server log data for this information. We want to introduce an alternative method of capturing content data that avoids direct feeds from primary corporate Web servers and provides an independent source of Website activity. We call this facility the *null logging server*. It's particularly applicable to capturing data from a highly distributed corporate Website with a diversity of individual departmental servers.

The null logging server is a Web server whose primary mission is not to deliver content, but to accept log data. See Figure 5.4. It is a conventional Web server in that it responds to HTTP requests, but it doesn't deliver meaningful data in response to those requests, just a minimal null response. Assume that such a server has only one content file, a one-pixel transparent image called *nullpic.gif*. We embed into a catalog page the following HTML tag:

```
<IMG
SRC="http://logserver.mega-merc.com/nullpic.gif?
type=catalog&sku=bear089">
```

A tag like this would normally be used to fetch an in-line image for display on the Web page. In our case, however, we don't care about the returned image. The log server returns an image, but it's a null image. We're using the tag to send a query string to the null logging server that results in a log entry containing data destined for the Webhouse. In this case the information we want to log is the type of page (catalog) and the SKU which the page shows (bear089).

In the null logging server's log file we will find an entry something like the following:

```
walter.tnet.com.15040922815083660 - - [09/Jun/1999:15:25:25 -0700]
"GET /nullpic.gif?sku=bear089&color=brown&size=10inch
HTTP/1.0" 200 64" "Mozilla/4.04 [en] (WinNT; I)"
```

This log entry provides us with a host name, cookie value, time, and content information (the type of page and the SKU referenced).

This logging method can be rolled out in a diversified corporate Web hosting environment very quickly by simply convincing (or requiring) departmental or divisional Webmasters to include the null log server tags in their content. These can be placed manually in static pages or automatically in dynamically generated pages. The processing of these log requests will add very little to page download times and essentially none if placed at the bottom of a page. The only cautionary note is that if the null logging server is not available, the page will show a broken link icon at the point where the logging tag is embedded.

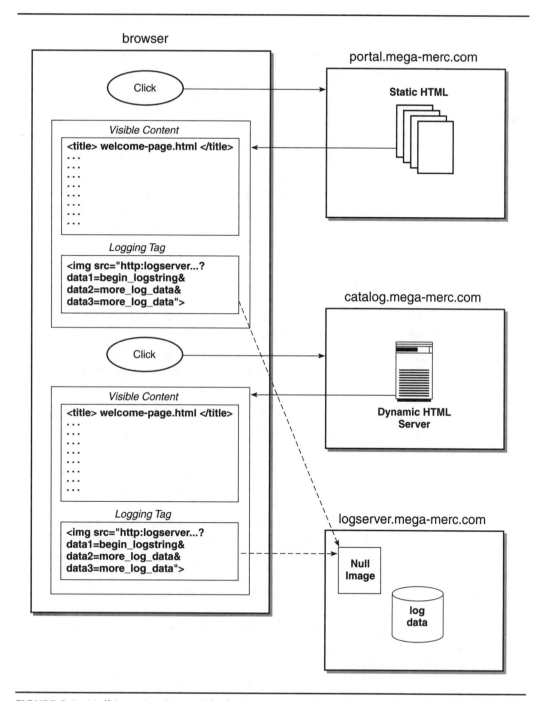

FIGURE 5.4   Null Logging Server Block Diagram

Although this may seem like a high-overhead approach, the actual returned data can be just a few bytes long. If the null server HTML tag is placed last in the target page, the page will be visible even if there is a delay in retrieving this tiny GIF file.

PERSONAL DATA REPOSITORY

Eventually a user's trust level or business requirements will evolve to the point where he is willing—or required—to identify himself to one of an enterprise's Websites. There are a number of very strong arguments for consolidating personal data, including demographics and credit information, into one and only one location within the enterprise. Regardless of which of an enterprise's subsidiary Websites first collects user information, we recommend that it be forwarded and maintained in a central repository, not at a departmental or divisional level. There are many reasons for this:

- Information such as addresses and telephone numbers stays current for all internal accessors.
- Access can be much better controlled and audited if the information to be protected is in one location and not distributed throughout an enterprise.
- The user is asked only once for personal information.
- Websites can quickly respond to changing legal requirements for privacy control.
- The user's access privileges to controlled or premium content can be monitored and granted on an enterprise-wide basis when needed.

It should be clear that an enterprise-level cookie server and a central personal data repository can be combined into a single database-driven application, accessible by all of an enterprise's Web servers. This architecture will serve the user in terms of improved privacy, the department in terms of sharing information between business units, and the data warehouse team in terms of maintaining consistent cookie and user IDs across data marts and enterprise-level data warehouses. At the same time, the team should recognize the extreme sensitivity of the personal data repository. If the cookie server is outside the firewall, then these functions should be physically separated to preserve the security of the personal data repository.

BUILDING TRUST

In order to get a visitor to share personal information with a Website and especially to get him to state this information accurately requires a level of trust to be built between the user and the Website. Note that we used the term *Website* in the previous statement. Although a Website is an inanimate object, this is exactly where the user will focus his trust, or lack thereof. And if one Website in an enterprise collection is deemed untrustworthy, other sites in the same enterprise will become untrustworthy by association. Once this happens, it becomes very difficult to entice the user back into a trusting position.

There are a number of things that you can do to ameliorate a user's fears and build his confidence in your ability to safeguard his personal information:

- Don't demand information unless it is specifically required for a *bona fide* business purpose such as an order or a request for a sales call.
- Ask only for the information needed. In the early stages of a trusted relationship, avoid seeding forms with fields for demographic data that don't obviously relate to the business transaction at hand. Demographic data can be obtained later, after the visitor is satisfied that they and you have a trusted relationship.
- Don't ask for an e-mail address unless you need it. Don't spam the e-mail address obtained during a trusted exchange—even with your own mailings—without explicit permission from the user. Give him a simple, foolproof way to get off mailing lists.
- Never include personal information in clear text in a cookie. If the user sees personal data in a cookie, they will conclude that you don't know how to keep secrets.
- Subscribe to privacy auditors like TrustE and the Better Business Bureau, and embrace their tenets in your privacy policies.
- Include a link to your privacy policy in each navigation block.
- On all forms requesting personal information assure the user that the information will be sent encrypted, using secure services. Don't depend on the user's ability to spot the little lock icon on the browser.

Special Issues in Collecting Information from Children

Collecting information from children is a special problem on the Internet, and it follows that the storage, safeguarding, and proper use of such information is equally important in all data warehouse initiatives. There is no faster way to for a Website to become untrustworthy than to collect information from children without the knowledge and consent of their parents.

Although not a new problem, the Internet is directing an intense spotlight on this issue. Until the advent of the Web, there wasn't a simple way to obtain information from children without asking them in person. Now we can ask such questions easily on a Website. Children will respond if asked since they lack the critical thinking skills that might cause an adult to hesitate before answering a personal question.

The fact that cookies identify computers, not individuals, adds to the problem. Demographic information provided by children can be tied to a specific computer, and another family member might already have provided a trusted identity to the same site. If that site has set a browser cookie on the machine, the child's naïve response can be immediately tied to the parent-provided identity.

The risks and potential liability inherent in this situation are obvious. It is extremely important to prohibit promiscuous access to user identities. Within your enterprise, you should use an anonymous user ID for demographic databases that can't be traced back to specific family or individual identity. It also is important to avoid incorporating any information in the data warehouse that isn't provided with permission by an adult.

SUMMARY

In this chapter we have examined specific initiatives that need to be taken with enterprise Websites to ensure that the information which they provide can be conformed into a data mart or data warehouse. We discussed the problem of having distributed Web servers in an enterprise environment and described several initiatives that will allow the data warehouse team to conform log information from diverse Web hosts into a single data warehouse.

CHAPTER 6

Building Clickstream Data Marts

We have come to the point in the book where we are ready to build the core structures of the data Webhouse. In this chapter we will build a set of specific data marts that support clickstream analysis. We begin with a brief review of dimensional modeling to make sure you remember the vocabulary and motivation behind the dimensional data mart structures. This lightning tour is intended to be a refresher, and to make sure that the main vocabulary is presented in one place. For a proper complete introduction to dimensional modeling and complete explanations of the dimensional modeling vocabulary, please see *The Data Warehouse Toolkit* by Kimball (Wiley, 1996) and *The Data Warehouse Lifecycle Toolkit,* Kimball et al. (Wiley, 1998). In the glossary of this book, we identify as many of the terms as we can and indicate where they are best described.

We then describe all the separate dimensions that connect to the clickstream, and we show you how to connect the rest of your existing enterprise data warehouse to the clickstream. We then make good on our promise in Chapter 3 to answer all the hard Web-oriented business questions.

A LIGHTNING TOUR OF DIMENSIONAL MODELING

Dimensional modeling is a discipline that seeks to model data for the purposes of understandability and performance. Dimensional models are the preferred format for the *presentation* of data in the data warehouse.

Dimensional modeling is an alternative to the traditional entity-relation (E/R) modeling discipline that most of us grew up with. Both dimensional models and entity-relation models have their proper place in the data warehouse. Table 6.1 summarizes the differences between the two modeling techniques.

All dimensional models are built around the concept of measured *facts*. Most of our production computer systems are engaged in capturing some kind of measured fact. A fact may be the sale of a product at a retail cash register, the price of a stock at a point in time, the amount of insurance coverage entered into a new policy that is being created, the balance of an account, or the change in your salary as a result of your promotion. All of these facts are numerical. Some of them are true at an instant in time, and others represent an accumulated measurement over a span of time.

We collect measured facts from our production computer systems and put them into tables called, appropriately, fact tables. It is no coincidence that a fact table is usually in close synchrony with a corresponding production system.

It is clear from this discussion that a fact table record contains one or more numerical measurements taken at some instant from a production computer system. What else does the fact table record contain?

Use	Dimensional Model	Entity-Relation Model
Transaction Processing	No	Yes
Data Cleaning Target	No	Yes
Final Data Staging	Yes	No
Ad Hoc Querying	Yes	No
Reporting	Yes	No
Data Mining	Yes	No
Forecasting	Yes	No
Drilling Across Distributed Data	Yes	No
Aggregate Aware Data Storage	Yes	No
Corporate Data Model	Yes, if not E/R	Yes, if not DM
Standard, Predictable Structure	Yes	No
Distributed Architecture & Administration	Yes	No
Explicit End User Tool Support	Yes	No
Compatibility with OLAP	Yes	No
Slowly Changing Dimensions (SCDs)	Yes	No

TABLE 6.1   A Comparison of the Uses of Dimensional Modeling and Entity-Relation Modeling

If the production system takes one million measurements, then usually we have one million records in the corresponding fact table.

The right way to approach this question is to ask "what is true in the context of the measurement?" Let's consider one of the examples from the first paragraph. If the measured fact is the amount of automobile insurance coverage entered into a new policy that is being created, then we might know the following context for this measurement:

- Date of this insurance transaction
- Customer
- Insurance agent
- Covered item (the car)
- Coverage type (e.g., comprehensive liability coverage)
- Transaction Type (e.g., create coverage)
- Policy format (e.g., a specific kind of policy containing a known set of legal paragraphs)

Our goal in dimensional modeling is to surround the measured facts with as much context as we can.

We call each of the items in the context list *dimensions*. We have identified seven dimensions for this insurance example.

When we think about these dimensions, it is clear that they aren't stand-alone numerical facts like the amount of the coverage requested by the customer. Rather, these dimensions are each rich textual descriptions of something that exists at the moment the fact table record is defined. Even the date is a rich textual description. It is a day of the week, a month name, a fiscal period, a holiday (yes/no), and a season.

The customer dimension is a classic, obvious set of text descriptors. A really good description of the customer may have 100 or more components, most of them textual, and some of them numeric attributes that largely behave like text.

Given how rich and open-ended the dimensional descriptions are, we clearly don't want to put all of the dimension descriptions in every record representing a measured fact. So we hang all the textual descriptions off in separate dimension tables, and just place a nice little foreign key in the real fact record. Each foreign key connects to its corresponding primary key in a dimension table. Our insurance transaction schema looks like Figure 6.1.

This characteristic data model looks a little like a star because the fact table is at the center, and all the dimension tables are arranged around it like a halo. Database engineers call this a *star join*, which is a term dating back to the beginnings of the relational database movement.

The *grain* of the fact table we have just created is "one record for each transaction." The grain is the formal definition of what is a single fact table record. Declaring the grain is hugely important to dimensional modelers. All dimensional designs must start by declaring the grain, and then deciding which facts and dimensions fit that grain. Once the grain is declared, then all facts should fit that grain. In our example, the only facts that should go in this table are facts directly defined in the context of the single policy creation transaction. Usually when the grain of the table is a single transaction, we have one fact, which we call "amount." We look in the transaction dimension to determine the meaning of the amount. Insurance transaction amounts might include the premium

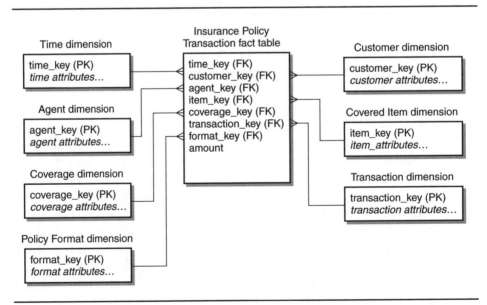

FIGURE 6.1   An Insurance Transaction Dimensional Model with One Fact Table and Seven Dimension Tables

charge for a specific coverage or the deductible for this specific coverage. It would be a major mistake to include facts not related to the grain such as the total premium paid by this customer to date on earlier versions of this policy. Other facts like these belong in their own fact tables, defined with different grains.

 Start the design of a fact table by making a clear declaration of the grain. Then add dimensions and measured facts consistent with that grain.

When the grain has been declared, the dimensional modeler searches for dimensions that take on a *single value* in the context of the measurement. Looking over the list of dimensions in our example, we see that at the instant of the transaction, we have well defined single values for the date, the customer, the agent, the covered item, the coverage, the transaction type, and the policy format.

There is an interesting open-endedness to dimensional modeling. We may decide to build our insurance fact table exactly as in Figure 6.1. We have seven dimension keys and one fact. But suppose we realize after our database is up and running that there is a well-defined location for the transaction. Perhaps it is a location where the broker meets the customer to discuss the policy. We assume that the broker can meet the customer at many possible locations, not just a single office. In this case, there is no reason why we can't add the location dimension to the design. Let's assume we can populate this new location dimension for all the old records in the database as well as new records received each day. We have added the new dimension in a *graceful* way. When we say that the addition of the dimension is graceful, we mean specifically that all old applications continue to work without being perturbed by the addition of the new dimension. Other graceful extensions of the design include adding more facts at the fundamental grain of the table, as well as adding more descriptive attributes within any of the dimensions.

The open-endedness of dimensional modeling implies that a good data warehouse designer is always on the prowl, looking for more information to add to the grain of existing fact and dimension tables. A good designer gets fact and especially dimension data from lots of sources. Some of the sources are official, blessed sources residing on the production computer system, and some of the sources are less formal or are perhaps purchased from third-party data suppliers.

Stringing Stars Together

Over a period of time, many similar-looking dimensional models (star schemas) will be built around the enterprise, representing diverse sources of data, and representing the interests of different groups wishing to analyze the data. This kind of distributed, independent development is generally very healthy, and is often the only way that individual projects can be brought to completion. For the moment, let's call each of these dimensional models a *data mart*. Individual groups building data marts can often decide on their design goals, secure funding, choose their technology, and implement their solution much faster than a centralized effort that tries to model and gather all the corporate data before anyone gets any benefit.

But such a distributed effort must be very vigilant to avoid the dreaded *stovepipe* problem. A stovepipe is a data mart that is incompatible with other data marts and is built in such a way that it is not flexible enough to participate in the overall fabric of the enterprise data warehouse. A stovepipe data mart is especially bad because usually the only solution to fix the stovepipe problem is to take the offending data mart offline and re-implement it. Not only is this an unfortunate waste of resources, but users will be unhappy when the new reports begin to flow out of the fixed data mart, because they will look different, and all their old queries will not work.

So if our goal is to build a distributed set of data marts (a data Webhouse) with no center, how do we proceed? How do we manage a data Webhouse? Is there any kind of architectural coherence to a large data Webhouse? Surely something must be centralized, or it's hard to imagine that it could work. If, in a real environment, many of the participants in a big data Webhouse are using different database technologies, how can we tie the pieces together at run time in order to deliver answers to queries, and structured reports and analyses?

Basic Architectural Coherence

A big data Webhouse spanning multiple organizations and multiple businesses has to have some kind of predictable uniformity. There must be a set of standards that allow the disparate parts to recognize each other and to communicate. New parts of the data Webhouse must be able join onto the existing data Webhouse and participate effectively.

Fortunately, this challenge of connecting distributed parts of the data Webhouse together is not a new challenge. We can bring much of existing data warehouse experience to bear on this issue. For several years, we have understood how to connect distributed data marts. First, we commit to using a standard dimensional framework for the actual presentation of all data in all parts of the data Webhouse. Second, we designers sit down at the beginning of the data Webhouse construction and agree on a series of conformed dimensions and conformed facts that span all the parts of the data Webhouse. A *conformed dimension* is a dimension that means the same thing and has the same structure across multiple data marts. A *conformed fact* is a definition of a measured fact that is consistent across multiple data marts. Note the subtle distinction between conformed dimensions and conformed facts. A conformed dimension is copied verbatim among the separate data marts. A conformed fact is not. Generally a specific instance of a fact exists in only one location in the data Webhouse. It is the definition of the fact that is consistent across data marts. This allows us, for instance, to compare and combine revenue facts across data marts.

Conformed dimensions and conformed facts implement a Data Warehouse Bus architecture. The Data Warehouse Bus architecture is the basis for a fully distributed data warehouse system, such as the data Webhouse.

What Is Physically Centralized and What Is Not

We have already identified a major centralized component of the data Webhouse, namely the *definitions* of the conformed dimensions and the conformed facts. But these definitions are logical, not physical! For instance, in most data Webhouses, we will decide on conformed dimensions such as Calendar (the Time dimension), Customer, and Product. When we actually assign responsibility for constructing the conformed dimensions, it is very likely that different groups will finally publish each of these dimensions. We have seen many organizations where the maintenance of the master customer list is performed by one group and the maintenance of the master product list is performed by another.

Thus the responsibility for each of the conformed dimensions is vested in a single group we call the *dimension authority*. Such a dimension authority has responsibility for defining, maintaining, and publishing a particular dimension to all the data mart clients that connect to or use the data Webhouse. The actual act of publishing is actually a kind of synchronous replication because all the downstream parts of the data

Webhouse need to have an identical copy of the dimension at the same time. See Figure 6.2.

The replication of the conformed dimensions outward from the dimension authorities to the downstream client data marts may be the basis for an odd misperception attributed to distributed data warehouses that are not highly centralized. The noncentralized data warehouse is accused of unnecessarily duplicating data. As we will see in the next few paragraphs, it is only the dimension data that needs to be duplicated, and this data *must* be duplicated. No matter what your architectural persuasion, a common structure like a dimension will always be physically duplicated in a large data warehouse environment anyway, unless the entire data warehouse sits in a single table space in a single vendor's DBMS. Total physical centralization is not very realistic. Most companies have many physical table spaces on many computers.

The fact table data, which may be more than 90 percent of a data warehouse, is explicitly not duplicated. A strong characteristic of the Data Warehouse Bus is the isolation of the fact table data at unique locations. *Local fact providers* live all across the data Webhouse. A local fact provider is a group that owns and controls a specific source of data. For example, one group may own the order entry system legacy data and this group makes the order data available to the data Webhouse. Another group may own the customer communications legacy data. Each local fact provider converts their own production keys for the calendar,

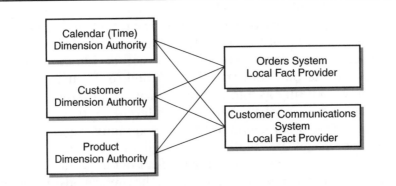

Five separate groups contribute to a part of a distributed Data Webhouse. The three groups on the left publish conformed dimensions. The two groups on the right publish unique fact tables to the Webhouse, and use the conformed dimensions.

FIGURE 6.2 The Relationship Between Dimension Authorities and Local Fact Providers

customer, and product dimensions from their system into the keys defined by the Data Warehouse Bus architecture. The process for building and administering the surrogate keys to support the Data Warehouse Bus architecture is outside the scope of this book.

Defining the conformed facts is an essential step that accompanies defining the conformed dimensions. A good example of a numeric, additive fact that usually must be conformed across separate data marts is *revenue*. If revenue is measured in several data marts, then it is essential that the technical definition of each of these revenues is exactly the same, so that a financial expert would agree that the separate revenues can be added and divided legitimately. If two types of revenue cannot be conformed, then they must be labeled differently, to warn the end user and the application developer not to combine them as if they were the same measure.

> A distributed data Webhouse has a centralized definition of conformed dimensions and conformed facts. The dimension tables are created centrally and then distributed across the organization, while the fact tables are often created independently by distributed departments and should not be copied to multiple locations.

There is no reason to duplicate fact table data anywhere in the data Webhouse. These huge tables only need to have one physical copy. All the disparate end user clients needing the fact data open connections directly to the one physical copy maintained by the local fact provider group. This process is described in the following section.

Making a Distributed Application Work

A data Webhouse based on a distributed set of divergent database technologies can be made to work as a seamless whole. The secret is "answer set accretion." This is just a fancy name for old-fashioned drill-across. The query tool or report writer simply opens connections to each of the fact table providers and retrieves separate answer sets constrained and labeled by the conformed dimensions. The use of the conformed dimensions guarantees that the separate answer sets can be combined in the application server above the DBMS, usually with a single-pass sort-merge operation because the row headers in each answer set row will be drawn from the same domains.

Answer set accretion is *not* the union of separate SQL answer sets. Such a union combines the rows of the separate answer sets. We want to combine the columns of the answer sets under the headers of each answer set row, using outer join logic.

Notice that the technique of fetching the answer sets back from the separate fact providers hides the separate identities of the underlying DBMSs. Once the answer sets have been retrieved into the application server, it doesn't matter where they came from. An additional bonus is that the fetching operations against the different remote fact tables can be performed in parallel, since they are probably on different machines. From this discussion it should be obvious why any updates to a conformed dimension need to be replicated simultaneously to all the affected data marts across the Webhouse. If a dimension is inconsistently represented in different parts of the Webhouse, there could be a brief period of time where a drill-across report would return weird, irreproducible results.

The Will to Make It Work

Ultimately, a successful distributed data Webhouse hinges on the will to use conformed dimensions and conformed facts. When the Data Warehouse Bus is in place, the technology to perform answer set accretion is straightforward. A number of front end tool providers can do this if the conformed dimensions and facts exist.

 The challenge of defining the conformed dimensions and facts is more organizational and political, rather than technical.

It usually isn't enough just to get all the affected data mart teams together in one room, although that is a heck of a good start. At some point in such a meeting, a senior authority, like a company CIO, needs to affirm the absolute intention to build the common definitions. If the groups in the room are from different companies in some kind of supply chain, then there must be a combined commitment to make the task of conforming work.

Now that we have completed our lightning tour of dimensional modeling, we are ready to build the clickstream data mart. We start with the clickstream dimensions.

CLICKSTREAM DIMENSIONS

Before we design specific clickstream data marts, let's collect together as many of the dimensions as we can think of that may have relevance in a clickstream environment. Any single star join schema will not use all the dimensions at once, but it is nice to have a portfolio of dimensions waiting to be used. In some ways, this mimics the process a data mart team might go through. A data mart team probably has a specific source of data in mind that they want to cast into a dimensional data mart framework. Reviewing the list of available conformed dimensions is a very helpful step early in the design. The dimension authorities, in effect, are inviting data mart teams to attach their data. Presumably, a rich, verbose, well-maintained dimension, like a customer dimension is a kind of attraction for the data mart team. Now the team needs to figure out how to attach their data to such a dimension.

Calendar Date Dimension

The first dimension we will deal with is the Calendar Date dimension. The Calendar Date dimension has one record for each day on the calendar. We will use this dimension whenever we have a date stamp or a date/time stamp. In the case of the date/time stamp, we will separate the calendar day from the time-of-day and make separate dimensions out of each. We create two dimensions for date/times for a couple of reasons. First, it simply isn't practical to make a single dimension out of all the minutes or seconds or microseconds over a several-year period. Second, even if we tried to make such a single dimension, it doesn't make a lot of sense from an applications point of view. We have names and labels for days, and we have names and labels for time periods within days, and these names and labels are somewhat uncorrelated. So we will split date/times into two dimensions.

We make an explicit Calendar Date dimension rather than just relying on an SQL or OLAP date type, because there are many calendar attributes that are not included in these language-oriented, industry-standard definitions. These special attributes include seasons, holidays, local work days, fiscal periods, and other special events that are determined by the calendar and are specific to your business. Special calendar attributes may also include foreign holidays or foreign seasons, but if you are intending to model a complex multinational calendar, read Chapter 10 on international data models for the kinds of extensions you need.

Here is our recommended Calendar Date dimension:

Date key	(surrogate values, 1..N)
Date type	(e.g., regular, unknown, unmeasured, corrupted, inapplicable, hasn't happened)
Calendar type	(Gregorian, Japanese, Chinese, Islamic, Talmudic)
Full SQL date	(legitimate value if type=regular, null otherwise)
Day of week	(Monday, Tuesday, etc.)
Day number in week	(1..7)
Day number in month	(1..31)
Day number in year	(1..366)
Day number in epoch	(a Julian number beginning at some point, could be negative)
Workday	(workday, holiday, use the words rather than yes/no for reporting)
Holiday	(none, or name of holiday)
Weekday	(weekday, weekend, use the words rather than yes/no)
Last day in month	(normal day, last day, used as a constraint convenience)
Week number in year	(1..53, week #1 is the first full week in the year)
Week number in epoch	(aligns with week number in year)
Month	(January, February, etc.)
Mon	(Jan, Feb, etc.)
Month number in year	(1..12)
Month number in epoch	
Quarter in year	(4Q1999, 1Q2000, etc)
Year	(no two digit years in this field!)
Fiscal period	(your fiscal period designation, could be several fields)
Season	(your season, or holiday period, could be several fields)

Event   (special indicator for a unique and note-
                              worthy period in time, e.g., Hurricane Hugo)

The calendar date dimension is tiny, even for a table spanning 30 years. If the nominal width of a single record is 150 bytes, then the total size of the table before indexing is $150 \times 365 \times 30 = 1.6$ MB. Adding a typical factor of three for copious indexing of every field, we still only have a total table size of about 6 MB.

The key for the calendar date dimension, and all the other dimensions in our designs, is a surrogate key. That is, the key is an anonymous integer. The first record in this dimension may as well have key value = 1. The second record will have key value = 2, and so on. The point of a surrogate key is that there is absolutely no semantics in the value of the key. It is just a vehicle for joining the dimension table to a fact table. But we don't make surrogate keys for religious reasons. We make surrogate keys so that we can deal with some important administrative situations that are unique to the data warehouse. These situations don't usually arise in an OLTP environment, and OLTP database designers often don't see the need for data warehouse surrogate keys. The first situation that arises in the data warehouse is if the object being referred to is unknown, unmeasured, corrupted, inapplicable, or hasn't happened yet. In all these cases, a semantically meaningful production key cannot be applied, yet the data warehouse has to provide a key. It is not acceptable for the data warehouse to provide a "fake" key drawn from the set of possible production keys. For instance, if a date is unknown, then we should not assign some real date in the future that is interpreted by applications as being "unknown" rather than the date named. We sort out the regular records from the exception case records by referring to a *type* key (in this case date type) that is found in all dimension tables.

A second reason for surrogate keys is that this insulates the data warehouse from changes in key administration in the production data. This may not be a big issue with dates, but it is a big issue with most of the other dimensions. For instance, if you are using a stock keeping number as the key for a product dimension, what are you going to do when your company acquires a new product line with weirdly formatted stock keeping numbers? Or even worse, when these new stock keeping numbers overlap the ones you already have . . .

A final reason for surrogate keys is the need to handle slowly changing dimensions (SCDs). Suppose that we want to revise our description of a customer. Perhaps the customer has moved or is now married. We are reluctant to throw away the old profile because it was true and valid up to a point in time. But if we have used some kind of production customer ID for the key to our customer dimension, we face the dilemma of overwriting the dimension record. The solution is to use a surrogate key, and put out a new customer record when we need to. See the sidebar on slowly changing dimensions later in this chapter.

A corollary to this surrogate key discussion is a kind of discipline in your applications. Never build in any dependence on the surrogate keys directly in your queries or applications. Do not constrain directly on a key value. Do not assume the surrogate keys are assigned in some meaningful sequential order. You have plenty of other fields in every dimension that can be used for constraining, navigating, and ordering. Leave the keys themselves out of your application logic.

As a philosophical issue, we have included several navigational fields in the Calendar Date dimension that strictly speaking aren't necessary. The last day in month field can, in principle, be determined by an end user application using complex logic. Doing this would be a serious mistake. The last day in month field is a great example of shifting the applications burden to the database storage, and relieving the query logic. The extra logic in an end user tool for some of these calendar navigation situations could easily sink the whole project by making the applications run slowly and making them hard to maintain.

Time of Day Dimension

The Time of Day dimension is a companion to the Calendar Date dimension. This is a simple dimension that lets us refer to named spans of time during the day. Individual hours are the most obvious example, but depending on the business we are in, we may have names for other time spans, like Swing Shift, Lunch Hour, Peak Periods, Closing, or News Hour Ad Slot. The Time of Day dimension can be built at the minute or even the second level. There are 1,440 minutes in a day, and 86,400 seconds in a day. Actually, December 31 frequently is given a leap second if you want to be fussy, but unless you are synchronized to the National Bureau of Standards, you probably won't encounter these leap seconds in your data.

We can argue that many interesting Web events may be time stamped to within a millisecond, and therefore a Time of Day dimension must have a granularity of 1 millisecond. This would yield a Time of Day dimension with 8,640,000 rows. While this is possible, it probably isn't worth it. You have to ask whether the analyses can reliably compute differences between events on a millisecond basis. And especially if you are merging events from multiple Web servers, it is very unlikely that your data is consistent to within a millisecond across servers. If the extremely precise time stamp is only being used to sort events in the proper order, then another nondimensional entry in the fact table, such as a session sequence number, could be used instead.

We take the approach of building the Time dimension with a granularity of one second, yielding 86,400 rows in the dimension. This will allow many interesting timing analyses. If the technology improves and a finer granularity is warranted, then the dimension can be gracefully expanded in place with more records for the finer grain. Remember that *graceful* means that existing applications continue to run without being affected by the change.

Our recommended design for the Time of Day dimension is:

Time key	(surrogate values, 1..N)
Time type	(e.g., regular, unknown, unmeasured, corrupted, inapplicable, hasn't happened)
Seconds since midnight	(0..86399)
Minutes since midnight	(0..1439)
SQL time stamp	(e.g., 13:30:58)
Hour	(0..23)
Minute	(0..59)
Second	(0..59)
Time span	(Swing Shift, Lunch Hour, etc. Possibly several fields for different purposes)

The Time of Day dimension is tiny. If the nominal width of a single record is 40 bytes, then the indexed data size is $86,400 \times 40 = 3.4$ MB. If indexing adds a factor of three, then the total size of this dimension is about 13 MB.

Notice that we don't need to specify the time zone for this Time of Day dimension, or for the Calendar Date dimension. The time zone is very important, but we will specify the time zone in the actual schema when we assign these dimensions to *roles*. Stay tuned.

Customer Dimension

The Customer dimension in some ways is the most important dimension in the data Webhouse. If your Customer dimension is accurate, complete, and verbose, then you have some very strong handles on understanding your business. But one of the challenges in a Webhouse environment is knowing just who it is that is clicking on your Website. We might have called this dimension User or even Machine, but with so much of our motivation aimed at the notion of the visitor on our Website being a human being to whom we would like to provide some value, we will imagine that the user or the machine is always a "customer." Hopefully, you can adapt your particular situation to this mindset.

We will build our Customer dimension so that it can be extended as we learn more and more about who the customer actually is. There are many physical ways to handle this kind of extensible design in real databases. If you know that you will never be able to supply the fourth group of extended attributes listed next, then leave them out of your physical design for the time being. You can always add these extended attributes *gracefully* at a later time. But let us imagine that we start at the top of the following design, and fill in as many fields as we can, like pulling down a window shade.

Our recommended design for the Customer dimension follows.

Group 1 fields always present in a Website hit:

Customer key	(surrogate values, 1..N)
Customer type	(e.g., regular, unknown, unmeasured, corrupted, inapplicable, ephemeral IP address, constant IP address, ephemeral machine cookie, constant machine cookie, identified non-customer, identified customer)
ISP address	(multivalued, since customer may connect from work, home, or travel; needs associative table between ISP address table and customer dimension)
Cookie ID	(same cookie ID for connection from work, home, or travel)
Last change datestamp	(SQL date of last change to this record; see sidebar on slowly changing dimensions)
Last change reason	(predefined set of change reasons; see sidebar on slowly changing dimensions)

Group 2 fields if we have a useful customer name and have assigned a Customer ID:

Customer ID	(ID assigned by us if we know anything more than the cookie ID)
Identifier	(hopefully a full, real name, but may be a pseudonym)
Name type	(pseudonym, unverified real name, verified real name)
Salutation	(Mr., Mrs., Ms.)
First name	
Middle names	
Last name	
Cultural greeting style	(American, European, Latin, Islamic, Japanese, Chinese, and many others)
Gender	(Male, Female, Declined to state, Unknown)
IP city	(City derived from customer's IP address)
IP state	(State or area within country derived from IP address)
IP country	(Country derived from IP address)

Group 3 fields if customer has shared basic address and demographics:

Customer type	(Residential, Commercial)
Degrees	(e.g., MS, Ph.D, and other honarary titles)
Ethnicity	
Company name	(this and following five fields null if not a commercial customer)
Department name	
Job title	
Primary Telephone	
Primary FAX	
E-mail	
Website	
Building	

Floor

Mail stop

Address type   (e.g., headquarters office, secondary field office, parcel delivery address)

Intended use   (e.g., domestic mail, foreign mail)

Street number

Street name

Street direction

Post office box

Locality

City

State

Postal code

Region

Country

Assembled address block   (A complete postally valid address in the correct sequence with line breaks)

Currency   (currency type used by this individual at this location)

Marital State   (Married, Single, Declined to State, Unknown, etc.)

Age range   (one of a set of predefined age range buckets)

Profession   (one of a set of predefined professional profiles, also optionally supplied)

Interest   (this can take many forms, and can consist of several fields)

Written greeting   (assembled written greeting in the right cultural style)

Verbal greeting   (assembled verbal greeting in the right cultural style)

Personal individual ID   (unique identifier tying together records referring to one individual)

Commercial entity ID   (unique identifier tying together records referring to one commercial entity)

SLOWLY CHANGING DIMENSIONS

Earlier in this chapter, when justifying the use of surrogate keys, we described the need to track slowly changing dimensions (SCDs). Tracking the changes in a dimension is one of the basic responsibilities of a data warehouse, and this function often distinguishes the data warehouse from a transaction processing system. It is really important for the data warehouse to have accurate old descriptions of customers, products, and other dimensions so that the analyst can see why decisions were made in the past.

Slowly changing dimensions come in three flavors. The Type 1 SCD occurs when the data warehouse team takes the new description and overwrites the old, without adding a new record or changing the key. Obviously, this changes the past history of any attribute that is overwritten. But in many cases, such as the correction of bad data, this is the desired outcome. The Type 2 SCD occurs when a true physical change has occurred as of a specific point in time, such as a change in a product description or a change in a customer profile. In this case, we create a new dimension record, with a new data warehouse key. The creation of the new data warehouse key, often called *surrogate key generation,* is an important step in the back room of nearly every data warehouse. Type 2 SCDs are the most common type, and they "perfectly partition history". The Type 3 SCD occurs when an alternate, simultaneous description of something is available. In this case an extra "old value" field is added in the affected dimension.

The Customer dimension designed in this chapter has two fields that support SCDs explicitly. The Last Change Datestamp and the Last Change Reason are navigational aids that let you perform very accurate time slice analyses of your customer base if you are constantly making changes to this dimension.

The Customer dimension presents a challenge because it is often so big. The customer dimension defined in this chapter has at least 59 fields, many of which are lengthy text fields. A single record in this Customer dimension could easily be 1,000 bytes. 50 million records would be 50 GB, not counting the voluminous indexes needed to support flexible querying through this dimension. Fully indexing each field in the Customer dimension would add approximately a factor of 3 to the size of the dimension table.

A full-fledged treatment of this slowly changing Customer dimension could grow this dimension by a significant factor. If we updated each customer record twice per year, we would be replicating the original size of the dimension that often.

If you have one million records in your customer dimension, you don't need to worry much about this problem. But if you have 50 million records in your Customer dimension, and they all are as verbose as our design recommends, *and* if you track the historical changes, then you should consider dividing the dimension into static and dynamic parts. For instance, perhaps the Group 4 fields are the source of the changes in the profiles, because you are constantly revising the profiles and clusters, and additionally you want to preserve the history. In this case, you should break off the Group 4 attributes and make a separate demographics profile dimension.

Group 4 fields if customer has ever made a purchase:

Recency	(date of last purchase)
Frequency	(number of purchases, lifetime)
Intensity	(total value of purchases, lifetime)
Projected Lifetime Value	(total projected lifetime value of customer)
Cluster	(one or more fields labeling the customer's overall demographic cluster)
Purchase profile	(one or more fields describing the purchase profile of the customer)
Credit profile	(one or more fields describing the credit profile of the customer)
Return profile	(one or more fields describing the customer's propensity to return products)
On Line Support Profile	(one or more fields describing the customer's use of on-line support)
Phone Support Profile	(one or more fields describing the customer's use of phone support)

Page Dimension

The Page dimension describes the page context for a Web page event. The grain of this dimension is the individual page *type*. Our definition of "page" must be flexible enough to handle the evolution of Web pages from the current mostly static page delivery to highly dynamic page delivery in which the exact page the customer sees is unique at that instant in time. We will assume even in the case of the dynamic page that there is a well-defined function that characterizes the page, and we will use that to describe the page. We will not create a page record for every instance of a dynamic page because that would yield a dimension with an astronomical number of records. These records also would not differ in interesting ways. What we want is a record in this dimension for each interesting distinguishable type of page. Static pages probably get their own record, but dynamic pages would be grouped by similar function and type.

When the definition of a static page changes, because it is altered by the Webmaster, the record in the page dimension can either be overwritten or can be duplicated as described in the sidebar on SCDs. This decision is a matter of policy for the data Webhouse, and it depends on whether the old and new descriptions of the page differ materially, and whether the old definition should be kept for historical analysis purposes. In Chapter 5 we described the process of the Website designers and the Webhouse developers collaborating to assign descriptive codes and attributes to each page served by the Web server, whether the page is dynamic or static. This crucial and problematic step is at the foundation of the implementation of this Page dimension.

Our recommended design for the Page dimension is:

Page key	(surrogate values, 1..N)
Page source	(e.g., static, dynamic, unknown, corrupted, inapplicable)
Page function	(portal, search, product description, corporate information, and many more)
Page template	(sparse, dense, and others)
Item type	(product SKU, book ISBN number, telco rate type)
Graphics type	(GIF, JPG, progressive disclosure, size pre-declared, or combination of these)
Animation type	(similar to Graphics type)
Sound type	(similar to Graphics type)
Page file name	

The Page dimension is small. If the nominal width of a single record is 100 bytes, and if we have a big Website with 100,000 pages, then the unindexed data size is $100 \times 100,000 = 10$ MB. If indexing adds a factor of three, then the total size of this dimension is about 40 MB.

Event Dimension

The Event dimension describes what happened on a particular page at a particular point in time. The main interesting events are Open Page, Refresh Page, Click Link, and Enter Data. As dynamic pages based on XML become more common, the Event dimension will get much more interesting because the semantics of the page will be much more obvious to the Web server. Each field in an XML document can be labeled with a user-defined tag. We will want to capture that information in this Event dimension.

Our recommended design for the Event dimension is:

Event key	(surrogate values, 1..N)

Event type   (e.g., Open Page, Refresh Page, Click Link, unknown, corrupted, inapplicable)

Event Content   (application dependent fields whose content will be driven from XML tags)

The Event dimension is tiny. If the nominal width of a single record is 40 bytes, and if we have 1,000 distinct events, then the indexed data size is $40 \times 1000 = 0.04$ MB. If indexing adds a factor of three, then the total size of this dimension is only about 0.16 MB.

Session Dimension

The Session dimension provides one or more levels of diagnosis for the user's session as a whole. For example, the local context of the session might be Requesting Product Information, but the overall session context might be Ordering a Product. The success status would diagnose whether the mission was completed. The local context may be decidable from just the identity of the current page, but the overall session context probably can only be judged by processing the user's complete session at data extract time. The customer status attribute is a convenient place to label the customer for periods of time, with labels that are not immediately clear either from the page or the immediate session. Useful statuses include High Value Reliable customer, or New Customer, or About to Cancel, or In Default. All of these statuses may be derived from auxiliary data marts in the data Webhouse, but by placing these labels deep within the clickstream, we are able to directly study the behavior of certain types of customers. We do not put these labels in the Customer dimension because they may change over very short periods of time. If there are a large number of these statuses, then we would consider creating a separate Customer Status dimension rather than embedding this information in the Session dimension.

This dimension is extremely important because it provides a way to group sessions for insightful analysis. For example, this dimension would be used to ask:

- How many customers consulted our product information before ordering?

- How many customers looked at our product information and never ordered?

- How many customers began the ordering process but did not finish? And where did they stop?

Our recommended design for the Session dimension is:

Session key	(surrogate values, 1..N)
Session type	(e.g., classified, unclassified, corrupted, in-applicable)
Local context	(mainly page derived context like Requesting Product Information)
Overall session context	(mainly trajectory derived context like Ordering a Product)
Action sequence	(summary label for an overall sequence of actions observed during the session)
Success status	(whether the overall session mission was achieved)
Customer status	(labels such as High Value Reliable or In Default)

The Session dimension is tiny. If the nominal width of a single record is 80 bytes, and we have 10,000 identified session combinations, then the indexed data size is $80 \times 10,000 = 0.8$ MB. If indexing adds a factor of three, then the total size of this dimension is about 3 MB.

Referral Dimension

The Referral dimension describes how the customer arrived at the current page. The Web server logs usually provide this information. The URL of the previous page is identified, and in some cases additional information is present. If the referrer was a search engine, then usually the search string is specified. It is not worthwhile to put the raw search specification into our database, because the search specifications are so complicated and idiosyncratic that an analyst couldn't usefully query them. We assume some kind of simplified and cleaned specification is placed in the specification field.

Our recommended design for the Referral dimension is:

Referral key	(surrogate values, 1..N)
Referral type	(e.g., intra site, remote site, search engine, corrupted, inapplicable)
Referring URL	(e.g., www.organization.site.com/linkspage)
Referring site	(e.g., www.organization.site.com)

Referring domain	(e.g., site.com)
Search type	(e.g., simple text match, complex logical match)
Specification	(the actual spec used: useful if simple text, questionable otherwise)
Target	(where the search found its match, e.g., in meta tags, or body text, or title)

The Referral dimension may be fairly large. If the average width of a single record is 100 bytes, and if we have 1,000,000 referral records, then the indexed data size is $100 \times 1,000,000 = 100$ MB. If indexing adds a factor of three, then the total size of this dimension is about 400 MB. This is a hard dimension to estimate without actual data, since the variability in size comes from the length of the Referring URL, and the search Specification, which may not be present.

Product (or Service) Dimension

The Product dimension describes the product or service that is the subject of a page or is the target of an event. The Product or Service dimension will only be applicable in certain situations. For those organizations that are not engaged in e-commerce, this dimension probably doesn't attach to the clickstream at all. In many other cases, this dimension attaches permanently to the clickstream and takes on meaningful values in many contexts.

Product dimensions are very well understood by the data warehouse design community. They range from the very explicit stock keeping unit (SKU), which lists hundreds of thousands of retail products, to much smaller and less elaborate lists of services provided by, for instance, a consulting company. A good product dimension has a large number of attributes describing each product. Some of the attributes may create a merchandise hierarchy that allows groups of products to be rolled up into ever larger clumps. Other attributes have nothing to do with the merchandise hierarchy but are simple useful descriptors.

Some businesses may desperately need a product dimension but have never faced the issue of building a serious product table. On the Web at the time of this writing, auction companies really need a good product table to describe all the things they auction. Their top-level categories do not provide enough of a breakdown to make it easy to find what you want. Similarly, telecommunication companies often do not have a very good idea of their list of services. They just don't think that way. Their rate structures have evolved over the years, so that there may be hundreds of thousands of separate rate plans for commercial customers, without very many unifying subcategories and categories.

Given the wide variability of possible Product/Service dimensions, we choose to show two designs at the opposite ends of the spectrum. Let's first imagine that our business is an electronics retailer, selling hardware and software "off the shelf."

Our recommended design for the Product dimension for the electronic retailer is:

Product key	(surrogate values, 1..N)
Product type	(e.g., regular, not measured, corrupted, inapplicable)
SKU number	(the bar code)
Description	(possibly unique description of individual product with version and release)
Brand	(brand name)
Manufacturer	(manufacturer name)
Category	(retailer's rollup)
Department	(retailer's rollup)
System type	(component, software, hardware, complete system)
Packaging	(piece, plastic bag, shelf box, floor box, other)
Package Width	
Package Depth	
Package Height	
Package Stacking Height	
Package Weight	
Standard Cost	(in this table only if constant over long period, otherwise in other fact table)
Standard Price	(in this table only if constant over long period, otherwise in other fact table)
Buyer	(in this table only if constant over long period, otherwise a Buyer dimension)

The Product dimension for a big retailer can be reasonably large. If the nominal width of a single record is 200 bytes, and the retailer has

500,000 SKUs, then the indexed data size is $200 \times 500{,}000 = 100$ MB. If indexing adds a factor of three, then the total size of this dimension is about 400 MB.

Now let's imagine that our business is a data warehouse consulting company. Our recommended design for the Services dimension for the consulting company is:

Service key	(surrogate values, 1..N)
Service type	(e.g., regular, not measured, corrupted, inapplicable)
Service code	(the internal code used by billing and tracking systems, if visible to managers)
Description	(e.g., requirements gathering, end user training, extract system development)
Category	(e.g., warehouse development, management consulting)
Sector	(e.g., telco, banking, health care, manufacturing, government)

The Services dimension for a consulting company is tiny. If the nominal width of a single record is 80 bytes, and there are 500 service codes, then the indexed data size is $80 \times 500 = 0.04$ MB. If indexing adds a factor of three, then the total size of this dimension is only about 0.16 MB.

Causal Dimension

The Causal dimension describes what the conditions of the marketplace are at the moment the measurement is made in the fact table. The Causal dimension tries to provide hints or "causal factors" that may explain why the customer is interested in our company or in a particular product or service. Maybe we have been running an ad on the Web or on television. Maybe we are offering our products or services with a temporary price reduction. Maybe a special "exogenous event" occurred in the marketplace that affected everyone's perception. For instance, the 1992 earthquake in Los Angeles caused thousands of people to seek earthquake insurance coverage. The surge in demand wasn't due to any marketing initiatives: it was due to a causal event.

Modeling causal events is not an exact science, but by using common sense, a lot of market dynamics can be explained. An individual causal event record simply needs to provide for the various causal factors that your particular industry is sensitive to. If you are an electronics retailer with a Web presence, then a reasonable set of causal factors would include temporary price reductions, newspaper ads, Web ads, radio ads, in-store displays, manufacturer promotions, and "other." Given this perspective, our recommended design for a Causal dimension is:

Causal key	(surrogate values, 1..N)
Causal type	(e.g., specific causal factor, no causal factor, corrupted, inapplicable)
Price treatment	(e.g., regular, 2-for-1, 10% reduction, $2 off)
Newspaper ad type	(e.g., large daily, small daily, large weekend, small weekend)
Web ad type	(e.g., search engine constant, news portal time slice)
Radio ad type	(e.g., 24x daily news station, 10x weekend classic music)
Store display type	(e.g., end aisle display, shelf tag)
Mfgr Promo type	(e.g., discount coupon, rebate coupon, bundled extra product)
Other causal event	(e.g., war, hurricane, competitor discount)

The Causal dimension is tiny. If the nominal width of a single record is 150 bytes, and if you have identified 5,000 interesting causal combinations, then the indexed data size is $150 \times 5,000 = 0.75$ MB. If indexing adds a factor of three, then the total size of this dimension is about 4 MB.

Business Entity Dimension

The Business Entity dimension describes a business entity that is associated with a fact record. We deliberately don't specify what the role of the business entity is at this point in the design. A business entity can play a number of different roles, sometimes playing more than one simultaneously. A business entity can be a supplier, a business partner, a referrer, a service provider, a customer, or something else. In this dimension, we exploit the fact that regardless of the role played, the business entity has the same kind of basic description. In the next section, when we build actual complete schemas, we may be able to plug the business entity dimension into one or more roles in the schemas.

In the following, we do not attempt to describe any organization hierarchies. If another entity owns the one we are describing, we do not record that information directly in the Business Entity record. Organization hierarchies can be represented by means of *hierarchy helper tables* that are associative tables used with conventional dimensions.

Our recommended design for the Business Entity dimension is:

Entity key	(surrogate values, 1..N)
Entity type	(e.g., commercial, government, individual, unknown, corrupted, inapplicable)
Entity Name	name of organization
Industry category	(e.g., Standard Industry Classification (SIC) codes with text equivalents)
Primary Contact Name	
Primary Telephone	
Primary FAX	
Contact E-mail	
Website	
Building	
Floor	
Mail stop	
Address type	(e.g., headquarters office, secondary field office, parcel delivery address)
Intended use	(e.g., domestic mail, foreign mail)
Street number	
Street name	
Street direction	
Post office box	
Locality	
City	
State	
Postal code	
Region	
Country	
Assembled address block	(A complete postally valid address in the correct sequence with line breaks)
Currency	(currency type used by this company at this location)

The Business Entity dimension can be quite large. A typical big manufacturer deals with perhaps 100,000 business entities. However, the biggest utilities deal with several million business entities. If the nominal width of a single record is 500 bytes, and if we assume 1 million business entities, then the indexed data size is $500 \times 1,000,000 = 500$ MB. If indexing adds a factor of three, then the total size of this dimension is about 2 GB.

Clickstream Tracking Keys

In addition to the dimensions naturally arising from the clickstream data, a host of production IDs will surface in various situations. The host ID is a URL that identifies a source or a target. The various session IDs may have relevance in constructing the session dimension during the extract-transform-load phase, but are probably not meaningful in the final session dimension. Similarly, the various kinds of user IDs will be crucial during the extract-transform-load phase, but will not be of direct interest to a final visitor dimension. Table 6.2 summarizes the various kinds of source IDs that are usually encountered in the underlying data.

Data Element	Description	Persistence	Source
Host	IP address or fully-qualified host name	session	the IP address of the computer on which the browser is running
Temporary session ID	unique identifier for an http session consisting of one user from one client to one host server	session	Web server—possibly as a session cookie
Session ID	unique identifier assigned for an http session consisting of one user from one client to one host server	unlimited	clickstream post-processor
Session cookie	Cookie placed into a browser's temporary storage (memory) space	from the first contact to a Web server, until the user's browser is deactivated.	Web server

TABLE 6.2 Tracking Keys *(continues)*

Data Element	Description	Persistence	Source
Persistent cookie	Cookie placed in a browser's cookie file by a Web server	Until the cookie expiration date/time	Web server or Web-based application
Anonymous user ID	unique identifier for a user whose actual identity has not been validated.	session	session application server, perhaps as a session cookie
Persistent user ID	unique identifier for a computer	cross-session	session application server, via persistent cookies, or from a profiling service.
Validated household ID	unique identifier for the household or business setting in which a specific computer is located	unlimited	link from persistent cookie to household database
Validated user ID	unique identifier for login to user database	unlimited	link from application

TABLE 6.2 Tracking Keys *(continued)*

THE CLICKSTREAM DATA MART

A data mart is a suite of fact tables together with a set of connected dimension tables that serves the needs of a particular business group. As a practical matter, a data mart should start out by being as closely related to a single source of measurement (fact) data as possible. In this way, the first version of the data mart can be brought on-line as expeditiously as possible. But before this first version of the data mart is implemented, the following items must be identified, in the order shown:

1. The business issues to be addressed by this data mart.
2. The source of the numeric measurement (fact) data.
3. The grain of each proposed fact table.
4. All dimensions needed by all proposed fact tables.
5. A *plan* and a *commitment* for conforming these dimensions across the enterprise.
6. All numeric facts to be included in each fact table.
7. A plan and a commitment to conform any facts appearing in more than one fact table across the enterprise.

Once the first dimensional models have been built and published to the user community, the data mart team has a rational agenda for expanding the data mart to include more sources of data, and to connect the data mart to the other data marts comprising the enterprise data warehouse.

In Chapter 3 we took the first step of identifying a wide range of business issues to be addressed by our clickstream data mart. Taking our own advice to heart, we will start somewhat conservatively, building a reasonably simple first dimensional model, and then gradually proposing more ambitious models that could be implemented in a staged and graceful way. We will use the example of the electronics retailer so that we can choose specific facts for the fact table.

A Clickstream Fact Table to Analyze Complete Sessions

The first fact table in our clickstream data mart will be based solely on the clickstream data derived from our own Website logs. This satisfies step 2.

With an eye toward keeping the first fact table from growing astronomically, we choose the grain to be *one record for each completed customer session*. This is step 3. This grain is significantly higher than the underlying Web server logs, which record each microscopic page event. But perhaps we have a big site recording more than 100 million raw page events per day, and we want to start with a more manageable number of records to be loaded each day. We assume for the sake of argument that the 100 million page events boil down to 5 million complete user sessions. This could arise if an average user session touched 5 pages, and there was an average of 4 basic events recorded per page, including requests for GIF and JPEG graphic images.

The dimensions that are appropriate for this first fact table are Calendar Date, Time of Day, Customer, Page, Session, and Referrer. This is step 4. Finally we add a set of measured facts for this session including Session Seconds, Pages Visited, Orders Placed, Units Ordered, and Order Dollars. This satisfies step 6. The completed design is shown in Figure 6.3.

There are a number of interesting aspects to the design shown in Figure 6.3. You may be wondering why there are two connections from the Calendar Date dimension to the fact table, and two connections from the Time of Day dimension to the fact table. This is a case where both the Calendar Date and the Time of Day must play two different roles.

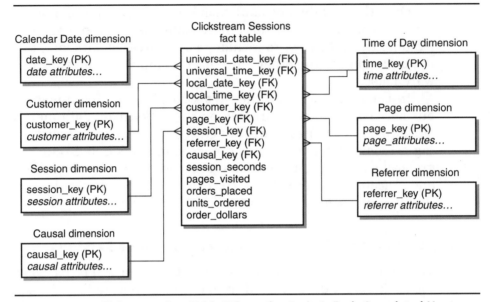

FIGURE 6.3 A Clickstream Fact Table Where the Grain Is Each Completed User Session

Because we are very interested in measuring the precise times of sessions, we must make sure we meet two conflicting requirements. First, we want to make sure we can synchronize all session dates and times across multiple time zones internationally. Perhaps we have other date and time stamps from other Web servers or from non-Web systems elsewhere in our date warehouse. To achieve true synchronization of events across multiple servers and processes, we must record all session dates and times, uniformly, in a single time zone such as GMT. We interpret the session date and time combinations as the beginning of the session. Since we have the dwell time of the session as a numeric fact, we can tell when the session ended, if that is of interest.

The other requirement we will meet with this design is to record the date and time of the session relative to the customer's wall clock. The best way to represent this information is with a second pair of Calendar Date and Time of Day foreign keys. Theoretically, we could represent the time zone of the customer in the Customer dimension table, but constraints to determine the correct wall clock time would be horrendously complicated. The time difference between two cities (such as London and Sydney) can change by as much as two hours at different times of the year depending on when these cities go on and off daylight savings time. This is not the business of the end user application to work out. It is the business of the database to store this information so that it can be constrained in a simple and direct way.

The two Calendar Date dimension tables are actually views on a single underlying table. The field names are massaged in the view definition so that they are slightly different when they show up in the user interface pick lists of end user tools. Similarly, the two Time of Day dimension tables are actually two views on a single underlying table. Note that the use of views makes the two instances of each table semantically independent.

The inclusion of the Page dimension in Figure 6.3 may seem surprising given that the grain of the design is the customer session. However, in a given session, a very interesting page is the entry page. We interpret the Page dimension in this design as the page the session started with. In other words, how did the customer hop onto our bus just now? Coupled with the referrer dimension, we now have an interesting ability to analyze how and why the customer accessed our Website. A more elaborate design would also add an exit page dimension.

We may be tempted to add the Causal dimension to this design, but if the Causal dimension is intended to focus on individual products, it would be inappropriate to add to this design. The symptom that the Causal dimension does not mesh with this design is the multivalued nature of the causal factors for a given complete session. If we are running ad campaigns or special deals for several products, how do we represent this multivalued situation if the customer's session involves several products? The right place for a product-oriented causal dimension will be in the more fine grained table we build in the second fact table example. Conversely, a more broadly focused market causal dimension that described market conditions affecting all products would be appropriate for a session-grained fact table.

The session seconds fact is the total number of seconds the customer spent on the site during this session. There will be many cases where we can't tell when the customer left. Perhaps the customer typed in a new URL. This won't be detected by conventional Web server logs (although if the data is being collected by an ISP who can see every click across sessions, then this particular issue goes away). Or perhaps the customer got up out of the chair and didn't return for an hour. Or perhaps the customer just closed the browser without making any more clicks. In all these cases, our extract software needs to assign a small and nominal number of seconds to this part of the session, so that the analysis is not distorted unrealistically.

The fact table shown in Figure 6.3 has thirteen fields. Since all the foreign key fields are surrogate keys, none of them needs to be represented in more than four bytes. Similarly, all the measured facts are either integers or scaled integers. Again, four byte fields are reasonable for estimation purposes. Thus our fact table is about 52 bytes wide.

With this fact table we can investigate at least two of our original major interests from Chapter 3 including:

- How to drive marketing activities by recognizing the identity of the customer and by clustering the customer by clickstream attributes.
- How to decide whether to encourage or support a referring cross-link.

These two major areas lead to dozens of specific analyses, since we can cluster and constrain through our wonderful Customer dimension. We can use the Session dimension to tell if the Website visit was productive, and we can use the Page dimension to see how the user came to our site. In addition to the two major areas of analysis, we can also investigate in detail.

- When do customers use our Website, and what is their local time when they do?
- When does maximum simultaneous loading occur on our Website from users in many different time zones?
- How long do customers spend on our site, and how many pages do they visit?
- How do customers reach our site?
- What fraction of our site visits are successful, and what fraction result in product sales?
- What is the total volume of product sales done on the Web?

If we collect 5 million new fact records each day for our hypothetical large Website example, then we are adding 260 MB of data (before indexing) to the fact table each day. Over the course of a year, this would amount to 260 MB × 365, or 94.9 GB of unindexed data. This is big, but not ridiculously so. Three years of data, together with indexing overhead would perhaps consume 600 GB of disk space. Given the pace of

Web marketing and Web technology, it seems reasonable to plan on keeping only three years of data.

Note that the dimension tables, with the possible exception of the Customer dimension, are small by comparison with the main fact table. A fully indexed 50 million row Customer table could occupy 200 GB of storage, about one-third the size of the fact table. All the other dimension tables are negligible by comparison.

We purposely built this first fact table in our clickstream data mart to focus on complete user sessions and to keep the size of the data mart under control. As you can see from the preceding list, we can perform a lot of interesting analyses. But to make progress with the rest of the major analysis objectives described in Chapter 3, we need some companion fact tables in the data mart. The next table we will build drops down to the lowest practical granularity we can support in the data Webhouse: the individual page event.

A Clickstream Fact Table to Analyze Individual Page Use

In this second fact table, we will define the granularity to be the individual page event in each customer session. With simple static HTML pages, we may be able to record only one interesting event per page view, namely the page view itself. As Websites employ dynamically created XML-based pages, with the ability to establish an ongoing dialogue through the page, the number and type of events will grow.

It is likely that this fact table will become astronomical in size. We will resist the urge to aggregate the table up to a coarser granularity because that step inevitably involves cutting off dimensions. Actually, the first fact table we built for this data mart represents just such an aggregation. It is a worthwhile fact table, but the analyst cannot ask questions about user behavior or individual pages. When the individual page-oriented data set gets too large, then in order to preserve the ability to analyze detailed behavior, either the time span of the data must be restricted or statistical sampling techniques must be used to reduce the data size. Although disk storage capacity has been doubling even faster (every 12 months, supposedly) than processing power, our propensity to collect reams of data seems to be doubling at an even faster pace. . . .

Having chosen the grain in step 3, we can choose the appropriate dimensions in step 4. Our list of dimensions includes Calendar Date, Time of Day, Customer, Page, Event, Session, Session ID, Product, Causal, and Referrer. The completed design is shown in Figure 6.4.

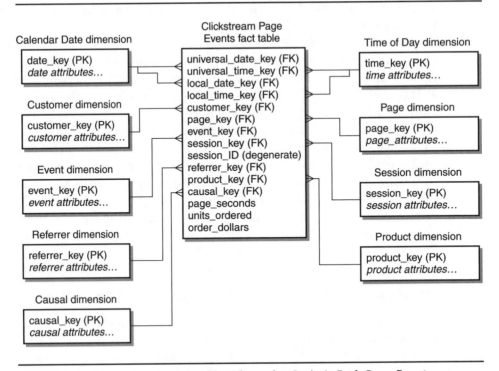

FIGURE 6.4   A Clickstream Fact Table Where the Grain Is Each Page Event

The design in Figure 6.4 looks rather similar to our first design. This similarity between fact tables is typical of dimensional models. One of the charms of dimensional modeling is the "boring" similarity of the designs. But that is where they get their power. When the designs have a predictable structure, all of the software up and down the data warehouse chain, from extraction, to database querying, to the end user tools, can exploit this similarity to great advantage. Query and reporting tools for example may be able to adapt to a whole family of dimensional designs without any reprogramming.

The two roles played by the Calendar Date and Time of Day dimensions have the same interpretation as in the first design. One role is the universal synchronized time, probably expressed in GMT, and the other role is the local wall clock time as measured by the customer. In this fact table, the date/time combinations refer to the individual page event that is being described by the record we are building.

The Page dimension refers to the individual page whose events we are recording. This is the main difference in grain between this fact table and the first one we built. In this fact table we will be able to see all the pages accessed by the customers.

The Event dimension describes what happened on the page. See the definition of this dimension earlier in this chapter.

The Session dimension describes the outcome of the session. The Session ID is a "degenerate" dimension that does not have a join to a dimension table. This degenerate dimension is a typical dimensional modeling construct. The Session ID is simply a unique identifier, with no semantic significance, that serves to group together the page events of each customer session in an unambiguous way. We did not need a Session ID degenerate dimension in our first fact table because each record in that table already represented a complete session. We recommend that the Session dimension be at a higher level of granularity than the Session ID, because the Session dimension is intended to describe classes and categories of sessions, not the characteristics of each individual session.

We show a Product dimension in this design under the assumption that this Website is owned by a Web retailer. A financial services site probably would have a similar dimension. A consulting services site would have a Service dimension. An auction site would have a Subject or Category dimension describing the nature of the items being auctioned. A news site would have a Subject dimension, although with different content than an auction site.

We accompany the Product dimension with a Causal dimension so that we can attach useful marketplace interpretations to the changes in demand we may see for certain products. See the discussion of the Causal dimension earlier in the chapter.

For each page event, we record the number of seconds that we believe elapse before the next page event. We call this Page Seconds to contrast it with Session Seconds that we used in the first fact table. This is a simple example of paying attention to conformed facts. If we called both of these measures simply "Seconds," then we would run the risk of having these seconds added or combined inappropriately. Since these seconds are not precisely equivalent, we name them differently as a warning. In this particular case, we would expect the Page Seconds for a session in this second fact table to add up to the Session Seconds in the first fact table.

Our final facts are Units Ordered and Order Dollars. These fields will be zero or null for many of the records in this fact table, simply because the specific page event is not the event that places the order. Nevertheless, it is highly attractive to provide these fields, because they tie the all important Web revenue directly to behavior. If the Units Ordered and Order Dollars were only available through the production order entry system elsewhere in the data Webhouse, it would be inefficient to perform the revenue-to-behavior analysis across multiple large tables. In many database management systems, the existence of these kinds of null fields are handled efficiently, and may take up literally zero space in the fact table.

We can quickly estimate the size of this fact table. If we use the earlier example of 100 million raw Web log events each day, we probably end up with about 20 million meaningful page events per day after we discard the requests for GIF and JPEG images. Each record in the page event fact table has 15 fields, which we estimate occupies 15×4 bytes, or 60 bytes. Thus the total fact table data to be added each day is 20 million $\times$ 60 bytes, or 1.2 GB per day. This would amount to 365×1.2 GB = 438 GB per year, before indexing. Again, while this is a large number, it is within reach of today's technology.

As we move to more dynamic page delivery, with better semantic labels on each of the actions (thanks to XML), we will undoubtedly increase the volume of data available. Perhaps we keep the granularity of the present table at approximately one page view per record, rather than making a record for each discrete customer gesture. It is too early at this time to make a definitive prediction of whether we will descend all the way to the individual gesture with a third and even more granular fact table. Even if our storage and query technologies keep up with the increased volume of data, we need to wait to see if there is sufficient analysis content in the lowest-level behavior data to make it worthwhile. Hopefully, you can see how to extend the techniques of this chapter to handle this case.

With this page event fact table, we can extend our ability to analyze customer behavior.

We can now shed considerable light on issues raised in Chapter 3, including:

- How to decide whether a customer is about to leave us,
- How to decide whether a particular Web ad is working,
- How to decide if custom greetings are working,
- How to (partly) decide if a promotion is profitable,
- How to improve the effectiveness of your Website, and
- Which products and services do we provide over the Web.

Aggregate Clickstream Fact Tables

Both of the fact tables we have built thus far in our clickstream data mart are pretty large. There are many business questions we would like to ask that are forced to summarize millions of records from these tables. For example, if we want to track the total visits and revenue from major demographic groups of customers accessing our Website on a month by month basis, we can certainly do that with either fact table. In the session-grained fact table we would constrain the Calendar Date dimension to the appropriate time span (say, January, February, and March of the current year). We would then create row headers from the demographics type field in the Customer dimension, and the month field in the Calendar dimension (to separately label the three months in the output). Finally, we would sum over the total Order Dollars, and count the number of sessions. This all works just fine. But it is likely to be slow without help from an aggregate table. If this kind of query is frequent, the database administrator will be encouraged to build an aggregate table such as shown in Figure 6.5.

We can build this table directly from our first fact table, whose grain is the individual session. To build this aggregate table, we group by month, demographic type, entry page, and session outcome. We count the number of sessions and sum all the other additive facts. This results in a drastically smaller fact table, almost certainly less than 1 percent of the original session grained fact table. This reduction in size translates directly to a corresponding increase in performance for most queries. In

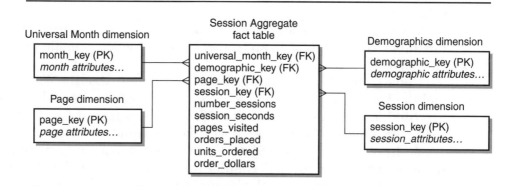

FIGURE 6.5 An Aggregate Clickstream Fact Table Where the Grain Is Demographic Type by Month by Entry Page by Session Outcome

other words, we would expect queries directed to this aggregate table to run at least 100 times as fast.

Although it may not have been obvious, we followed a careful discipline in building the aggregate table. This aggregate fact table is connected to a set of *shrunken dimensions* directly related to the original dimensions in the session grained fact table. The Month table is a conformed subset of the Calendar Day table. The Demographic table is a conformed subset of the Customer table. We assume the Page and Session tables are unchanged although a careful design of the aggregation logic could suggest a conformed shrinking of these tables as well.

SUMMARY

In this chapter we have delivered the central promise of bringing the Web to the warehouse. We began by defining a standard design template: the dimensional model. We showed how nearly all kinds of business measurements can be cast in this model, and we showed how dimensional models can be linked together. When dimensional models are linked together, complete Webhouses spanning many business functions can be implemented in an incremental and distributed style.

We proposed three specific dimensional models for Web data, each at a different grain. Perhaps the most useful grain is a record for each complete customer session. This grain is a good compromise between the extreme detail provided by the page event grain and the much more summarized monthly snapshot grain. The customer session fact table allows many decisions to made about what kinds of customers are being attracted to our Website, and whether these customers are being satisfied.

The most detailed record of behavior is found in the page event grain fact table. In this table we are recording every gesture made by every customer.

Underlying all of these designs is an assumption that the Webmaster and the Webhouse project manager have successfully defined a way to describe Web pages. The value of the Web logs rises tremendously when a good description can be associated with each page delivered to a customer.

We have now set the foundation for the last step in bringing the Web to the warehouse. In the next chapter we see how our completed Website behavior data marts fit into the larger framework of existing data marts derived from the other operational systems in our enterprise.

CHAPTER 7

Assembling Clickstream Value Chains

In Chapter 3 we showed many valuable business questions that could be answered with the help of the clickstream data. But several of these questions needed to link the clickstream data to other existing data marts within the organization. In the last chapter we described the framework, called the Data Warehouse Bus architecture, that makes all of this possible. The secret, of course, is to implement conformed dimensions and conformed facts across all the data marts.

In the first two fact tables we designed for the clickstream data mart, we defined a number of dimensions. A few of these dimensions probably have no relevance outside the clickstream context. These might include the Page, Event, Session, and Referrer dimensions. But several other dimensions absolutely will link to other far-flung data marts. These more public dimensions include Calendar Date, Time of Day, Customer, Product, and Causal.

Similarly, the conformed facts we must pay special attention to include Orders Placed and Order Dollars.

In this chapter we will propose a set of plausible designs for other data marts you may have in your environment. We highlight the dimensions and facts that are conformed jointly with the clickstream in order to emphasize the leverage gained with this approach and to remind you not to avoid this task! We show four examples of complete value chains representing multiple processes within a business, where each value chain includes a clickstream data mart as one of the processes.

THE SALES TRANSACTION DATA MART

The first outside data mart we describe is the Sales Transaction data mart. We have assumed in these chapters that the Website is capable of taking sales directly on-line. When the Web server receives a properly filled out page back from the customer containing a sale, we assume the Web server invokes a transaction on the production sales system. The production sales system is not concerned about Web pages or anything to do with the Web. The job of the production sales system is to book the order quickly and reliably. This system after all, is the retail cash register for the company.

We assume the production sales system also processes transactions from other sales channels in addition to the Web. This is one of the reasons why we probably want to query the sales transaction data mart conjointly with the clickstream data mart. We hope to see meaningful patterns of customers crossing over from non-Web to Web purchases, and how customers balance their purchases between our different channels.

The grain of our Sales Transaction fact table will be the individual line item sold on a sales ticket to a customer at a point in time. This table will record all possible sales made by our company, which we imagine spans store sales, telesales, and Web sales. The dimensions for these revenue transactions includes Date, Time, Customer, Channel, Product, Causal, and Ticket number (degenerate). The additive facts include Order Dollars, Units Ordered, and Dollar Cost. The design is shown in Figure 7.1.

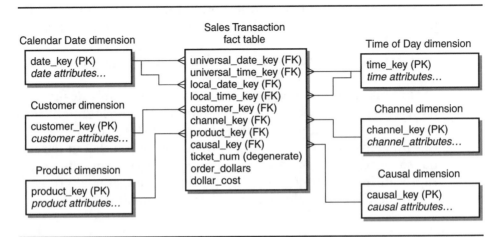

FIGURE 7.1   The Sales Transaction Dimensional Model

We have highlighted the five dimensions that are conformed within the enterprise and are shared by the clickstream fact tables as well as this revenue transaction fact table.

The Channel dimension tells us how we sold the product. The main choices are Store, Telesales, and Web. This dimension probably has a record for every store, every telesales desk, and every Web page that takes an order.

The degenerate Ticket Number dimension corresponds to the order entry system's view of a set of line items ordered or bought by the customer in a single episode. Hopefully, this means the same thing as a session in the case of Web sales, although that would take some careful coordination between the Web server that is maintaining the session and the order entry system.

The Dollar Cost field is useful because it allows the analyst to calculate gross profit, which is the difference between the Order Dollars and the Dollar Cost fields. Note that the Dollar Cost field must be an extended amount, not a unit amount, so that the gross profit calculation remains very simple.

If the Clickstream and Sales Transaction data marts are designed with these conformed dimensions, it is a simple matter to combine results from these data marts into a single query or report. Any constraint on a conformed dimension will mean the same thing in both data marts. Any row header used to label output rows will mean the same thing in both data marts. That means that answer sets can be combined on the same rows on the same pages of a report. The use of conformed facts, like Units Ordered and Order Dollars, means that calculations can be performed across the two data marts. For instance, we can reliably calculate what the percentage of Web sales from a particular referrer to all sales is. This calculation can only be done using the two fact tables.

THE CUSTOMER COMMUNICATION DATA MART

The customer communications data mart records all the communications with the customer outside the direct Web interactions. These communications include mailings and telephone interactions such as sales calls, support calls, and inquiry calls. The grain of the main fact table in this data mart is the individual communication with a specific customer at a point in time. This may well be a "factless" fact table, with no obvious measured fact. What we are trying to record is the existence of the event. Event tracking, which often leads to factless fact tables, is discussed in both of Kimball's books.

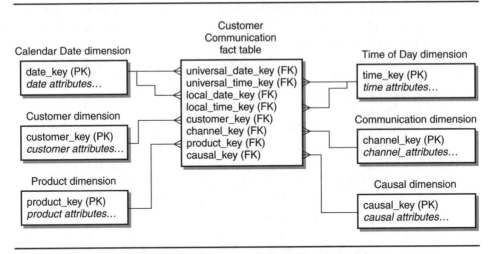

FIGURE 7.2   The Customer Communication Dimensional Model

The dimensions appropriate for this Customer Communication fact table include Calendar Date, Time, Customer, Product, Causal, and Communication Type. The complete design is shown in Figure 7.2.

The Communication Type dimension takes on values such as Mailing, Response to Mailing, General Inquiry, Support Inquiry, Help Desk Inquiry, Sales Inquiry, and Product Sale. This fact table can be used in conjunction with the clickstream and sales transaction data marts to track the effectiveness of ads, greetings, deals, mailings, support programs, and participation.

THE WEB PROFITABILITY DATA MART

After the data Webhouse team successfully brings up the initial Clickstream data mart and ties it to the Sales Transaction and Customer Communication data marts, the team may be ready to tackle the most challenging data mart of all: the Web Profitability data mart.

We will build the Web Profitability data mart as an extension of the Sales Transaction data mart. Fundamentally, we are going to allocate all of the activity costs and infrastructure costs down to each sales transaction. We could, as an alternative, try to build the Web Profitability data mart on top of the Clickstream data mart, but this would involve an even more controversial allocation process in which we allocated costs down to each session. It would be hard to assign activity and infrastructure costs to a session that had no obvious product involvement and led to no immediate sale.

A big benefit of extending the Sales Transaction fact table is that we will get a view of profitability over all our sales channels, not just the Web. In a way, this should be obvious because we know that we have to sort out the costs and assign them to the various channels anyway. For this reason, we will call the main fact table in our new data mart simply Profitability.

Thus the grain of the Profitability fact table is each individual line item sold on a sales ticket to a customer at a point in time. This is the same as the grain of the Sales Transaction data mart and includes all channels, which we assume are store sales, telesales, and Web sales.

The dimensions of the Profitability fact table are the same as the Sales Transaction fact table: Date, Time, Customer, Channel, Product, Causal, and Ticket number (degenerate). The big difference between the Profitability fact table and the Sales Transaction fact table is the breakdown of the costs. See the complete design in Figure 7.3.

Before discussing the allocation of costs, let us examine the format of the Profitability fact table. It is organized as a simple profit and loss (P&L) statement. Remember that the grain of this table is the individual line

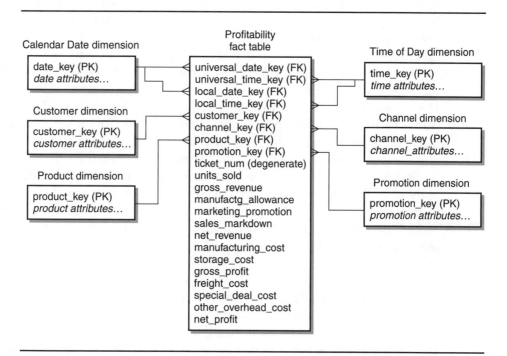

FIGURE 7.3   The Profitability Data Mart Dimensional Model

item (product) sold to an individual customer on a single sales ticket or within a single Web purchasing session. The first fact is our familiar Units Sold. All the rest of the facts are dollar values beginning with the value of the sale as if it were sold at the list or catalog price. Let us call this the Gross Revenue. We assume that sales often take place at lower prices, and we account for any such difference with a manufacturer's allowance, a marketing promotion that is a price reduction, or a mark-down done to move the inventory. When these effects have been taken into account, we can calculate the Net Revenue, which is the true net price the customer pays times the number of units purchased.

The rest of the P&L consist of a series of subtractions, where we calculate progressively more far reaching versions of profit. We begin by subtracting the product manufacturing cost (if we manufacture it) or equivalently the product acquisition cost, if we acquire it from a supplier. We then subtract the product storage cost. At this point, many enterprises call this partial result the Gross Profit. One can divide this Gross Profit by the Gross Revenue to get a ratio called the Gross Margin.

Obviously, the fields called Net Revenue and Gross Profit are calculated directly from the fields immediately preceding them in the P&L table. But should we explicitly store these fields in the database? The answer depends on whether you provide access to this fact table through a view or whether you allow users or applications to access the physical fact table directly. The structure of the P&L is sufficiently complex that, as the data Webhouse provider, you don't want to risk the important measures like Net Revenue and Gross Profit being computed incorrectly. If you provide all access through views, you can easily provide the computed columns without physically storing them. But if your users are allowed to access the underlying physical table, then you should include Net Revenue, Gross Profit, and Net Profit as physical fields.

Below the Gross Profit we continue subtracting various costs. Typically, the Webhouse team must source or estimate each of these costs separately. Remember that the actual entries in any given fact table record are the fractions of these total costs allocated *all the way down to the individual fact record grain*. Often there is significant pressure on the Webhouse team to finish the Profitability data mart. Or to put it another way, there is tremendous pressure to source all these costs. But how good are the costs in the various underlying data sets? Sometimes a cost is only available as a national average, computed for an entire year. Any allocation scheme is going to assign a kind of pro forma value that has no real texture to it. Other costs will be broken down a little better, perhaps to the calendar quarter, and by geographic region (if that is relevant). Finally, some costs may be truly *activity based*, and vary in a highly dynamic, responsive, and realistic way over time.

Website system costs are an important cost driver in e-commerce–oriented businesses. Although Website costs are classic infrastructure costs, and are therefore difficult to allocate directly to the product and customer activity, this is a key step in developing a Web oriented P&L statement. Various allocation schemes are possible, including allocating the Website costs to various product lines by the number of pages devoted to each product, allocating the costs by pages visited or allocating the costs by actual Web-based purchases.

 Before leaving this design, it is worthwhile putting it in perspective. When a P&L structure is embedded in a rich dimensional framework such as the one we have designed, we have immense power. We can see the breakdown of all the components of revenue and cost and profit for every conceivable slice and dice provided by the dimensions.

Although we began with the somewhat narrow task of reporting profitability of our Web business, we have emerged with far more. We can not only ask what is profitable, but we can ask *why*, since we can see all the components of the P&L. Our profitability questions include:

- How profitable are each of our channels (Web sales, telesales, store sales)? Why?
- How profitable are all our possible customer segmentations? Why?
- How profitable are our product lines? Why?
- How profitable are our promotions? Why?
- When are we most profitable? Why?

Of course, the symmetric dimensional approach we have taken allows us to combine constraints from as many dimensions as we can. This gives us compound versions of the profitability analyses like

- Who are the profitable customers in each channel? Why?
- Which promotions work well on the Web but do not work well in other channels? Why?

The data Webhouse team cannot be responsible for implementing activity-based costing (ABC) in a large organization. When the data Webhouse team is building a Profitability data mart, the team gets the best cost data available at the moment, and publishes the P&L. Perhaps some of the numbers are simple rule-of-thumb ratios. Others may be highly detailed activity-based costs. Over time, as the sources of cost improve, the Webhouse team incorporates these new sources and notifies the users that the business rules have improved.

A SUPPLY CHAIN FOR A WEB RETAILER

In this section we look at the overall design of a series of data marts implemented for a Web-based computer retailer. The data marts correspond to all the business processes needed by this retailer to run its business. We could illustrate this design by showing each schema as we have done in the previous examples, but the synergy among the designs would be difficult to see clearly. Instead, we use a data warehouse design technique called the matrix method.

The matrix method lists the data marts down the left side of the matrix and lists the dimensions used by the data marts across the top of the matrix. The cells of the matrix contain an X if the particular data mart uses a particular dimension. Note that the matrix describes data marts, not individual fact tables. Typically, a data mart consists of a suite of closely associated fact tables, all describing a particular business process. A good way to start the design of a series of data marts is to define *first-level* data marts that are, as much as possible, related to single sources of data. Once several of these first level data marts have been implemented, then *second-level* data marts can be built that require data from the first-level marts to be combined. The profitability data mart described in the previous section is usually a second-level data mart because all the components of revenue and cost turn out to be derived from separate first-level data marts.

Thus the entries in a given row of the matrix represent the existence of a dimension somewhere in the closely associated suite of tables defining a particular data mart.

Table 7.1 shows the completed matrix. The matrix has a number of striking characteristics. There are a lot of Xs. The average data mart uses six to eight dimensions. Some of the dimensions, such as Date/Time, Transaction, Status/Type, Organization, and Employee appear in almost every data mart. The Product and Customer dimensions dominate the whole middle part of the matrix, where they are attached to

	Date and Time	Part	Vendor	Transaction	Status and Type	Facilities Location	Carrier	Product	Customer	Media	Causal	Service Policy	Internal Organization	Employee	Clickstream dims (4)
Supplier Purchase Orders	✓	✓	✓	✓	✓			✓					✓	✓	
Supplier Deliveries	✓	✓	✓	✓	✓	✓	✓	✓					✓		
Part Inventories	✓	✓	✓	✓	✓			✓					✓		
Product Assembly Bill of Materials	✓	✓	✓	✓				✓	✓				✓	✓	
Product Assembly to Order	✓	✓	✓	✓	✓			✓	✓	✓			✓	✓	
Product Promotions	✓							✓	✓	✓	✓		✓		
Advertising	✓								✓	✓	✓		✓		
Customer Communications	✓			✓	✓				✓	✓			✓	✓	
Customer Inquiries	✓			✓	✓			✓	✓	✓		✓	✓	✓	
Web Visitor Clickstream	✓			✓				✓	✓	✓	✓	✓			✓
Product Orders	✓			✓	✓			✓	✓			✓		✓	
Service Policy Orders	✓			✓	✓			✓	✓			✓	✓	✓	
Product Shipments	✓			✓	✓	✓	✓	✓	✓				✓	✓	
Customer Billing	✓			✓	✓			✓	✓			✓	✓	✓	
Customer Payments	✓			✓	✓				✓				✓	✓	
Product Returns	✓			✓	✓			✓	✓	✓		✓	✓	✓	
Product Support	✓			✓	✓			✓	✓	✓		✓	✓	✓	
Service Policy Responses	✓			✓	✓			✓	✓	✓		✓	✓	✓	
Employee Labor	✓			✓	✓			✓					✓	✓	
Human Resources	✓			✓	✓			✓					✓	✓	
Facilities Operations	✓			✓	✓			✓					✓	✓	
Web Site Operations	✓			✓	✓			✓					✓	✓	

TABLE 7.1   A Data Mart Planning Matrix for a Web Retailer

the data marts that describe customer oriented activities. At the top of the matrix, suppliers and parts dominate the processes of acquiring the parts that make up products and building them to order for the customer. At the bottom of the matrix, we have classic infrastructure and cost driver data marts that are not directly tied to customer behavior.

We see the Web Visitor Clickstream data mart sitting squarely among the customer-oriented data marts. It shares the Date/Time, Transaction, Product, Customer, Media, Causal, and Service Policy dimensions with several other data marts nearby. In this sense it should be obvious that the Web Visitor Clickstream data mart is well integrated into the fabric of the overall data warehouse for this retailer. Applications tying the Web Visitor Clickstream will be easy to integrate across all of these data marts sharing these conformed dimensions because the separate queries to each data mart will be able to be combined across individual rows of the report.

The Web Visitor Clickstream data mart contains four additional dimensions not found in the other data marts. These dimensions are Page, Event, Session, and Referrer. However, the lack of other data marts with these dimensions does not pose a problem for applications. Instead, the ability of the Web Visitor Clickstream data mart to bridge between the Web world and the brick-and-mortar world is exactly the advantage that we are looking for. We can constrain and group on attributes from the four Web dimensions and explore the effect on the other business processes. For example, we can see what kinds of Web experiences produce customers who purchase certain kinds of service policies and then invoke certain levels of service demands.

Finally, it should be pointed out that the matrix serves as a kind of communications vehicle for all the data mart teams and for senior management to appreciate the need to conform the dimensions and conform the facts. A given column in the matrix is, in effect, an invitation list to the meeting for conforming the dimension!

A POLICIES AND CLAIMS CHAIN FOR INSURANCE

Manufacturers, distributors, and retailers are not the only businesses for which we can build a chain of data marts. Property and casualty insurance also has an elaborate chain representing all the steps in creating policies and then handling claims. A typical property/casualty insurance chain is shown in Table 7.2.

Again, we see a characteristic pattern between the data marts and the dimensions. The first seven data marts, up through Reinsurance, are concerned with creating insurance policies. The next six data marts are concerned with settling claims. We see that the claims processing data marts inherit all the dimensions of the claims, and then add a set of dimensions unique to the claim and the claimant.

After these two groups of data marts, we see that the Web Visitor Clickstream data mart spans nearly all the dimensions of both policies and claims. After all, who is the visitor on the insurance company Website? Certainly, we would expect the prospective customer to be studying the insurance company's offerings. We would expect the existing

	Date and Time	Agent	Customer	Coverage Type	Covered Item (e.g. a house)	Facility, Location	Policy Contract Type	Causal	Other Insurer	Claimant	Claim Type	Service Provider	Service Recipient	Lawyer	Other Employee	Internal Organization	Other Organization	Clickstream dims (4)
Agent Policy Sales	✓	✓	✓	✓	✓	✓	✓	✓									✓	
Rating	✓	✓	✓	✓	✓	✓	✓									✓	✓	
Underwriting	✓	✓	✓	✓	✓	✓	✓									✓	✓	
Policy Commitment	✓	✓	✓	✓	✓		✓									✓	✓	
Coverage Adjustments	✓	✓	✓	✓	✓	✓	✓	✓									✓	
Renewals and Cancellations	✓	✓	✓	✓	✓	✓	✓	✓								✓	✓	
Reinsurance	✓		✓	✓	✓		✓		✓							✓	✓	
Web Visitor Clickstream	✓	✓	✓	✓	✓		✓		✓	✓	✓	✓	✓	✓	✓	✓	✓	✓
Claim Capture	✓	✓	✓	✓	✓	✓	✓			✓	✓	✓	✓	✓	✓	✓	✓	
Reserve Estimation	✓	✓	✓	✓	✓	✓	✓			✓	✓	✓	✓	✓	✓	✓	✓	
Claim Investigation	✓	✓	✓	✓	✓	✓	✓			✓	✓	✓	✓	✓	✓	✓	✓	
Claim Settlement	✓	✓	✓	✓	✓		✓			✓	✓	✓	✓	✓	✓	✓	✓	
Subrogation	✓		✓	✓	✓		✓			✓	✓	✓	✓	✓		✓	✓	
Salvage	✓	✓	✓	✓	✓	✓	✓			✓	✓	✓	✓	✓		✓	✓	
Advertising	✓			✓	✓			✓									✓	
Promotions	✓			✓	✓	✓		✓									✓	
Customer Communications	✓	✓	✓	✓	✓	✓	✓	✓			✓	✓	✓	✓		✓	✓	
Customer Inquiries	✓	✓	✓	✓	✓	✓	✓	✓			✓	✓	✓	✓		✓	✓	
Customer Billing	✓	✓	✓					✓									✓	
Customer Payments	✓		✓														✓	
Employee Labor	✓						✓									✓	✓	
Human Resources	✓						✓									✓	✓	
Facilities Operations	✓						✓										✓	
Website Operations	✓						✓										✓	

TABLE 7.2   A Data Mart Planning Matrix for a Property/Casualty Insurer

customer to be inquiring about current policy coverages, and requesting renewals or alterations to those coverages. When a claim is made, we would expect a whole host of visitors to visit the Website, including the claimant, the service provider (such as a doctor or a car repair shop), and even various lawyers representing the parties. Even more than the retailer, we see that the Web Visitor Clickstream has the potential for recording just about all the important communications of the insurance company. Here's a case where designing the customer facing business processes to be Web-enabled is a major revolution for the insurance industry. The brick-and-mortar insurance companies who ignore the Web may face stiff competition from startups who offer "virtual" insurance services to all the parties in the insurance chain. Many analysts have remarked that insurance is really an information-processing business, not a tangible products business.

Again, we use the special clickstream dimensions of Page, Event, Session, and Referrer to drive our analyses of the whole insurance business. If we expect the insurance Website to provide the whole spectrum of services, we need to spend a lot of time studying what actually gets accomplished through the Web interfaces.

A SALES PIPELINE CHAIN

The third chain of data marts we will explore is the sales pipeline. Let's imagine that our company is a large hardware systems supplier. We sell expensive systems, mostly with a dedicated sales force that calls on the IT organizations within our customers. One of the main responsibilities of the vice president of sales for our company is to manage the sales pipeline. Roughly speaking, this pipeline takes in "unqualified prospects" and gradually turns them into paying customers. The original prospect is invited to seminars, is sent product literature, and eventually is personally called upon by the sales team. As a prospect progresses along the sales pipeline, the prospect learns more about our company, and we learn more about the prospect.

A good vice president of sales keeps all the levels of the pipeline full. There should always be more unqualified prospects than qualified prospects. Qualified prospects have only a certain probability of turning into customers. Even customers only have a probability of being repeat customers, or being customers who buy other product lines from our company.

In Table 7.3 we show the sales pipeline for our company. The first seven data marts at the top of the matrix define the sales pipeline. Sales pipelines have some interesting dimensions. The Prospect dimension describes a person or a company who has just come on to the radar of our marketing and sales teams. Initially, we may not know anything about a prospect except for a name. As we communicate repeatedly with the prospect, we gradually fill in more information. But a prospect is often not a customer. The two dimensions are quite different. When a

	Date and Time	Prospect	Area of Interest	Systems Environment	Marketing Employee	Sales Employee	Communication Mode	Location	Customer	Product	Contract	Internal Organization	Clickstream dims (4)
Prospect Contact	✓	✓	✓	✓	✓	✓	✓	✓	✓			✓	
Sales Referrals	✓	✓	✓	✓		✓	✓	✓	✓			✓	
Mass Communications	✓	✓	✓		✓		✓		✓			✓	
Web Visitor Clickstream	✓	✓	✓	✓					✓			✓	✓
Invited Seminars	✓	✓	✓	✓	✓	✓	✓	✓	✓	✓		✓	
Sales Calls	✓	✓	✓	✓		✓	✓	✓	✓	✓		✓	
Product Sales	✓					✓	✓	✓	✓	✓	✓	✓	
Support Contracts	✓					✓	✓	✓	✓	✓	✓	✓	
Consulting Contracts	✓					✓	✓	✓	✓	✓	✓	✓	

TABLE 7.3   A Data Mart Planning Matrix for a Sales Pipeline

prospect finally "graduates" and becomes a customer, we create a record in the Customer dimension and add a lot of much more specific and accurate information. Most of the time a customer record contains a pointer back to the associated prospect record. This pointer is valuable because it allows us to study how we developed a customer. It is possible that this back reference is multivalued, if we believe that a customer actually was developed out of more than one prospect. It is also possible that the prospect is indeed already a customer. This would be true if we were trying to cross-sell an existing customer on a new product or service. In all of these cases, we carry the Prospect dimension through the pipeline up to the point we actually make a sale, then we use just the Customer dimension.

Another interesting dimension in the sales pipeline is the area of interest. When a prospect first identifies themselves through the Website or in response to a mailing, they may describe their interests very broadly. Perhaps they are interested in "health care applications," or maybe "high performance RAID devices." It is important to capture the initially described area of interest no matter how broadly it may be stated. The area of interest is likely to be multivalued as well. But as the prospect moves down through the sales pipeline, the area of interest needs to be focused more and more on specific products and services that our company sells. When the prospect turns into a customer, the real product (and service) dimension attaches to the data. The transformation from an area of interest into a specific product is handled in much the same way that an identified prospect is transformed into a specific customer.

The status dimension is very important to the sales pipeline. A record in this dimension can combine several notions of status, but the most important status for managing the sales pipeline is the probability that the prospect will convert to a customer. This allows the vice president of sales to study all the stages of the sales pipeline to make sure that a balanced effort is being maintained to keep a steady flow of real customers. The status dimension in a fully Web-enabled business should track the progression of the customer from the first acceptance of a cookie to an advanced customer who is a repeat purchaser of multiple product lines. There could be a number of discrete steps in this progression, including:

- Unidentified New Visitor with Cookie
- Unidentified Repeat Visitor with Cookie
- Identified Visitor, No Purchases
- Known Purchaser
- Repeat Purchaser

A sophisticated version of the sales pipeline would attempt to "elevate" customers from simply being purchasers to being high-quality or high-yield purchasers.

In the middle of the matrix we see the Web Visitor Clickstream data mart. Like the other examples of chains, it is nicely integrated into the fabric of the overall pipeline data warehouse. It can share the Date/Time, Prospect, Customer, Area of Interest, Product, Prospect Source, Communication Mode, and Status dimensions with the other data marts. This will allow drill-across reports that tie different types of Website visits to all the steps of the sales pipeline.

A HEALTH CARE VALUE CIRCLE

The previous three examples of chains all had a strong notion of something moving through a series of sequential steps. A product moves from a manufacturer to a supplier to a retailer. An insurance coverage moves through the steps of policy formation and claims handling. A sales prospect moves through the stages of the sales pipeline. But not every distributed data warehouse has this notion of sequential steps.

An important example from the health care world is the group of companies and organizations that create and measure and reimburse health care charges. For example, a large HMO is really a consortium of health care providers like physicians, clinics, and hospitals, together with laboratories, pharmacies, and pharmaceutical manufacturers. This group extends finally to employers, insurance companies, and government agencies. A patient who receives a treatment does not encounter these organizations in any predictable order, but eventually all these organizations are interested in sharing the data generated by the same patient treatments. We can picture this situation as a "value circle" shown in Figure 7.4.

We can build a data mart planning matrix from the health care value circle in much the same way we built the previous three matrices. Our health care data mart matrix is shown in Table 7.4.

The data mart planning matrix for health care looks quite different than the previous three we have described in this chapter. Nearly every

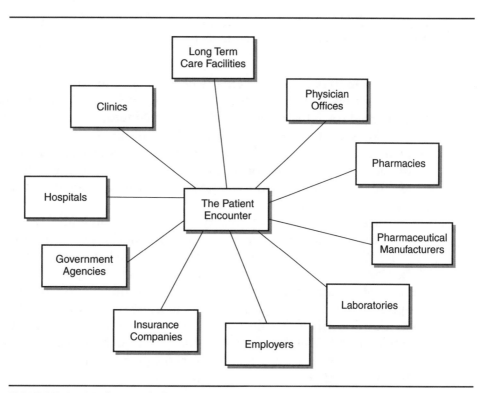

FIGURE 7.4   A Value Circle for an HMO

	Date and Time	Covered Employee	Patient	Payer	Provider	Treatment	Drug	Diagnosis	Location	Organization	Status	Internal Organization	Plan	Clickstream dims (4)
Hospitals	✓	✓	✓	✓	✓	✓	✓	✓	✓	✓	✓	✓	✓	
Clinics	✓	✓	✓	✓	✓	✓	✓	✓	✓	✓	✓	✓	✓	
Long Term Care Facilities	✓	✓	✓	✓	✓	✓	✓	✓	✓	✓	✓	✓	✓	
Physican Offices	✓	✓	✓	✓	✓	✓	✓	✓	✓	✓	✓	✓	✓	
Pharmacies	✓	✓	✓	✓	✓		✓		✓	✓	✓	✓	✓	
Pharmaceutical Manufacturers	✓	✓		✓	✓	✓	✓	✓	✓	✓	✓		✓	
Laboratories	✓	✓	✓	✓	✓	✓	✓	✓	✓	✓	✓	✓	✓	
Employers	✓	✓	✓	✓	✓	✓	✓	✓	✓	✓	✓	✓	✓	
Insurance Companies	✓	✓	✓	✓	✓	✓	✓	✓	✓	✓	✓	✓	✓	
Government Agencies	✓	✓	✓	✓	✓	✓	✓	✓	✓	✓	✓	✓	✓	
Web Visitor Clickstream	✓	✓	✓	✓	✓	✓	✓	✓	✓	✓	✓	✓	✓	✓

TABLE 7.4   A Data Mart Planning Matrix for an HMO

cell in the matrix has an *X*. This is because all the entities are sharing the same kind of data. All of them are analyzing and sharing patient treatment data. This data is highly dimensional, with twelve or more dimensions, as shown on the matrix. Some of the dimensions may even appear in a given fact table more than once, under different roles. For instance, a hospital procedure like an operation will have several provider roles, where the different physicians and nurses involved in the procedure are identified.

If the eleven organizations comprising the overall HMO want to share patient treatment data, then they need to conform all of the dimensions.

The Web visitor clickstream data mart clearly is tied into all of the data marts and all of the dimensions. A Web-based information system for this HMO supporting all of the patients, physicians, payers, bookkeepers, pharmacies, employers, and insurance companies would clearly be extraordinarily valuable. Perhaps even more than the previous three examples, this Website would need to have a comprehensive, well-controlled security system in place so that the right people could access the data they were entitled to and no one else.

SUMMARY

In the previous chapter we have provided a lightning tour of dimensional modeling as a refresher course and as a way to align our vocabulary. If this material was unfamiliar, it is strongly recommended that the reader consult Kimball's *Data Warehouse Lifecycle Toolkit* or its forerunner, *The Data Warehouse Toolkit*.

We carefully built two different granular levels of the Clickstream data mart and showed how they live in a richly dimensional framework. We described each dimension carefully, because all the power of the dimensional approach comes from careful attention to the dimensions themselves.

The first granular level was the individual customer session, and the second was the individual page event. We recommend starting with the session level before tackling the voluminous page event level.

In this chapter we described Sales Transaction, Customer Communications, and Web Profitability data marts, although we added a huge bonus. To do a proper job of evaluating Web profitability, we really needed to allocate costs to all of the channels of the business, and in doing so, we ended up with the immensely powerful enterprise Profitability data mart.

Now that we have a clear idea of our main data Webhouse deliverables (the data marts), it's time for us to step in a little closer and look at the detailed techniques for building and managing the Webhouse. In the remaining chapters, we will learn what the impact of evolving Web user interface designs will be on the data Webhouse, how to design for international deployment, how to design for serious security and serious scalability, and finally how to be a good data Webhouse manager.

CHAPTER 8

Implementing
the Clickstream
Post-Processor

Having identified the data that is available from the clickstream we can now take a look at how this clickstream data can be fed to our data warehouse. In many ways the clickstream can be handled by extract>transform>load (ETL) processes that we use for other more traditional data warehousing applications. There are, however, some important differences to note. In this section we will explore clickstream ETL requirements and develop a model ETL system that we've called the *clickstream post-processor*. See Figure 8.1.

As the state of the art of clickstream post-processing evolves over the next several years we expect that it will become possible to purchase commercial systems that fulfill some or all of the requirements

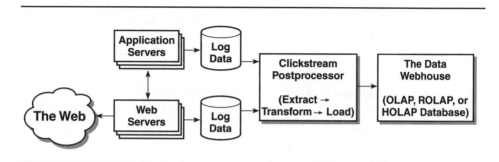

FIGURE 8.1   The Webhouse Extract-Transform-Load Architecture

we will outline here. This is a very complex software development project, and we anticipate that many organizations will be unwilling or unable to develop it from scratch. This chapter will provide a guide for what features should be included, whether the post-processor is developed in-house or procured commercially.

Clickstream post-processing ultimately prepares the clickstream data for loading into the data warehouse. Several goals must be met in the post-processing application, including the extraction of dimension keys for sessions, users, and hosts:

- **Filter out unneeded records.** Merge associated data and drop records that won't be passed through to the data warehouse. Reduce transaction volume as much as possible without compromising the integrity and completeness of data needed to support the design granularity of the warehouse.
- **Identify sessions.** Tag associated clickstream records with a unique session ID, and verify that event times are logically consistent with one another among the records that describe the session.
- **Identify users.** Match the user with an existing user ID, if possible. Otherwise, assign a unique anonymous user ID if identity is unknown.
- **Identify hosts.** Resolve (to the desired granularity) the IP addresses of clients and referrers. Retain country-of-origin and canonical domain data.

The numerical IP address of most Internet hosts can be resolved into their text equivalent using the nslookup program, which is available in most UNIX and Windows systems.

- **Consolidate data into a uniform format.** Put all of the clickstream data into a well-defined format that is acceptable to the data warehouse loader software.

All of these identification activities end up driving the capture of native keys for the Page Events dimension, which we defined in detail in Chapter 6. See Table 8.1.

Dimension Key	Resolved by
date_key	Page Event Extractor
customer_key	Session Identifier
event_key	Page Event Extractor
referrer_key	Host/Referrer Resolver
causal_key	Marketing (manual input)
datetime_key	[native]
page_key	Content Resolver
session_key	Session Identifier
product_key	Content Resolver

TABLE 8.1   Page Event Table Dimensions

POST-PROCESSOR ARCHITECTURE

It's possible to implement the clickstream post-processor either as a streaming, transaction-oriented application, a batch application, or some combination of these. In any case, the primary design constraints will inevitably boil down to *performance* and *scalability*. As we have mentioned previously (and will emphasize again) the log output from a successful Website is enormous. Each user click generates several log records that eventually reach the clickstream post-processor, because a single page click spawns separate requests for each object embedded on the page, such as GIF or JPEG graphical images.

A streaming post-processor architecture requires the clickstream transactions to be held in a staging area while transactions are consolidated and dimensions such as session ID are computed. In such an implementation, the staging area is likely to be an OLTP database. The consolidation and identification tasks will be performed by parallel application daemons that massage the raw transaction data, identifying sessions, hosts, and other dimensions.

A batch post-processor architecture implies a cascade of sort/merge steps with file-oriented data staging between steps. The consolidation and identification tasks are performed by serial applications that run between the sort and merge processes.

Figures 8.2 illustrates the process flow in a clickstream post-processor. This illustration is meant to show major processes, independent of whether the post-processor is implemented as a streaming or as a batch application. In either case we suggest an implementation that supports parallel data paths and multithreaded processes—parallel processing almost always enables scalability.

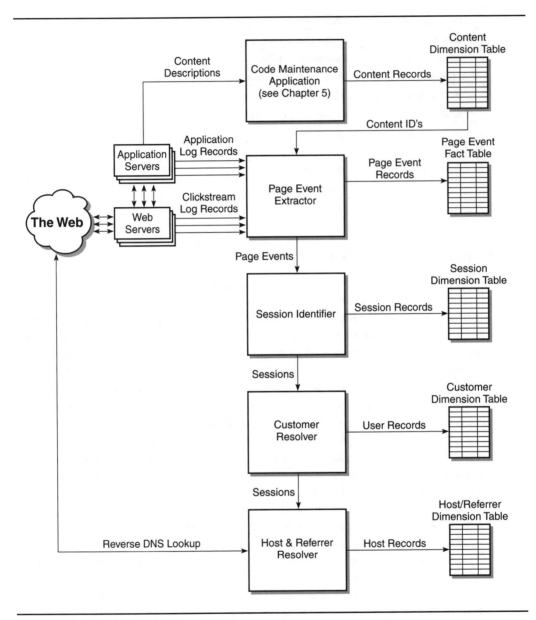

FIGURE 8.2 Inside a Clickstream Post-Processor

The Page Event Extractor

The page event extractor gathers log records from Web servers and from application servers, and merges them into *page events*. A page event may be navigational (e.g., go to a page) or static (e.g., click a button on a page). In either event, it is a page-specific event and will sit at the finest level of granularity in the Web-based data warehouse. The page event extractor potentially needs to have the ability to deal with a variety of different input data formats, from diverse Web and application servers within an enterprise. We have seen one instance in which page events are being extracted from 500 separate Web servers in a single enterprise by a page event extractor. Though we might be tempted at this point to discard log records for the retrieval of images (GIF and JPEG files) and other non-HTML items, this would be premature. We will need to retain these records for use by the session identifier in computing dwell time.

The page event extractor assigns an event dimension key that identifies the type of event represented by the record, such as opening a page or entering data. The extractor must also have the ability to reject data that it doesn't understand or which is inconsistent or incomplete, and to report these records in a form that will allow the data extract manager to rectify problems with the data sources that cause such rejections.

The page event extractor may actually add records to the clickstream. If our applications are not able to log significant events (like shopping cart checkout) to the clickstream log flow, the page event extractor will have to obtain these from the appropriate application server and add them as pseudo page events.

Inasmuch as the page event extractor culls information from a variety of sources, it has the responsibility of conforming data from these diverse sources. We've talked about this role in Chapter 5, but for the present, remember that Web servers may assign slightly different meaning to the same measurement. While one brand of Web server might log the time that an HTTP request was received, another might log the time that the request was actually satisfied. The event extractor is the best place to conform such information since it is the first downstream process to handle the server log data. Finally, the extractor writes the events it has identified out to a table or file in a common format for further processing.

The Content Resolver

The content resolver examines each page event record and attempts to relate the page event to site-specific content. In order to do this, the content resolver must have access to various content indexes supplied by the application server. More specifically, the content resolver is responsible for generating two of the event record's dimension keys: its *page key* and its *product key*. The page key identifies a specific Website static page ID or in a dynamic hosting environment, a template ID. This ID may be carried in the original log information, or it might need to be looked up by name in a site's content index.

The product key is germane to a retail environment but might have other meanings in different kinds of Websites. In a retail environment the product key might be a UPC obtained from an SKU/Product Name index. For booksellers we might use an ISBN obtained from a Title/Author index. And for a news publishing Website this might mean headline/story/revision indexes.

The Session Identifier

The session identifier's primary role is to collect and tag all of the page events that occurred during a single, identifiable user session. The session identifier is responsible for two of the event record's dimension keys: its *session key* and its *customer key*. This process also computes *dwell time*. All of these computations contain significant elements of uncertainty that the session identifier must attempt to resolve. Because of this, the session identifier is likely to be the most difficult single element of the Web-enabled data warehouse to program. Its algorithms for session identification, user identification, and dwell time computation will be complex and will of necessity, incorporate intelligent guesses rather than absolute computational certainty.

Several times in the preceding text we have referred to the HTTP protocol as being stateless. This is the point at which this lack of state becomes a severe problem to our data gathering and analysis tasks. It's relatively easy to declare the starting time of a session: For analytical purposes it's the moment of the first HTTP request from a user (or a specific IP address). Unfortunately, a Web user normally doesn't do anything as decisive as hanging up a phone. If there is no definitive session-ending event like a store checkout, you will have to rely on a site-determined best-guess *inactivity timeout*—for example, five minutes without an HTTP request-to put an outer bound on a session. If the user is silent longer than the timeout period, subsequent events are assumed to be from a follow-on session. Having bracketed the session from the first user request to a specific closure event or to the end of the timeout period, we can now consider the contents of the session itself. The session consists of all events that were logged for this user over the session duration. The session identifier assigns a unique arbitrary session key to the user session and tags all of the records that comprise the session with this key.

The session identifier must now determine to the precision possible, the identity of the user. As we discussed in an earlier chapter, even in the best of circumstances we are actually identifying the browser or PC, not the user, since there is virtually no way to determine who's actually sitting at the keyboard. The session identifier should use the most trustworthy information it has, from the following list of candidate user IDs. See Table 8.2.

At this point the session identifier has completed its primary tasks. After computing dwell time, it can elect to cull out log records that will not be carried further into the data warehouse. Typically, we will exclude detailed content log records at this point, eliminating records for the download of ancillary content like images.

Computing Dwell Time

After the session identifier completes its initial tasks, it will work on calculating dwell times—the likely time that a specific page was actively displayed on the user's screen. As shown in Figure 8.3, the dwell time can be calculated as the time between successive HTTP HTML requests (t_0 to t_3) minus the time it takes to serve the entire request—that is, the initial request plus downloads of ancillary content such as images and scripts (t_0 to t_2).

Most Trustworthy	Validated User ID from an application server
Somewhat Trustworthy	Validated User ID from a persistent cookie
Neutral	Anonymous User ID from a persistent cookie
Somewhat Untrustworthy	Server-assigned anonymous User ID (new cookie)
Least Trustworthy	Session-level User ID (unknown user)

TABLE 8.2   Candidate User IDs

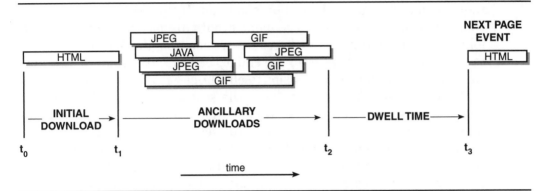

FIGURE 8.3   Computing Dwell Time

 If one or more of the ancillary downloads is streaming media, such as Real Audio or Video, then the dwell time should be computed using the beginning of the streaming media download regardless of whether the rest of the content is fully downloaded.

Web browsers and servers allow parallel requests, so several ancillary content requests might be serviced at the same time. Some Web servers (e.g., Apache) include an optional time-to-serve measurement in their log records. If time-to-serve is unavailable from log records, it must be estimated using the logged number of bytes in the object (plus an allowance for an HTTP header), and an assumed rate of uploading, perhaps augmented by page loading time estimates from a third-party Web performance measuring house such as Keynote. Once the time-to-serve has been determined, the composite page download time is easily calculated, as the completion of the request time plus time-to-serve for all elements of the page, minus the time at which the initial HTTP request was received. The dwell time for each successive page is computed the same way as shown in Figure 8.4. At the end of the session or visit, we have no way of determining the next HTML request. If there is one, it won't be directed to our Web server. So we must establish an assumed timeout after the last download as shown in the illustration.

When a download takes too long, the visitor is likely to stop the download and go to something else—even to another site. It is very important to capture these events because they represent one of the greatest sources

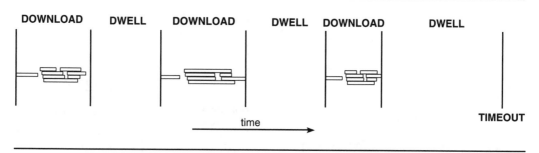

FIGURE 8.4   Dwell Time at the End of a Session

of user dissatisfaction. If a download is terminated, the dwell time is zero as shown in Figure 8.5.

Host and Referrer Resolver

Unless we specifically resolve them, the URLs for hosts and referrers are expressed as numeric IP addresses, not as host names. We will definitely want to resolve hostnames for referrers, and probably want to resolve (to some level) the addresses of hosts as well. Resolving host names requires the use of reverse DNS lookup across the Internet. See Figure 8.6. This is a very resource-intensive process for the net, and it can take several seconds to complete for each address resolved. Reverse DNS lookups can be multithreaded, so this isn't as much of a limitation as it may seem.

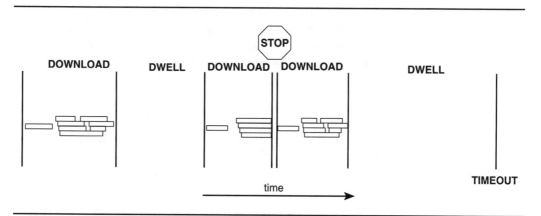

FIGURE 8.5   Zero Dwell Time

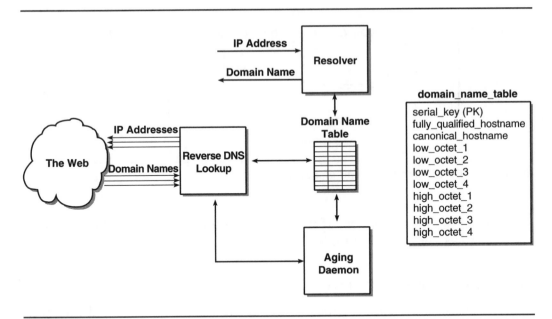

FIGURE 8.6 Domain Resolution

The master reference for IP and host names is held by the Internet Assigned Numbers Authority (IANA) and is in transition to the successor organization, the Internet Corporation for Assigned Names and Numbers (ICANN).

Most addresses will not need to be resolved beyond the second or third octet in their addresses. It is sufficient to know that an address begins with 152.176 to identify it as having originated on America Online and that if it begins with 207.217 it belongs to Earthlink. Further granularity of address resolution will generally provide no additional information, only a dynamically assigned network IP address. For most Website hits we don't need the actual host name, only the canonical name of the domain—that is, its highest resolved level.

 When specifying fields for IP addresses be sure to allow for 128 bits to accommodate the new IPv6 standard.

Our goals then, are to resolve hostnames only to the level needed—in most cases the network's canonical name and to reduce the amount of reverse DNS lookup as much as possible. To accomplish these, the host and referrer resolver will have the following characteristics:

- Use a resolution algorithm that attempts to resolve the host name using the fewest number of octets possible. Each row in the domain table should be able to represent either a unique IP address or a range of IP addresses.
- Maintain a local domain name table (it may have several tens of millions of rows) to avoid duplicate reverse DNS lookups.
- Age the contents of the hosts table and re-check old entries (6 months or more) to reaffirm their validity. Drop domain names or IP addresses that no longer are in use.

SUMMARY

In Chapter 4 we examined the clickstream from Web server and Web application logs as the primary data source for our Web-enabled data warehouse. In the intervening chapters we have described the detailed data targets in the final Webhouse for this clickstream data. In this chapter we have picked up the thread again and have followed the data through the extract/conform/load process we call the clickstream post-processor. Here we have looked at the specific features a post-processor should contain and presented alternative approaches for implementing them. We have now completed the process of bringing the Web to the warehouse and we are ready to turn around in the other direction and bring the warehouse to the Web.

PART TWO

Bringing the Warehouse to the Web

CHAPTER 9

Why Bring the Warehouse to the Web?

The data warehouse is the place where we publish the data assets of the enterprise. The data warehouse manager is a kind of executive publisher and editor-in-chief. The data warehouse manager gathers data inputs from a wide variety of sources. The inputs are laid on the "copy desk" and judged for relevance, correctness, and completeness. Problems in the data inputs are identified and corrected. The data inputs are cast in a common, recognizable format, and then they are published to the readers (end users) of the data warehouse.

The publishing steps of the data warehouse take place on a timely, regular basis. The readers of the data warehouse implicitly trust the content of the data, and that trust is taken very seriously by the data warehouse manager acting as the publisher and editor. Complaints stop at the data warehouse manager's desk.

For the past ten years or more, we have been building data warehouse infrastructure and refining our techniques. We have learned that the most time-consuming and difficult task of building a data warehouse is extracting, transforming, and loading the legacy data into the data warehouse. We have developed the techniques of dimensional modeling that are responsible for much of the success of delivering data through our data warehouses to end users. We have improved our database engines enormously so that they can efficiently process queries against our dimensionally modeled tables. And we have gradually improved the end user tools so that they are more usable.

During the 1990s we have had many data warehouse successes and a fair number of failures. In the authors' opinion, the failures were mainly due to:

- not responding to the urgent business requirements of the enterprise
- not building a system that could be used by the end users
- embarking on overly ambitious, expensive, centralized designs that could not be finished

The arrival of the Web at the end of the 1990s is hugely beneficial to the data warehouse movement. The Web amplifies and extends the publishing metaphor of the data warehouse. The Web offers many benefits that the data warehouse industry by itself could never have built. The Web is so compelling that data warehousing has no choice but to get on this express train.

But in joining the Web revolution, the data warehouse has to play by a number of new rules. The data warehouse must permanently shed some of its early conceptions and prejudices, and in some ways, reinvent itself. The second half of this book works through this new data warehouse perspective in some detail. In this chapter, we divide the discussion into two parts. The first part is the "pull," where we remind ourselves of all the ways the Web supports and strengthens the existing structures of the data warehouse. The second part is the "push," where we sign on to the new responsibilities imposed by the Web, and start laying the plans for the necessary changes in our data warehouses. When we are done, we will have the new and cleaner definition of the data Webhouse.

THE WEB PULLS THE DATA WAREHOUSE

In many ways, the Web seems to be made to benefit the data warehouse. As a medium, the Web sends everyone powerful, subliminal messages, some of which are surprisingly similar to traditional data warehouse goals. The subliminal messages that support the existing view of the data warehouse are:

- The Web is a great place to find information.
- The Web is full of interesting content.
- All our customers, business partners, and employees are already on the Web; you don't have to worry about connecting them.

- The Web goes everywhere in the world, and it matches our international needs and our mobility needs.
- Everything comes through the browser, so you already have the software you need.
- All the familiar software vendors are committed to content delivery over the Web.
  - Corollary: many existing applications should transfer seamlessly to the Web.
  - Corollary: the vendors' pricing models are increasingly Web driven.

This is only half the list of subliminal messages. These are the messages that make a compelling case for bringing the existing data warehouse to the Web, perhaps without making very many changes. This isn't a crazy perspective, and it is a reasonable place to start planning for the impact of the Web, but in the second half of this chapter we will pay attention to some other messages from the Web as well.

Perhaps the most basic supportive message the Web sends to the data warehouse is that the Web has conditioned millions of people to turn on their computers and browse for information. Since the primary function of the data warehouse is to publish information, the Web is a beckoning potential partner.

Similarly, the Web solves a huge problem that ten years ago loomed as a major headache to organizations contemplating large distributed data warehouses. The Web is the answer to universal connectivity. In fact, the Web has raced ahead of the data warehouse, and has already signed up and connected every possible end user! The Web has signed up millions of users in countries and markets we haven't even considered yet. Not only that, but the Web has placed a single end user tool on all these desktops, too. The end user tool, of course, is the standard browser (whether it's Netscape or Internet Explorer).

Software vendors have been scrambling to accommodate the Web since the mid-1990s. What started as a Web option is now becoming a forced migration to the Web. The next major release from virtually every software vendor will be fully Web-enabled, if it isn't already. The software pricing models, and the underlying business models of the vendors, have shifted dramatically from end user software licenses to Web server software licenses. It is likely that many software vendors will soon sell only Web-configured and Web-priced software.

Given all these advantages and the immense pressure on all computer users, IT organizations, and software vendors to convert to the

Web, there really isn't much choice. The data warehouse is coming to the Web.

Now read the rest of the story.

THE WEB PUSHES THE DATA WAREHOUSE

All those users already connected to the Web have developed some pretty specific expectations. We can continue the list of expectations we started in the previous section:

- The Web is easy to use. Anyone can press buttons and fill in little forms.
- The Web is supposed to be fast—never mind that it sometimes isn't! This expectation is nonnegotiable.
  - Corollary: I really value fast Websites and would prefer to use them.
- Websites are supposed to be up 24 hours a day, 7 days a week.
- I can find the status of almost anything on the Web and I expect it to be up-to-the-minute.
- All sorts of amazing things happen on the screen. Web interfaces are intensely graphical and dynamic.
- The ability to communicate with someone is marbled across almost every Web page.
- A Web page should be personalized to me, the user, as if I were having a dialogue with the Website.
- Since I can connect anywhere, by analogy I expect to drill across my distributed data Webhouse.
- What I want is an enterprise information portal.
- Security is a huge issue that must be dealt with before I feel comfortable trusting the Web.

We need to keep in mind that the Web is bigger and more important than the data warehouse. The Web is changing our basic cultural values, and the warehouse needs to hurry to stay aligned with these new values. Go back to the list we just finished, and instead of reading the list in the context of the Web, read it in the context of the data warehouse. What we are trying to say is that the Web is defining a whole list of new requirements for the data warehouse. The significance of this change is one of the reasons we call the new data warehouse the Webhouse.

It is very eye-opening to take the above list of expectations and apply them to the design of a data warehouse. We see that our new Webhouse needs to be unusually easy to use, able to deliver its results in ten seconds, available 24 hours per day, capable of delivering graphical results, personalized to our information needs, and highly secure. In the remainder of this chapter, we hint at the techniques we must develop to meet these needs, and then we spend the rest of the book developing these techniques in detail.

Tightening the User Interface Feedback Loop

The Web is an unforgiving crucible that measures user interface effectiveness directly. The clickstream supplies the evidence in a way that we can't avoid. We see every gesture the user makes, and some of the gestures aren't pretty. A user arrived at the page and left in 10 seconds. If they didn't click on the page, they didn't see what they needed. If they left the page before it finished painting, it was too slow. If they don't come back to the page, they can't use it. The Web is finally making usability important.

Up until now the user interface designers who work for software vendors have been somewhat insulated from their customers. They have not had such direct measurements of user activity. All too often, feature suggestions and usability suggestions have been collected by the field organization of the software vendor, and these suggestions have been considered by product marketing once or twice a year as new releases of the software are planned. The user suggestions have had to compete with new development initiatives sponsored by the developers and by headquarters executives. Individual ease-of-use suggestions have often been treated as insignificant by themselves, and worse, have been occasionally dismissed as a symptom of lack of training or understanding by the end users.

The Web places much more pressure on tools to be easy to use. Web tools and Websites in general are more accessible and can be compared more easily. Perhaps more important, user interface design has become more fashionable. New vocabularies for judging ease of use on Websites are emerging, and we will explore these new user interface perspectives in some detail in Chapter 10. As Website and data Webhouse designers, we want to tighten the feedback loop so that the clickstream gives us even more specific guidance about what is working with our user interfaces.

Mixing Query and Update

Web users are used to dealing with forms that display information and have buttons that do things. The pressure to design systems that mix query and update increases as the applications become more and more operational. An end user that is looking a single account balance or a single back order status, or a single stock price, is fairly likely to want to press a button to make a deposit, cancel the back ordered item, or sell some of the stock. Even before the big shift to the Web, the data warehouse was aggressively drawing in operational users.

If account balances, order statuses, and stock prices are maintained on production transaction processing systems, then an operationally oriented data Webhouse will be something of a hybrid. The Web server application may use the hot response cache to display current status, but if the user presses a button that actually posts a transaction, then the application probably connects directly to the OLTP system.

Beyond these architectural impacts, there is something about the Web itself that makes people expect to find "current status." This expectation impacts the design of any data warehouse exposed to the Web. That is why a true data Webhouse needs the hot response cache component.

Speed Is Nonnegotiable

Web users are impatient. Their attention is entirely on the screen. After more than ten seconds of waiting, the mouse begins to hover over the "back" button. Web users don't know about coffee cup response times and turning their backs to the screen. Part of this impatience comes from a natural fear that any long-running response on the Web is "wedged" and needs to be started over.

There has been a tendency in data warehouse circles to allow certain kinds of queries to run for 5 minutes, or 1 hour, even 72 hours. There is no excuse for a 72-hour query. Something is drastically wrong. Maybe the hardware is too small for the job, and the machine is thrashing virtual memory. More likely, the query processing is grossly inefficient and needs to be either rewritten or moved to a DBMS that has a better query analyzer.

One-hour queries and even five-minute queries are too long. As a data warehousing industry, we are probably less than halfway through a generation of software retooling that will yield dramatically better query performance. So, we as data Webhouse implementers can expect significant improvements in query response time, thanks to advances in software engineering. It also means, however, that over time we need to consider many different query technologies and not stay marooned with any vendor that is slow to add new query capabilities to their DBMS engines. Fortunately, the distributed, heterogeneous design techniques that the Web is forcing us to use anyway allow us to gracefully add interesting new technologies such as high-speed OLAP engines into an existing data Webhouse framework. We will be much more specific about how to employ these distributed techniques in the next chapter.

 The hot cache doesn't make the database run faster, but it does create the illusion of high performance by caching answers to predictable questions.

The Sun Never Sets on the Data Webhouse

The worldwide reach of the Web is one of its most remarkable characteristics. The Web invites every data warehouse to take on international proportions. Customers in remote countries click on our Website and order our products. Business partners and employees log in from remote locations at strange hours. See Figure 9.1.

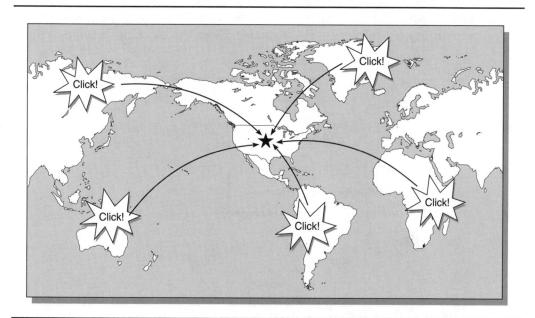

FIGURE 9.1   The International Webhouse

The data Webhouse can no longer go off-line for long periods to re-load data. Even short gaps in availability are undesirable. The modern data Webhouse must use advanced shadowing techniques to load data off-line and then switch the new data sets onto the main line without any interruption in service. We discuss the latest techniques for continuous data Webhouse availability in Chapter 12.

The multicultural nature of the Web also places a number of related database design requirements on the data Webhouse. In Chapter 10 we draw together all of the following threads:

- International character sets and UNICODE
- International sorting and reporting
- International names, addresses, and telephone numbers
- International currency handling
- International dates and times
- International privacy

Multimedia Merges into Communication

The data Webhouse must deliver its results into a multimedia environment. See Figure 9.2. Users expect graphics, animation, zoomable images, maps, video clips, and sounds. The Web provides much of the machinery for delivering these modes. Even the existing databases don't

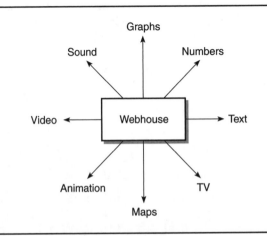

FIGURE 9.2   Multimedia Drives the Webhouse

need to be changed to accommodate the new data types. One can embed a file reference to a multimedia object in any database record, and then just instruct the final presentation tool to play that file reference if it is called for. The real issue for multimedia, strangely, is not technical, but rather is the issue of sourcing the multimedia material in digital form in the quantities needed to describe every data Webhouse object.

Another kind of "multimedia" that Web users expect is the e-mail link. Any reference to a person or an enterprise is expected to be "hot." Click on the name or the picture of the person or enterprise, and your next keystrokes are an e-mail message directed to them. Either the databases or the presentation tools must recognize an object that contains a mailable link and present it with the familiar blue underline in all contexts.

Finally, Web users will expect the data Webhouse to allow not only the display of multimedia types, but their query as well. Some kinds of multimedia are already being successfully queried. The Web's search engines have certainly shown that free text in an ocean of documents can be queried. At the same time, great progress is being made in querying maps. We know how to search for objects that are near each other, and objects that partially or fully contain each other. Data Webhouses need to incorporate text searching and geographic searching, starting now.

The searching of graphical images and sounds, however, is not as well developed. It seems safe to say that as more of these sources become available in systematic databases, clever techniques will be developed that will allow some forms of searches. Although today we may not be able to tell if a dog is in an image, we probably can pick out all the music selections that contain violin solos.

The ability to search all forms of information, not just structured text and numbers in records, makes the data Webhouse a true *enterprise information portal*.

The Web Is Mass Customization

Static Web pages based on fixed HTML encoding in most cases will be phased out in favor of dynamically created pages based on XML. If we have built our data Webhouse well, then the Webhouse is responsible for driving the personalization routines that paint unique pages for each user. The same personalization logic that serves our customers on the public Web server will also drive the data Webhouse user interfaces for business partners and employees.

Part of the charm of XML is that even if a Web page display for a particular user is entirely unique with a selection of fields and buttons not found on another user's display, the meaning of the fields and buttons can be well described. When the user interacts with their unique page, we can capture the interaction in a meaningful way, because XML provides semantic labeling for a Web page's contents. The record of this interaction makes XML-based clickstreams more descriptive and more actionable.

Sean Kelly used the term *mass customization,* and described it clearly in his book, *Data Warehousing: The Route to Mass Customization* (Wiley, 1996). Although the word customization has morphed into the word personalization in 1999, Sean's ideas were clearly an early expression of CRM. As he put it in 1996, "Genuine mass customization is an attempt to establish a real and informed dialogue with the customer and to demonstrate that the organisation has a knowledge of the behaviour of that customer over time."

If discrete page events and eventually XML-based descriptions of customer behavior are the raw data that drive mass customization, the data Webhouse is the engine that analyzes this customer behavior.

The Webhouse Is Profoundly Distributed

The data Webhouse requires a profoundly distributed architecture. See Figure 9.3. Increasingly, Web-enabled data warehouses will be sets of lightweight flexible data marts implemented on a widely heterogeneous mix of incompatible technologies. We need to take seriously the scientific issues of hooking these data marts together (it can be done), rather than arguing that these independent data marts shouldn't exist.

Centralized, monolithic designs will become more difficult to pursue in these widely distributed data warehouse environments in the same way that centralized designs are difficult in widely distributed computing environments and networks. The problem is that it is too expensive and time-consuming to do fully centralized database planning, and these idealistically motivated designs are difficult to keep in synch with dynamically changing real-world environments. Because our data Webhouse designs encompass not only our internal operations but also our business partners in the supply chain and even our customers, we simply can't mandate a fully centralized approach. There is no center.

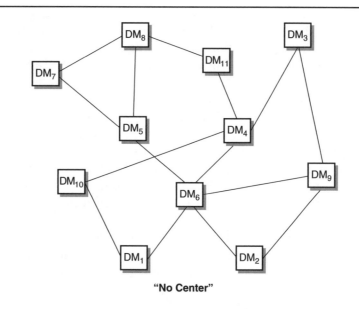

"No Center"

FIGURE 9.3   The Distributed Webhouse Has No Center

However, in moving more aggressively to a distributed design approach, we can certainly avoid the old stovepipe argument that distributed systems represent out-of-control separate efforts that can't be connected together. The solution to the stovepipe argument is a flexible framework of common definitions (conformed dimensions and conformed facts) that let us stitch the individual data marts together. Interestingly, we only need to centralize the actual definition, implementation, and replication of the conformed dimensions and facts out to the working data marts logically, not physically.

In Chapter 6, we built a set of data marts with conformed dimensions that address all the business requirements from Chapter 3. Then, in Chapter 15, we figure out who has management responsibility for the various parts of the distributed data Webhouse, and what is centralized and what is not.

We Must Face Security and Its Cousin, Privacy

We have saved our favorite topic for last. If you are a data Webhouse manager, you need to publish only to those who have a need to know. This was hard enough in a closed client/server environment, but it is a real challenge in a Web environment.

The biggest reason the data Webhouse manager needs to be concerned with security is that the data Webhouse manager is the only person in the organization able to judge the appropriate use of the data by the various requesting users. Who else understands the content of the data and simultaneously understands the business needs of the requesting end users?

The data Webhouse manager can exercise the most important part of his or her responsibility by defining a set of security policies that map user profiles into access profiles. This needs to be defined in one place, and obviously this specification must be done at a fairly high (i.e., abstract) level. If the data Webhouse manager needs to deal with more than a few hundred user profiles and access profiles, then the system will break down.

If you as a data Webhouse manager agree with this view, then how do you take it to completion? What decisions do you make for this to happen? And, perhaps the question that has been in the forefront of your mind as you have been reading this section: How do I avoid becoming a security expert?

The short answer is that you need a full-time, expert security and networking person on your data Webhouse team from the start of the project. This person will understand and specify a single log-in, single console security system that is built from the ground up as a Web-deployed security system. If the only thing the security person on your staff is doing is going around to separate DBMS machines and typing in GRANTs and REVOKEs for individual end users, then you need another security person. You have lost your security already. The right person will also implement an ongoing program of reviewing the user profiles and the access profiles and making sure that the current assignments seem appropriate. This person will also put in place a constantly updated threat assessment program to detect, repair, and prevent the inevitable stream of security issues that every Web-connected system faces.

The longer answer to building an appropriate data Webhouse security system is found in Chapter 13. See you there.

SUMMARY

The Webhouse has been thrust into the spotlight of our new Web-enabled business systems. The Webhouse needs to be available to compute custom responses, sometimes within seconds. The Webhouse has to take on a more operational flavor because its responses are needed to run the business. The Webhouse needs to be usable by a much wider constituency than before. The Webhouse needs to smoothly handle international dates, times, currencies, character sets, and even languages. The Webhouse needs to remain secure while operating in a chaotic public environment. All of these requirements add up to a significant change in what we were accustomed to call the data warehouse. The rest of this book develops the techniques that will be needed to build this new kind of system.

CHAPTER 10

Designing the User Experience

The 1970s witnessed the first great revolution in user interface design for computers. This revolution, which began at Xerox Palo Alto Research Center (PARC), was symbolized by the graphical windows interface, the mouse pointing device, and icons. In the late 1990s we are now beginning a second major revolution in user interface design. This second revolution, propelled by the inexorable forces of the World Wide Web, builds on the first revolution but defines the user interface in ways not envisioned by the designers of the 1960s and 1970s. The user interfaces we must build as we turn the millennium no longer have the goal of making the *computer* useful. Our new goal is to make the *Web* useful.

HOW THE SECOND REVOLUTION DIFFERS FROM THE FIRST

The first revolution was based on a new medium that allowed a personal relationship with the computer. This new medium was called, appropriately, the personal computer. Although early personal computers had character displays, the revolution really caught fire when the personal computer became equipped with a bitmap screen, a mouse, a windows user interface, and icons. This new interface allowed WYSIWYG (What You See Is What You Get). It was based on using the screen to recognize commands rather than remembering them, and to point rather than type.

The second revolution is based on an even newer medium that allows a person access to the services of the World Wide Web. Although early uses of the Web were based on character interfaces, the revolution really caught fire when a common format for hypertext links was adopted that allowed the development of a vast interconnection of information consisting of text, graphical images, and other media. The impact and the importance of the Web cannot be overstated. It is a force like a tidal wave. Within the next few years, most of the human beings on the planet are going to have some kind of access to the Web. Most businesses will be transformed and defined by the Web. It is the great homogenizer, the great communicator, and it is chaos.

The new Web user interface no longer promotes WYSIWYG, but rather it promotes IWIN (I Want It Now). It is based on gathering information, recognizing the choices that one expects, and getting the results instantly.

Although for the moment, the Web is still being delivered through client/server user interfaces, make no mistake about it: this is a new medium. The rules are changing, and most of these changes never could have happened without the force of the Web constantly pushing. The push is real and much more urgent because:

- **User interface feedback from the Web is personal.** Web logs allow us to see gestures of the individual customer. In many cases we know who the customer is, what the customer was trying to do on the Web, and whether they were successful. Developers in the first-generation personal computer world could go their entire careers without ever analyzing actual user protocols.

- **User interface feedback from the Web is immediate.** The success or failure of individual user sessions on the Web can be detected back at headquarters within seconds and analyzed at leisure by the next day. In the personal computer world, user gripes and usability issues could take a year to accumulate, only to have to survive the political release planning process.

- **User interface effectiveness on the Web is now tied directly to profit.** The user interface is no longer the product by itself; it is the portal to all possible products. By the time the customer used a product on a personal computer, he or she had already paid for it. Now on the Web, the user interface stands in the way of the purchase. Corporate revenue is directly tied to the effectiveness of the user interface. We are in the unprecedented situation where the CEO is pounding the table and demanding a better user interface!

THE USER INTERFACE IS NOW MORE URGENT

During the first user interface revolution, we all marveled at the personal computer, but strangely, we did not put effective pressure on the user interfaces to improve. The computer marketplace still has not provided a good feedback loop for improving user interface design. User needs and user dissatisfaction have not been communicated directly to the developers responsible for the design. Product evolution has been driven either by marketing, who wants more features for the feature list, or by development, who wants more robust infrastructure. How often have we waited for a complete release cycle where a computer product was being "rearchitected" without adding features? Lost in all of this have been the concerns of the user. Advances in usability can only come from a thousand tiny improvements. Up until now, when each of the user interface improvements needed to compete in the vendor's annual release planning meeting, they often didn't have a powerful spokesperson or a critical mass.

SECOND GENERATION USER INTERFACE GUIDELINES

Having made the case for better user interfaces, is that all there is? What does the Web demand from the user interface that is different? The following list of user interface criteria has emerged as a kind of standard checklist for Web user interface design. What is striking is not only that these items are so important, but that many of these were not in the top part of the list in the first generation of user interface guidelines. We follow each guideline first with technical advice for the general Website designer, and then with additional technical advice for the data Webhouse architect who is tasked with delivering data warehouse services over the Web.

In every case, we assume the general Website user interface design guidelines have been applied to the Webhouse query, reporting, and analysis interfaces as well. It is a mistake to classify the user of the Webhouse as an employee who can be abused by giving them a degraded quality user interface. In many cases, even the assumption that the Webhouse user is an employee is wrong. The Webhouse user may be a business partner or a traditional customer.

Ensure Near-Instantaneous Performance

Ten seconds is a long time on a Web page. A page has to deliver the first screenful of its useful content in less than ten seconds. It is acceptable if the page keeps loading for more than ten seconds, if the page has made good on the promise of providing useful, engaging content before the ten seconds have passed.

The ten-second requirement is a reflection of the intensity of Web use. Web users frequently have a very specific need and a very specific focus. If that need can even be partially addressed in the first few seconds, the user feels like progress is being made, and will forgive the Website if the page continues to load more content. This technique is even more effective if the additional material is further down the page and off the screen.

The instantaneous performance requirement really isn't negotiable. Websites in general and data Webhouses must continuously exploit the techniques given here to improve performance. Performance is a multifaceted effort, where many of these techniques must be applied simultaneously.

Website Architect Design Responses

- **Design for a 28.8 Kbps modem.**   Every aspect of Web page presentation must be designed around the lowest common denominator slow communication line. Pages that paint quickly on a high-speed company intranet may be unusable when accessed over the Web. It is crucial to preserve the same user interfaces, the same applications, and the same security mechanisms regardless of where the page is being accessed from. See Figure 10.1. Some of the large differences in communication bandwidth in different situations may be handled by the progressive disclosure techniques described next.

- **Measure page performance on a continuous basis.**   Page performance must be continuously monitored in a scientific way. This means maintaining a database of page download times from various different perspectives, including the company intranet, a dedicated extranet (if you have one), and various locations on the Web. Make sure you are getting the page from the intended Web server, not from a cache somewhere. Make sure you measure page performance at peak usage times on the Web. See Figure 10.2. The download time in seconds should be known for every page on the Website. Pages that paint in more than ten seconds require corrective action.

- **Paint navigation buttons immediately.**   Navigation buttons that allow the user to return to the homepage, progress to various likely following pages, perform a search, or engage the Help system, should all paint in the first second or two. See Figure 10.3. This is just the first step of progressive disclosure.

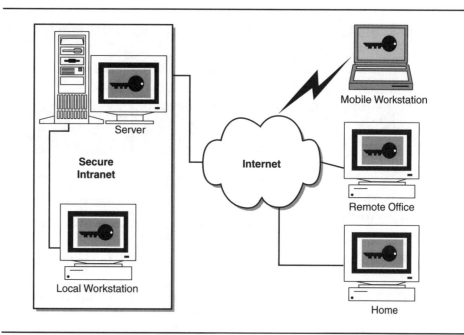

FIGURE 10.1   The Same User Interfaces, Applications, and Security Everywhere

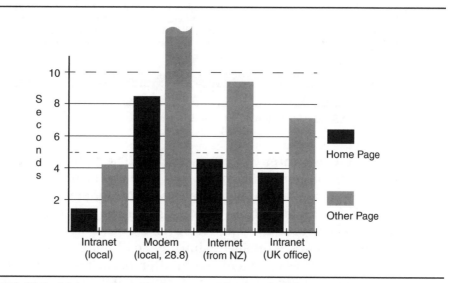

FIGURE 10.2   Measure Page Performance from Multiple Web Locations

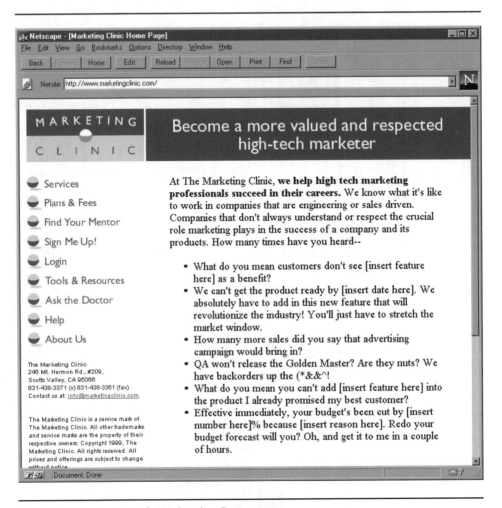

FIGURE 10.3   Basic Web Navigation Buttons

- **Disclose content progressively.**   The page is designed to paint useful content immediately. The user can begin reading the text to understand the content of the page before other items, such as graphic images, finish painting. Large graphic images can be painted progressively at increasing resolutions so that they can be recognized before they are finished painting. See Figure 10.4. Information appearing off screen should paint after all the main useful information on the first screen appears. If graphic images are an important deliverable of the Web page, then presenting the images as thumbnails that can be expanded is a reasonable compromise. But beware of painting dozens of thumbnails on one page, especially if the user must wait to find the specific thumbnail of interest. Sometimes, depending on the context, the textual name of the picture can be painted in the space where the graphic image is to appear. The user can often click the rectangle showing text and navigate effectively to the next page without waiting for the entire page to download. A corollary of this approach is to make the rectangles containing the images size themselves correctly on the screen in the first second or two so that the page doesn't jerk around unpredictably as the various graphic images appear.

- **Remove unnecessary and slow graphic images**.   Some Web page designers try to dress up a page as a kind of art project or maybe as a form of entertainment. Unnecessary graphic images that slow the presentation of a page really should be identified and removed. Hopefully, the systematic measurement of page performance is used to reveal these opportunities for improvement.

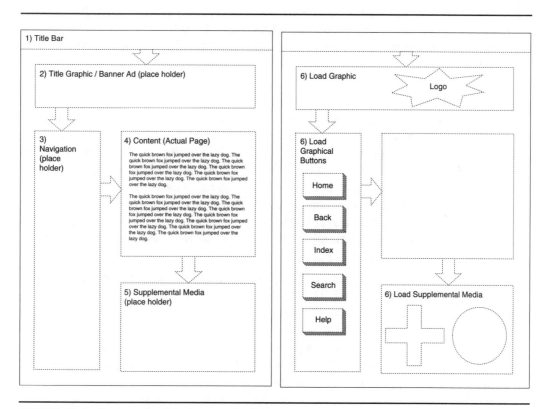

FIGURE 10.4   Progressive Disclosure of a Page

PAINTING HTML PAGES QUICKLY

If the HTML describing the page contains a predeclaration of the sizes of the graphic images, the browsers will reserve the spaces for the graphic images on the page and continue painting the page. If the browsers don't know the sizes of the images, then they wait to fetch the image before painting any more text. So if the browser has the size declarations in advance, the browser can finish painting the main page and then separately fetch the contents of the graphic images in parallel. Meanwhile, all the text on the page has been fetched, positioned, and displayed to the user. This technique is the key to progressive disclosure of a Web page. This technique needs to be applied both to static pages with hard-coded HTML as well as dynamically generated pages being conjured up by the application server in real time.

Additionally, each graphic image has an alternative "ALT" specification consisting of plain text. This was originally meant for browsers that have chosen to turn off all graphics. But even for fully graphically enabled browsers, this ALT text will display in the space reserved for the graphics until such time as the connection to the actual graphics source has been established. The effect for the user is that a useful text message can briefly be displayed while the graphics retrieval is being set up. In this situation, the graphics area can even be "hot." So perhaps the ALT text can say something quite useful like "Click Here to see the detailed product description." The user can see this and perform the click, all before the graphics image has been fetched.

■ **Implement page caching.** Page caching can be used in several places to improve Website performance. A static page, whose content is determined in advance of the user's session, can be cached by the ISP so that a true Web page fetch is avoided. If the user is connected to a high-speed intranet on which the page cache is located, the performance improvement can be huge. Page caching, of course, introduces headaches for anyone who is trying to analyze the user's Web behavior, because these caches located at the user's location may not be accessible to the real Website.

Another kind of page cache that is under the control of the Website is the proxy server. The full complexity of proxy servers was discussed in Chapter 4. This may simply be a redundant hardware device that operates in parallel with the "real" Web server to balance the load of incoming page requests. A proxy server has the advantage that it can duplicate both static as well as dynamic pages. The main issue for the data Webhouse is how to reliably merge the Web server logs of multiple proxy servers to reconstruct the user's complete session.

- **Cache data.**   Data caching is distinct from page caching, and can be thought of as a kind of precomputed query that is stored for rapid retrieval. The hot response cache discussed earlier in this book is the prime Webhouse example of data caching. The objective is to avoid using a database to compute the query in real time. In situations where common queries can be anticipated in advance, this kind of storage vs. speed tradeoff is a good idea. Examples might include a precomputed customer greeting that offers a cross-selling opportunity or a request for the status of an order or an account.

- **Cache reports.**   Report caching is a larger form of data caching, which involves more than simply fetching data from a database. Again, like data caching, the report cache can be implemented in the Webhouse's hot response cache. Full report generation may involve merging data from multiple sources or perhaps running complex analytic models. In all of these cases, if the report can be anticipated in advance, and especially if the report will be accessed by more than one user, a cache results in obvious performance improvements.

- **Improve Web server bandwidth.**   The Website designer cannot control the bandwidth at the client's location in many cases, if the access is over the Web. But the Website can choose among some significant alternatives at the location of the Website itself.

- **Improve server throughput.**   There are many things that can be done within a single Web server to improve performance. Faster CPUs, faster disks, more physical memory (to reduce memory swapping), and more network interface bandwidth are obvious hardware related areas to address performance. The delivery of a single Web page can often be parallelized to take advantage of multiple CPUs. This parallelization can be managed at several different levels, but ultimately is controlled by software in the operating system or in the application that divides the computation tasks explicitly.

Data Webhouse Architect Design Responses

- **Adapt all of the preceding general Web design responses to the specific needs of the data Webhouse.**   Each of the Web performance techniques discussed earlier is appropriate to the data Webhouse, even though the data Webhouse as of the time of this writing is usually more oriented toward querying and reporting and more oriented toward organization employees than traditional "walk through the door" customers. It is very important that the Webhouse designer have the same usability concerns for these Webhouse users as the Website Webmaster has for the traditional customer. In each of the following sections we will repeat this admonition to apply all of the general techniques as well as the specialized Webhouse techniques. The marriage of the Web with the warehouse makes this overlap increasingly important.

- **Select appropriate DBMS software.**   Since in this book, we argue that the most effective database designs for all forms of querying in the data Webhouse are dimensional designs, then it is obvious that the Webhouse designer wants to choose DBMS software that is adept at evaluating dimensional queries. Such DBMS software should have powerful strategies for handling multitable join queries, but it should also have explicit data definition commands for declaring dimensional models. In other words, if the database is a star join, the DBA should be able to declare that fact to the DBMS at table creation time. If this declaration is possible, it is an indication that the DBMS's optimizer is much more likely to make sensible decisions about evaluating star join queries than a DBMS for which no such declarations can be made. The choice of appropriate DBMS software makes a huge difference. The gap between the most adept DBMSs and the slowest is more than a factor of ten, all other hardware issues being equivalent.

   We should not limit our thinking to relational DBMSs to support data Webhouse queries. For small applications typically involving less than 10 GB of input data, and less than 250,000 members in any given dimension, proprietary OLAP systems offer huge performance and analytic advantages over traditional relational databases.

- **Use table indexes.**   The traditional mechanism for boosting query performance, once hardware and software have been selected, is the use of indexes. Indexing schemes, such as bitmap indexes, that offer highly symmetric access to the many dimensions in a fact table, are increasingly important for dimensional database environments. The more symmetric the access, the more able the database is to resist "ad hoc attacks" from the user community where the choice of dimensions and the nature of constraints is unexpected and continuously varying.

   Bitmap indexes play an important role in the dimension tables as well as the fact tables. Dimensional attributes of very low cardinality can be used very effectively with bitmap indexes. Although the selectivity of a single constraint on a single dimensional attribute may be low, the combined effect of several such constraints can be highly selective.

- **Partition files.**   The ability to physically partition extremely large database files is a key capability of DBMSs that provide effective support for fact tables of the size of typical clickstream designs. File partitioning allows the administrator to break off a chunk of a single large file and place it on a different disk drive or storage medium, and allows the administrator to drop or create an index on that portion of the file. Meanwhile, all applications continue to treat the large file as a single, unbroken logical object. File partitioning affects query performance because the current, frequently accessed portions of a big table can be placed on a very fast disk and can be indexed with powerful indexing options. File partitioning affects up-time, because a small most-current portion of the file can be taken off line for the daily update process and then rapidly be returned to active querying. File partitioning affects many of the big administrative processes like indexing and restoring, because most of the activities are confined to small portions of the big table rather than the whole table. This is the way a modern DBMS administrator handles the "whale in the swimming pool."

- **Use aggregations.**   Broad queries against millions of records are the hallmark of the data Webhouse. Some of these queries will be very precisely constrained in a way that is impossible to anticipate in advance. Other queries will deliberately scan huge numbers of low level records while producing value banding reports where various reporting buckets accumulate record counts. Although for these two cases, aggregations are generally impossible, there are a large number of queries that request data in one or more predictably aggregated forms. A data Webhouse aggregation strategy anticipates as many of these higher-level queries as possible and "heads them off at the pass" by diverting these queries to aggregate tables. Aggregate administration and the architecture of aggregate navigation are both discussed in Kimball's earlier books.

- **Increase real memory.**   Real RAM memory almost always improves performance because it increases the in-memory working set size and reduces the need to swap data to and from the disk. RAM access is roughly 100 times faster than normal disk access.

- **Exploit parallel processing.**   Many activities in the data Webhouse can be directly sped up by increasing the degree of parallelism. Once the hardware and software have been chosen, the remaining options for exploiting parallelism are at the applications level. Multipass SQL is a technique for decomposing complex reports and complex comparisons into several separate queries, each of which is simple and fast. In almost all of the situations where multipass SQL is employed, the separate queries can be executed in parallel, on the same machine or on different machines. The ability to control this kind of parallelism depends on the query and reporting application. Generally, the application systems that allow the construction of explicit "icon flows" where the data is graphically depicted as flowing down separate pipes from the distinct queries, are the kinds of systems where parallel processing can be directly managed by the application architect. Application systems where the multipass SQL is performed implicitly are harder to control.

Meet User Expectations

Every Web page has the responsibility of providing all the natural choices the user expects and to make them immediately visible and recognizable. The designer needs to carefully list all the choices that might be expected when a user arrives at a Web page. The choices break down into several categories, including sets of predictable navigation choices, application-specific choices, help choices, and communication choices.

Website Architect Design Responses

- **Site navigation choices.** User interface design for the Web must be determined by the conventions of the Web itself, not the individual Website. The user's perception of the Web is that it is a seamless whole, not a collection of independent media. See Figure 10.3. Basic site navigation must be provided by every Web page in a standard and predictable way. Site navigation buttons include:
  - Drill-down choices from current page
  - Overall Website home page
  - Overall Website major subject choices
  - Website map button
  - Website search box
  - Alternate language versions of the Website
  - Trouble resolution button
  - Website sponsor corporate information

The first five items should appear in an obvious way when the page is first opened. The last three items can appear at the bottom of the page and in smaller typeface. It is acceptable if the page must be scrolled before the last three items appear.

- **Application-specific choices.** Application-specific choices for linking to further pages should be grouped and laid out so that the overall organization is immediately evident. See Figure 10.5. Again, the links should appear immediately and the placement of the links should not move on the screen as slow loading graph images are progressively painted.

- **Help choices.** If the user is expected to understand a sequential process on the Website like placing an order or making a bid, more than one Help choice is appropriate. See Figure 10.6. Enough Help buttons, clearly labeled, should be provided to deal with 80% of the problems experienced by the users. An FAQ button is a good idea.

- **Communication choices.** Users may wish to communicate with the parent company who owns the Website. Perhaps this breaks down to general management, marketing, order tracking, account dispute resolution, and Website issues. All of these communication options

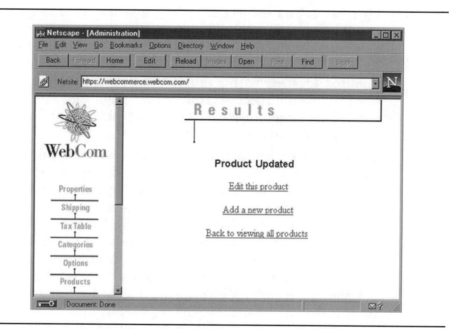

FIGURE 10.5   Application-Specific Choices

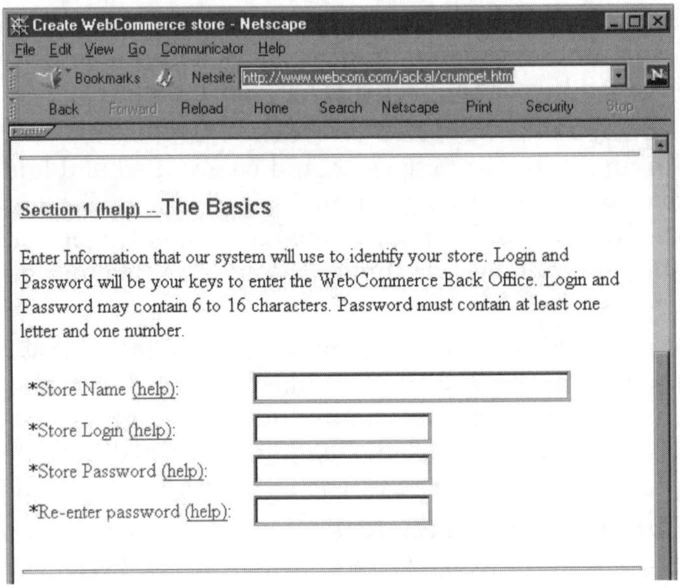

FIGURE 10.6 **Help Choice Buttons**

give the user a comfortable feeling that the Website cares about the user. However, the communications interface must be supported with *very* responsive follow up. If the user sends an e-mail to one of these functions, that e-mail should be automatically responded to within minutes, together with a promise that a real human being will follow up within a specified time frame. Then that follow up needs to occur. This kind of responsiveness is exactly what builds good will. Good will appears on the balance sheet.

■ **Buttons and headlines must be serious and immediate microcontent.** Jacob Nielsen, a well-known expert on Website design (see his Website at www.useit.com), argues persuasively that Web page headings are quite different than article headlines in a newspaper, although they look similar at first glance. See Figure 10.7. Web page headings need to communicate immediately and unambiguously. The first word is important. Web page titles have more stringent communication requirements than headlines or titles in a newspaper because a Web page provides much less two-dimensional context than a newspaper. This requirement for immediate effective communication means no humor or plays on words in buttons or

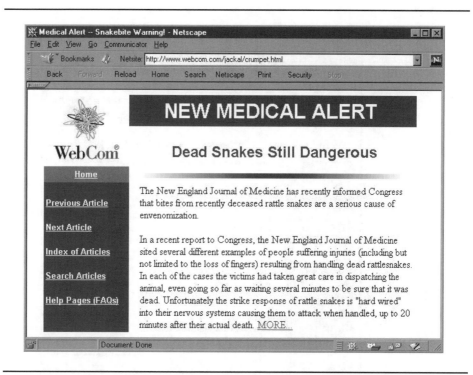

FIGURE 10.7   Serious and Immediate Microcontent

headlines. There should be no slang or language that would confuse people of different cultural backgrounds.

- **Indicator of off-screen material.**   It may seem obvious, but the user should always be advised in some way that there is more material that isn't showing on the current screen. This is especially true if important navigation choices may be available that don't show. The basic window scroll bar does provide this information but it can be overlooked. A large, colored down arrow at the bottom of the window might be good.

- **Use a customer survey to learn what the users are looking for.** Keep any survey short. If possible, give the user something in return, like the results from the very question they are asking. See Figure 10.8. Learn from unexpected answers. Don't take the user to another page, especially if their responses require some of the session context. Most questions can be handled by multiple choice, which makes tallying easier. But give the user an "other" box in which to enter an

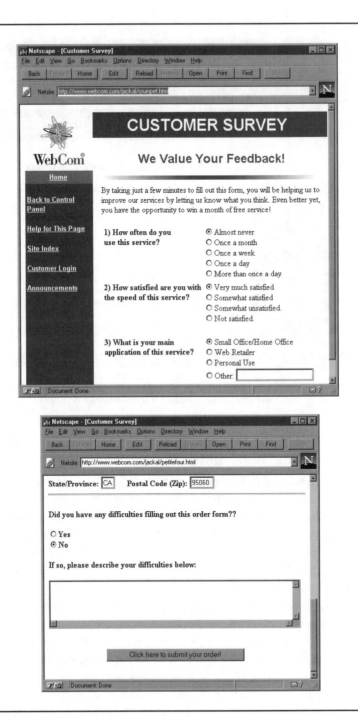

FIGURE 10.8 A Sample Customer Survey

unexpected response. Follow up change suggestions with acknowledgment, and follow up actual changes you make with notification.

Data Webhouse Architect Design Responses

- **Report library.**   Users expect to navigate the available reports to choose the one they want. See Figure 10.9. This is just a Webhouse variation on the application-specific choices discussed earlier. An explanation of the meaning of a report should be available at the time the user is reviewing the choices. A precomputed sample of the report that is available instantly is a good idea, especially if the report itself takes a long time to return to the user's screen. If the report does take a long time, a link to it should be e-mailed to the user, so the user can close their browser window or log off their computer.

- **Common and most recently used projects.**   An extension of the report idea is the concept of a project, which is a folder of queries,

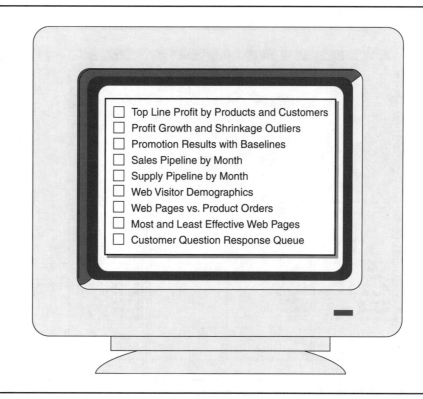

FIGURE 10.9   A Sample Report and Project Library

reports, spreadsheets, graphs, and formatted presentation output. An individual user's projects should be available like a folder for access from any Web browser (with appropriate security), as well as common projects that can serve as templates.

- **Dimension browser.** Dimensions are the entry points into a data warehouse. Most of the meaningful constraints in a query or a report are placed against attributes in dimension tables. Many interesting variations in report content such as drilling down are created by selecting dimension attributes to become row headers. See Figure 10.10.

  Users can create queries and reports much more effectively if they can understand and visualize what is in a dimension. But visualizing a huge product dimension or a huge customer dimension is a challenging user interface problem. All of these situations would benefit from a dimension browser interface that:

  - Shows the distinct values of a number of selected dimension attributes simultaneously

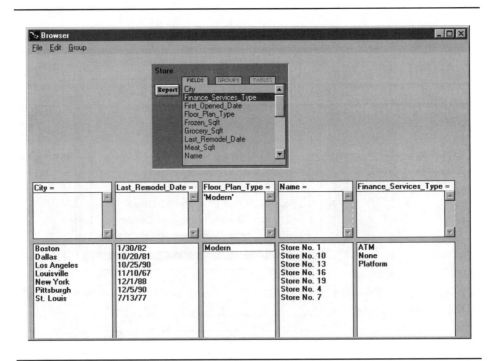

FIGURE 10.10 A Sample Dimension Browser

- Allows a constraint to be placed on any dimension attribute and then displays the adjusted lists of values for all the attributes accordingly
- Protects the user from accidentally displaying a huge list of attribute values by substituting a COUNT instead of the list of values
- Allows the constraints posed by the user to be saved as a "named constraint" to be used in subsequent queries

- **Business metadata interface.** Every Webhouse environment needs a metadata interface that allows the user to understand the organization's data assets. See Figure 10.11. The metadata interface should display the names and definitions of all the available data elements in the Webhouse. The definitions should be organized into brief introductions, detailed technical derivations, and current extract status reports. The list of data elements available to any given user should be consistent with the user's security privileges.

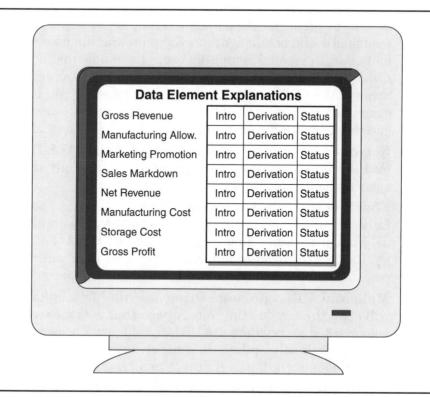

Data Element Explanations

Gross Revenue	Intro	Derivation	Status
Manufacturing Allow.	Intro	Derivation	Status
Marketing Promotion	Intro	Derivation	Status
Sales Markdown	Intro	Derivation	Status
Net Revenue	Intro	Derivation	Status
Manufacturing Cost	Intro	Derivation	Status
Storage Cost	Intro	Derivation	Status
Gross Profit	Intro	Derivation	Status

FIGURE 10.11   A Sample Business Metadata Interface

Make Each Page a Pleasant Experience

Users will notice a Website where each page is well laid out, is easy to read, has no problems, and has no distractions. Cosmetic problems with a Web page lend a suggestion of incompetence and lack of caring about quality and the customer relationship. Web page hosts are quickly learning that users ignore advertising and distractions, especially when they are on a navigational page. Even more strongly, users will avoid pages with blinking, invasive, gratuitous attempts to get attention. The designer needs to judge every page by its potential for distraction and decide whether the distraction is justified.

Website Architect Design Responses

- **Use fonts and colors only to communicate effectively.**   Typographers learned hundreds of years ago that less is more when it comes to laying out a book, a magazine, or a newspaper. When the font draws attention to itself, it has failed in its mission to convey the content effortlessly and pleasantly to the reader. When laser printers became available for the personal computer, we saw a phase of really wretched document designs as everyone experimented with multiple fonts. Most personal computer users have now instinctively recognized that overuse of fonts is an irritation. We are definitely going through the same experience with Web page design. Hopefully, the same natural evolution will occur, and we will see fewer sites with garish background colors and cute but difficult-to-read fonts.

- **Remove** cute gimmicks, **blinking graphics, ALL BOLD TEXT, and the use of exclamation points!!!!**   Hopefully, this design response is self explanatory.

- **Check entire site for broken links.**   All sites should be regularly scanned for broken links. A broken link is like a glaring typo in a document. It sends a message that quality is not the highest priority. Large sites need to automatically scan their entire set of Web pages. Third-party services and tools exist to automate this process.

- **Make old URLs do something useful.**   Old links to your site will exist throughout the Web. A page that gets a lot of hits will be bookmarked everywhere. Its URL should never become invalid even if you periodically update its content. Invalidated URLs are called *linkrot*. Persistent URLs continue to attract links.

- **Avoid page content that requires a sophisticated browser configuration.**   A Website accessible to the general public should not require the latest browser release. Studies show that users update to the current release of the major browsers only at the rate of 1% or 2% per week. In other words, it may take several years before the user community has substantially migrated even to today's browser. Additionally, a Website that requires complex Java scripts or other multimedia applets is taking a tremendous chance that users will be turned off, or get frustrated, or will opt out. Most users will not return after even a single bad experience with an unusual technology configuration. Even worse, a kind of resentment is fostered when a site does not make the effort to reach the user's level.

- **Paint links in standard colors, avoid underlines.** The color conventions for links are extremely important and should not be tampered with. An untouched link should show in the standard blue color, and a link already visited should show in the standard purple color. Because links are so important to easy use of the Web, colored text and the use of underlines of any kind are both highly risky.

- **Do not play music unexpectedly.** A few sites play music unexpectedly. This is one of those gratuitous distractions. These Websites also don't realize that they have sent the user a very unsettling message. They have "invaded" the user's computer with the music, and it feels a little like a virus. A button that plays music on demand is wonderful, but music that just emanates from nowhere is a no-no.

- **Do not overlay screen with an interruption.** A few sites still overlay the primary viewable page with an interruption that asks a question or reminds the user of an "opportunity." These sites will suffer from Darwinian selection.

- **Regularly seek third-party feedback.** In the previous guideline on expected choices, we recommended conducting surveys directly with the users of the Website. In this guideline we recommend soliciting professional third-party feedback about your site. You want an outsider's unbiased and fresh opinions regarding confusion, distraction, unintuitive options, directness, recognition of next actions, clarity, consistency of the user interface to Web standards, honesty, lack of marketese, correctness, smoothness of procedures, follow-up, ability to handle exceptions, and ability to communicate. You can also conduct your own usability studies. Jacob Nielsen recommends not asking the opinions of focus groups for these issues, because the issues are most closely related to an individual's cognitive reactions. Thus it is better to watch a single user interact with your site, and then debrief them about the experience.

- **Decide if a customizable site is better than a personalized site.**   A customizable site allows the user to set preferences for what the site displays. A personalized site tries to guess what these preferences should be. There is a subtle difference. At the time of writing of this book, there is a growing sense that customizable sites are more effective, and that the users feel more ownership in the experience. Customizing a site is something like customizing your desktop on your personal computer. The details seem a little trivial, but the sense of organizing things the way you want them is a way of developing trust, familiarity, and a personal investment.

Data Webhouse Architect Design Responses

- **Simplify the reporting interface.**   Data warehouse reporting tools have often been complex and intimidating. Part of this has been the lack of separating the power user from the casual user. The power user starts with blank slates and creates complex logic. The power user likes the computer and views computer use as an end in itself.

  The casual user only wants to run a report or an analysis and then think about the result. The casual user feels most comfortable just selecting a previously built report and displaying it. The casual user is willing to change one or two parameters to get a new variation of an existing report, but the casual user's appetite for complex specifications is almost zero.

  The Webhouse is helping to sort out the power users from the casual users because it has forced the vendors of report writing and analysis systems to take much more seriously the delivery of a report with just a single button push. The message from the Web again and again is that simplicity wins. The best simple interfaces get exponentially more use. Simple means uncluttered and direct. Maybe the best and simplest interface is a blank screen with two or three buttons in the middle that read "Push Me For Report #1", and "Push Me For Report #2."

- **Provide convenient capture.**   The Webhouse user lives in a world of reports and spreadsheets and graphs and presentations. The spreadsheets and presentations must be based on the user's standard personal computer tools. This compels the Webhouse reporting tools to provide convenient capture of the results on the screen for use in all the other tools. Selected rows and columns of reports should be selectable and copyable to spreadsheets and documents. A list of customers found in an exception report should be capturable in one user interface action so that follow-on queries constrained to that list of customers can be performed in other databases.

- **Equip all registered Webhouse users with standard reporting applets.**   The Webhouse architect has a major advantage that a general Website does not have. The Webhouse architect knows who all the users are and can systematically equip these users with powerful reporting and analysis applets. These users presumably have a powerful motivation for complying, since they are employees, business partners, or really serious customers. Employees and business partners can additionally be required to have a standard hardware and software configuration. Usually at this juncture a specific choice must be made between Microsoft (Internet Explorer and ActiveX controls) and non-Microsoft (Netscape and Java Beans). Registered Webhouse users can also be updated with consistent software that offers improved features or improved security.

Streamline Processes

Business processes must be designed from the ground up to work seamlessly on the Web. Ordering a product, tracking the delivery of a product, paying for a product, returning a product, and requesting support for a product should all be part of the same overall process. The customer should not need to enter their name in several places. Each process should know about the existence and status of the other processes. A customer should be able to resume a session after an interruption. A customer engaged with any one of these processes should be able to link to the other processes. The limited display surface of Web interfaces makes this requirement more urgent because the processes usually need to be seen alternatively rather than all at once.

Website Architect Design Responses

- **Work with legacy system designers to architect a seamless application suite with uniform Web interfaces.**   The real point of this overall design guideline is that the Web forces a kind of business reengineering that streamlines the processes to make them easier for the customer to navigate. This is the point Patricia Seybold develops so effectively in her book *Customers.com*. So this paragraph can only be the tip of a very big iceberg. It is hard or impossible to merely attach a set of clever Web pages onto a poorly designed set of business processes that weren't designed to communicate with each other.

- **Remove barriers to accessing a page.** An important page on your Website should be easy to reach. Nothing is more annoying than to have to click through five or six layers of pages to get to the page you know you want. Consider some of the experiences you may have had finding the page for a software driver download, or a particular detailed product specification. Why aren't the interfaces to those pages on the vendor's home page? And shouldn't the request be satisfied in one or two clicks? That leads us to the next item.

- **Count the clicks and count the windows to judge whether the process is streamlined.** Although counting clicks seems a little simplistic, it is really quite meaningful. Cognitive studies have showed that each click is a "subgoal" that a user is forced to establish on the way to the real overall goal. Too many clicks are too many subgoals. Another useful insight is that each new window is a distraction comparable to the phone ringing. A new window forces the user to read new content and temporarily set aside the original reason for interacting with the Website. So if nothing else, a user interface strategy that minimizes clicks and minimizes new windows is a good user interface. Count the clicks and windows needed to find a product, order a product, and request the status of a product on your Website.

- **Resume a session, park a basket.** A user needs to be able to interrupt a session and return to it later. Some of the best product-selling Websites have begun to support this need. Amazon, for instance, allows a shopping basket to accumulate over many sessions. But this concept should extend to many other kinds of interactions with the Web. Full support for resuming a session and parking a basket will have to come from a combination of features in the user's Web browser as well as support for personalized on-going processes at the Website.

Data Webhouse Architect Design Responses

- **Build an explicit value chain for reporting and analysis around the application suite using conformed dimensions and facts.** If the hard work of streamlining business processes has been made in your organization, then the data Webhouse architect should be in a much better position to build a set of reporting databases around these processes. When the Webhouse architect calls for conformed dimensions and conformed facts, the architect is really just asking that the common definitions of customers, products, calendars, and other major entities are rationalized across all the processes.

- **Provide easy drill-across reporting.**   Conformed dimensions and conformed facts allow any number of reporting systems to drill across separate data sources and assemble integrated reports. If the business has been streamlined and a set of conformed dimensions and conformed facts have been established, then the only remaining step is to expose the data sources to reporting systems that are capable of performing the drill across function. Kimball's *The Lifecycle Toolkit* describes this process in detail.

- **Provide a single user interface for reporting against all parts of the business.**   The existence of streamlined processes, conformed dimensions, and conformed facts sends an engraved invitation to the end user departments within your organization to adopt a single user interface for reporting against all parts of the business. Many of the technical issues of defining data structures, providing aggregates, replicating data to remote parts of the organization, and defining security profiles are made easier by limiting the number of reporting technologies.

- **Provide complete report library descriptions and FAQs.**   The single user interface for reporting should be accompanied by a single master report library, with descriptions of each accessible report, and with a FAQ (frequently asked questions) section. The master report library can be an extension of the more basic metadata described earlier.

- **Provide single login and single console access to the Webhouse.** A big advantage of taking a Webhouse perspective is that by solving the general authentication and authorization issues associated with coming in from the Web, you may be able to achieve a single comprehensive solution to all the data Webhouse use in your organization. The secret is a single login and single console system for all the users of the data Webhouse, regardless of the status and regardless of their location. This security architecture topic is so important that we devote all of Chapter 13 to it.

Reassure Users

Users can be reassured by a Website when they can visualize where they are in the process. In a linear process that is hard to visualize, the status of the process should be carried along from page to page. For instance: "You have three items in your basket. You can check out and arrange payment at any time, or complete filling your basket. Your basket will be saved if you leave the site."

Website Architect Design Responses

- **Provide a map of the processes.**   A standard navigation button can give the user a summary of what they have done so far and what still needs to be done. See Figure 10.12. This feedback can also tell the user which process they are using and what other processes are available.

Data Webhouse Architect Design Responses

- **Provide status and lineage of data.**   Using the Webhouse to access data or request a report can be thought of as just another business process supported by the Website, even if this process is limited

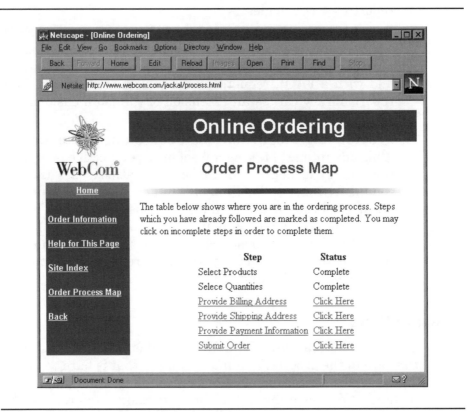

FIGURE 10.12   A Map of the Process

to employees and business partners. The users of the Webhouse have the same need to be reassured as regular outside users of a Website. Perhaps the need to be reassured is greater because of the complexity of the different data Webhouse tasks, and the lack of feedback at critical times as to what is going on. Users of the Webhouse want to see the load status of yesterday's business results. They want to understand the actual origins of the data they are looking at (the "lineage"). Requests for status and lineage are a kind of real time request for metadata.

- **Provide status of running reports.**   Users of the Webhouse may be much more tolerant of long running reports if they can easily see the status and degree of completion of these reports.

- **Active notification.**   Users of the Webhouse greatly appreciate being notified when critical data becomes available. Better yet, if they are confident that they will be notified, they won't waste time calling people or probing the system to see if the information is available.

- **Allow "NAs encountered" option in reports.**   A powerful feature that is possible in some report writers is to detect the existence of Not Applicable data during the computation of a business result. This can often mean that data is missing or a zero has been implicitly substituted for real data because it wasn't available. When Not Applicable underlying data is encountered, these report writers can append a footnote to the report stating that NAs were encountered.

- **Time stamp dimensions.**   A time-stamped slowly changing dimension can provide reassurance that the analysis of a prior situation, such as the granting of credit, is being understood in the correct contemporary context.

- **Time-stamp reports.**   All reports should be stamped with the date and time they were computed, for obvious reasons.

Provide a Means for Resolving Problems

A good Web user interface allows the customer to backtrack, correct previous entries, determine status, and ultimately talk to a human being. Being denied all access to human contact is a major mistake. It is a clear statement of not wanting to talk to a customer, and not taking seriously the customer's opinion. A corollary of allowing problem resolutions is providing complete information. People call about product features when the Website fails to provide a complete description of the product on-line.

Website Architect Design Responses

- **Allow backtracking, rollback, and play forward.** Backtracking is more than pressing the back button on the browser, although that may be the way the user will invoke the backtracking operation. Backtracking means returning to a previous step in the process, maybe because the user realized that different information was required. Then the process is resumed from that point forward. Although this sounds complex, there are some user interfaces (such as Adobe's Photoshop) that make this kind of backtracking very natural and very powerful.

- **Keep old transactions.** Users frequently would like to look at old sets of transactions. What books have I ordered in the past 12 months, and when did I order them? When did payment arrive and when were they sent?

- **Make it easy for users to report errors.** Users can be very helpful in reporting quality problems, but it must be a positive and easy action for them. Maybe this qualifies as another basic navigation button, at the bottom of the window. But this capability requires the next guideline.

- **Religiously acknowledge, track, and follow up all user inputs.** User inputs will dry up quickly if significant energy is not put into acknowledging the inputs, tracking the status of the inputs, effectively addressing the inputs, and always communicating these steps to the original user who provided the input. Does this sound like a lot of work? Yes! But each effort made to pay attention to the user and to validate the user's opinion is rewarded with a loyal user who will be a good customer.

- **Show how many requests have been acknowledged and what the current acknowledgment delay is.** If you are going to commit to being responsive, you may as well make it obvious. When the user sees that requests are being acknowledged and that the response delay is reasonably short, they will try the automated problem resolution system. But most people are very cynical because their questions have been ignored in other situations.

- **Use active spell checking to assist searches.** A search that is frustrated because it yields no useful results rapidly becomes a candidate for problem resolution. Sometimes the problem is that a literal character string is just too literal. Maybe "2" should be "two." Maybe "child" should be "children." Search engines should provide one or more options for widening a search in systematic ways that the user can invoke if they are dissatisfied with the results of the initial search.

Data Webhouse Architect Design Responses

- **Provide adequate end user support.**   The use of a data Webhouse, and the use of data in general, requires a significant commitment to direct support. At the beginning of a data Webhouse rollout, it is reasonable to plan for one MBA-class support person for every 20 end users at first, maybe gravitating to 1 for every 50 end users eventually. Scenarios for staffing these support functions are described in Kimball's *Data Warehouse Lifecycle*.

- **Show which aggregations were being used and which could be created or are currently off line.**   Sometimes a user may be dismayed by unexpectedly bad performance. It is very desirable for the user to ask "what's going on?" One of the most important diagnostic explanations of performance is to tell the user which aggregations are normally available and which are actually being used. See the next paragraph.

- **Show system load and percent of completion.**   The other most useful diagnostic explanation of performance is to show the current loading on the system and to estimate, if possible, the percentage of completion of the user's current request.

Build Trust

The designer should clearly state and observe the Website's policies for using the customer's identity. Customers will build trust gradually, the same way they build trust in a physical retail store. If the customer has repeated good experiences and feels that the trust has not been abused, a good relationship can grow. Because of the multitude of choices on the Web and the reluctance of customers to trust a remote anonymous entity, a trust relationship that has been abused may be impossible to recover.

Website Architect Design Responses

- **Do not abuse privacy with unexpected disclosures or e-mail spam.**   Show high integrity by stating a clear privacy policy and sticking to it.

- **Link to privacy statement on front page.**   One of the basic navigation links on the home page of every Website should be the privacy statement. It is okay if the privacy statement link is in small type at the bottom of the home page, but it should be there.

- **Use pictures of people.**   Pictures of the people at the Website company can be a very powerful way to engender trust, if done tastefully. The best examples we have seen of this are relaxed, high-quality photos of individuals that simply look "friendly." See Figure 10.13. Do not use press photos that you would use for keynote speeches. Imagine instead that the user is looking at the picture just before deciding whether to trust you with his or her credit card.

- **Clearly distinguish ad content from editorial content.**   Customers want to know and trust where information comes from. Make sure you police your "testimonials." As retail sites offer information

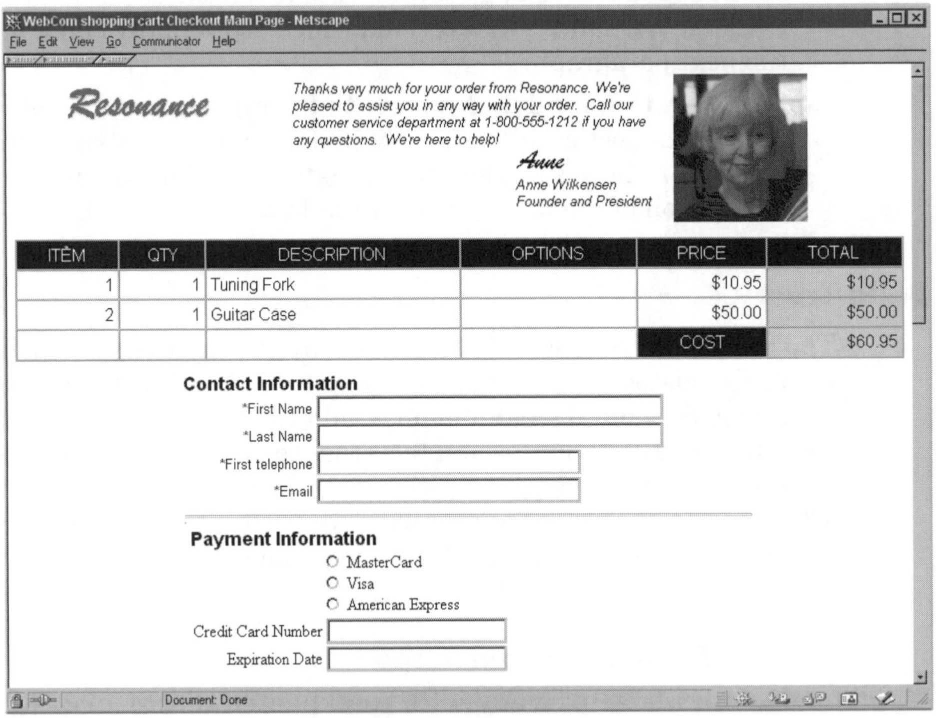

FIGURE 10.13   Pictures of People *(photo from PhotoDisc, Inc.)*

services as part of the Website offering, the customer's trust is being abused if some of the services actually turn out to be ads. You need to disclose the degree of commercial influence on searches. Jacob Nielsen summarizes these issues nicely by stating that trustworthiness is communicated by design quality, up-front disclosure, correct and current content, and connectedness with the rest of the Web. When he talks about connectedness, he means that if you are willing to acknowledge the rest of the world, including perhaps your competitors, then you will engender trust because you sound realistic.

Data Webhouse Architect Design Responses

- **Implement two-factor security everywhere.** Access to the facilities of the data Webhouse from anywhere on the Web is definitely an exercise in trust, both by the Website exposing the Webhouse to the void, and to the employee or business partner who wonders if their actions could be compromised. In Chapter 13, we recommend uniform adoption of two-factor security for all the registered users of Webhouse services. Two-factor security involves verifying (1) what you know (a password), and (2) what you possess (a piece of plastic).

- **Track human resource changes for employees and contractors.** The data Webhouse manager is hopefully in the position of managing authentication and authorization from a single console. This gives the data Webhouse manager the ability to track changes in employee status and changes in contractor status very responsively. If someone is (how do we say this delicately) let go, then that person's rights to access the Webhouse need to be terminated immediately. Ideally, the data Webhouse manager works closely and continuously with the human resource manager to make these changes of status reflected in the information access privileges of the Webhouse.

- **Manage information boundaries among employees, contractors, and customers.** Our recommendation in Chapter 13 to manage security from a single console is only partially driven from a concern for the administrative load on the Webhouse security manager. We are far more concerned with the misadministration of security, especially in a complex mixed environment with employees, business partners, and customers. Much of the data in the Webhouse must be carefully partitioned so that only the right people have access to it. A breakdown in the authorization system for accessing data will scare customers and can easily provoke lawsuits. In Chapter 13, we recommend careful attention to the creation and enforcement of security roles. The use of roles needs to be coupled with vigilant monitoring of all information objects to make sure that users with the appropriate roles have access to them.

- **Manage Webhouse security directly.**   No one is better qualified to marry the data with the users from a security perspective than the data Webhouse manager. The security responsibility for the Webhouse must not be ignored, and it must not be handed to a service organization that has no way of understanding the content of the Webhouse data or the legitimate access needs of all the users. A large Webhouse environment requires a full-time security manager dedicated to the data Webhouse project.

Provide Communication Hooks

A good Web user interface provides multiple links to people and sites. A good Web user interface provides copyable URLs that can be saved and printed on one line of an e-mail or a document.

Website Architect Design Responses

- **Use expected communication choices.**   Part of the expected choices we discussed earlier was a set of communication links to key individuals of functions behind the Website. These links included the *Webmaster* for complaints and suggestions about the Website itself, *technical support* for help with products or services, *administrative support* for help with ordering and billing, *marketing and sales* for complex orders that cannot be handled over the Web, and *headquarters* for general questions and information.

- **Provide useful links to others.**   A modern Website that understands what it means to be part of the Web does not ignore the rest of the world. Users expect useful references to other entities besides the local Website itself.

- **Remove links that invalidate the "back" button.**   Some sites still have links that send the user into a trap from which there is no escape. The "back" button stops working and the user must effectively terminate the browser session and start over to get away from the offending Website. Fortunately, this kind of behavior is self-limiting, since users will avoid sites that create objections or seem to try to trap them.

- **Use copyable URLs.** URLs need to be copied frequently in their full-text form. Most references to a site embedded in e-mail must copy the full URL. When the URLs become longer than a single text line in a document or in an e-mail message, they become prone to corruption. URLs to static pages should remain short.
- **Use URLs as the medium of distribution.** Rather than send a report, send the URL to the report.

Support International Transparency

The Web is profoundly an international marketplace. A Website with a strong international presence should provide multiple language versions of its site to serve major foreign markets. This implies support for international languages, character sets, addresses, phone numbers, currencies, dates, and times. This topic is amplified in Chapter 12.

Website Architect Design Responses

- **Suport UNICODE throughout.** All Websites should support the UNICODE character set so that multicultural names, addresses, and currencies can be represented gracefully. We remind the reader in Chapter 12 that the omission of accents and the garbling of names and addresses is insulting to our international partners and customers, and makes us look insensitive and stupid.

- **Choose appropriate home language.** Any Website that can possibly attract visitors or do business with customers who do not speak English should strongly consider alternate language choices for the Website. If provided, this option should be a basic navigation choice on every page. Remember that only a fraction of a Website's visitors will enter the Website from the fundamental root page. Many others will jump into the middle of a Website because of a bookmarked URL or a search engine reference.

- **Establish clear usage guidelines for addresses and phone numbers.** In the United States, we are often not sensitive enough to the complexities of international addresses and international telephone dialing. In all cases where we provide this information, we need to provide the complete address or the complete dialing sequence and to distinguish between domestic access and international access.

Data Webhouse Architect Design Responses

- **Anticipate multinational reporting requirements.**   In Chapter 12 we discuss international reporting requirements in some detail. In multinational organizations there is a complex tradeoff between expressing business results in local terms and expressing business results in a single central language or style. The key differences revolve around the choice of dates, times, currencies, languages, and collating sequences.

SUMMARY

The length and variety of this chapter illustrate the main dilemma of user interface design. An effective user interface is judged by the total experience the user has with the system. A user interface is not highly leveraged by a single feature or a single technology. A great user interface is the result of a thousand little improvements, spread over all the subjects in this chapter. A great user interface also depends on the taste and judgment of the designer. We have made no attempt to quantify taste and judgment in this chapter or even to suggest specific guidelines for taste. Perhaps all that can be said about taste and judgment is to give all these decisions to a single competent designer and then stand back and let him or her finish the job without interference. Designs that require taste and judgment should be done autocratically, not by committee.

At the beginning of this chapter we pointed out that user interface design is becoming more important and more urgent. On the Web, we see much more clearly how the user interface drives the success of our Website.

The data Webhouse is the place where we analyze the clickstream and try to decide what the customers are doing, and whether they got what they want. In many cases, the diagnosis of what went right or what went wrong will point to some aspect of the user interface. This chapter should prove to be a guide for understanding some of the customer behavior, especially if direct user feedback can augment the clickstream detail.

We also tried in this chapter to argue convincingly that the analytic use of the Webhouse by employees, business partners, and customers is nothing more than another Website process that must meet the needs of the users. Although the deployment of Webhouse services over the Web is a specialized application, it is subject to all the guidelines and strictures of regular Website services. The data Webhouse is just one more little boat being swept along by the Web tidal wave.

In the Chapters 12 and 13 we focus on specific techniques required by Web applications. Chapter 12 details all of the international considerations for Web delivered applications with special focus on the delivery of Webhouse services, and Chapter 13 provides a comprehensive architecture for controlling Webhouse security.

CHAPTER 11

Driving Data Mining from the Webhouse

Data mining is one of the hottest topics in data warehousing. Virtually every IS organization believes that data mining is part of their future and that it is somehow linked to the investment that they have already made in their data warehouse. But behind all the excitement is a lot of confusion. Just exactly what is data mining? Is data mining just a generic name for analyzing data, or does one need special tools and special knowledge to do data mining? Is data mining a coherent body of knowledge or is it an eclectic set of incompatible techniques? Once we understand data mining, can we automatically use the Webhouse to mine the data or do we have to perform yet another extraction to a special "platform?"

In this chapter we define the main categories of data mining and show what transformations need to be done on your Webhouse data to make it ready for data mining.

Before descending into the details, let's paint the big picture:

- Data mining is a collection of powerful analysis techniques for making sense out of very large data sets. In the right situations, data mining can be extraordinarily valuable.

- There is no one data mining approach, but rather a set of techniques that often can be used in combination with each other to extract the most insight from your data. If you invest in data mining, you will probably end up with several data mining tools from several different vendors.

- Each data mining tool can be viewed logically as an application that is a client of the data warehouse. Like a query tool or a report writer, the data mining tool often sits on a separate machine, or in a separate process, requesting data from the data warehouse, and occasionally using the data warehouse as a convenient resource to house and store results from running the data mining tool.

- The goal of the Webhouse is to provide "ready-to-go observation sets" for data mining. These observation sets usually take the form of complex drill-across reports involving multiple levels of aggregation. The Webhouse is used intensively to populate these observation sets, which are then stored in a designated location for high-speed, repetitive access by the data mining tools.

THE ROOTS OF DATA MINING

Although the marketplace for data mining currently features a host of new products and companies, the underlying subject matter has a rich tradition of research and practice that goes back at least 30 years. The first name for data mining, beginning in the 1960s, was statistical analysis. The pioneers of statistical analysis, in our opinion, were SAS, SPSS, and IBM. All three of these companies are very active in the data mining field today and have very credible product offerings based on their years of experience. Originally, statistical analysis consisted of classical statistical routines such as correlation, regression, chi-square, and cross tabulation. SAS and SPSS in particular still offer these classical approaches, but they and data mining in general have moved beyond these statistical measures to more insightful approaches that try to explain or predict what is going on in the data.

In the late 1980s, classical statistical analysis was augmented with a more eclectic set of techniques with names like fuzzy logic, heuristic reasoning, and neural networks. This was the heyday of AI, or artificial intelligence. Although perhaps a harsh indictment, we should admit that AI was a failure as packaged and sold in the 1980s. Far too much was promised. The successes of AI turned out to be limited to special problem domains, and it often required a very complicated investment to encode a human expert's knowledge into the system. And perhaps most seriously, AI forever remained a black box that most of us normal IS people couldn't relate to. Try selling the CEO on an expensive package that performs "fuzzy logic."

Now in the late 1990s, we have learned how to take the best approaches from classical statistical analysis, neural networks, decision trees, market basket analysis, and other powerful techniques and to package and talk about them in a much more compelling and effective way. Additionally, we believe that the arrival of serious data warehouse systems is the necessary ingredient that has made data mining real and actionable.

THE ACTIVITIES OF DATA MINING

The best way to talk about data mining is to talk about what it does. A useful breakdown of data mining activities includes:

- clustering,
- classifying,
- estimating and predicting, and
- affinity grouping.

For the discussion of this taxonomy we are indebted to Michael Berry and Gordon Linhoff for their wonderful book, *Data Mining Techniques for Marketing, Sales, and Customer Support* (Wiley, 1997).

An example of clustering is looking through a large number of initially undifferentiated customers and trying to see if they fall into natural groupings. This is a pure example of "undirected data mining" where the user has no preordained agenda, and is hoping that the data mining tool will reveal some meaningful structure. The input records to this clustering exercise ideally should be high-quality verbose descriptions of each customer with both demographic and behavioral indicators attached to each record. Later in this chapter we will see that preparing these high-quality verbose descriptions is the central task of the Webhouse. Generally, it will be expensive and slow to produce these descriptions because we may have to drill across many fact tables in a value chain, but once these descriptions are complete, we make them available as a kind of finished report for high-speed consumption by the data mining tools.

Clustering algorithms work well with all kinds of data, including categorical, numerical, and textual data. It is not even necessary to identify inputs and outputs at the start of the job run. Usually, the only decision that must be made by the user is to ask for a specific number of candidate clusters. The clustering algorithm will find the best partitioning of all the customer records (in our example) and will provide descriptions of the "centroid" of each cluster in terms of the user's original data. In many cases, these clusters have an obvious interpretation that provides insight into the customer base.

Specific tools that can be used for clustering include standard statistics, memory-based reasoning, neural networks, and decision trees. See Berry and Linhoff's book for a very readable introduction to each of these types of tools.

An example of classifying is to examine a candidate customer (for instance) and to assign that customer to a predetermined cluster or classification. Another example of classifying is medical diagnosis. In both cases a verbose description of the customer or patient is fed into the classification algorithm. The classifier determines which cluster centroid the candidate customer or patient is nearest to or is most similar to. Viewed in this way we see that the previous activity of clustering may well be a natural first step that is followed by the activity of classifying. Classifying in the most general sense is immensely useful in many data warehouse environments. A classification is a decision. We may be classifying customers as credit worthy or credit unworthy. Or we may be classifying patients as either needing treatment or not needing treatment.

Specific tools that can be used for classifying include standard statistics, memory-based reasoning, genetic algorithms, link analysis, decision trees, and neural networks.

Estimating and predicting are two similar activities that normally yield a numerical measure as the result. For example, we may find a set of existing customers that have the same profile as a candidate customer. From the set of existing customers we may estimate the overall indebtedness of the candidate customer. Prediction is the same as estimation except that we trying to determine a result that will occur in a future time. Estimation and prediction can also drive classification. For instance, we may decide that all customers with more than $100,000 of indebtedness are to be classified as poor credit risks. Numerical estimates have the additional advantage that the candidates can be rank ordered. We may have enough money in an advertising budget to send promotion offers to the top 10,000 customers ranked by an estimate of their future value to the company. In this case an estimate is more useful than a simple binary classification.

Specific tools that can be used for estimating and predicting include standard statistics and neural networks for numerical variables, and all of the techniques described for classifying when only predicting a discrete outcome.

Affinity grouping is a special kind of clustering that identifies events or transactions that occur simultaneously. A well-known example of affinity grouping is market basket analysis. Market basket analysis attempts to understand what items are sold together at the same time. This is a hard problem from a data processing point of view because in a typical retail environment there are thousands of different products. It is pointless to enumerate all the combinations of items sold together because the list quickly reaches astronomical proportions. The art of market basket analysis is to find the meaningful combinations of different levels in the item hierarchy that are sold together. For instance, it may be most meaningful to discover that the individual item "Coca Cola 12 oz" is sold very frequently with the category of "Frozen Pasta Dinners."

Specific tools that can be used for affinity grouping include standard statistics, memory-based reasoning, link analysis, and special-purpose market basket analysis tools.

PREPARING FOR DATA MINING

In the previous section we talked about an important set of data mining activities, which included clustering, classification, predicting, and affinity grouping (market basket analysis). Hopefully your appetite is whetted, and you are anxious to use one of the data mining tools to begin mining. But are you ready? Does anything have to be done to your data, or can any data warehouse automatically be used for data mining? The answer is that often a significant amount of work needs to be done to prepare your data for data mining. In fact, you may spend more effort getting the data ready for data mining than you will spend actually doing the data mining. This section explores many of the data transformations you will need to perform.

Data Transformations for Webhouses in General

There is a set of basic data transformations you are probably already doing if you have a data warehouse. You are performing these transformations in your data extract system that pulls data from your legacy system, and you may be housing the data in your operational data store for cleaning and reformatting. The cleaned data is exported from the operational data store into one or more of your subject-oriented data marts. Although there may be many transformation steps in your data extract system, the ones of particular interest to data mining are:

- **Resolving inconsistent legacy data formats,** such as ASCII and EBCDIC, and resolving inconsistent data encoding, geographic spellings, abbreviations, and punctuation. Hopefully, you are already cleaning your data at this level, because if you aren't, then you can't even ask for SQL groupings or produce simple reports with meaningful row and column headers.

- **Stripping out unwanted fields.** Legacy data contains many fields that are meaningless from an analysis point of view, such as version numbers and formatted production keys. If you haven't stripped these out, the data mining tool may waste cycles trying to find patterns in these fields or trying to correlate these fields to real data. Especially if these fields are numeric, a data mining tool may interpret the fields as measurements or magnitudes.

- **Interpreting codes into text.** A classic form of data cleaning that should be done in all data warehouses is augmenting or replacing cryptic codes with textual equivalents written in recognizable words. Hopefully, these codes are already in your dimension tables (not your fact tables) so that adding the explanatory text is an easy, graceful change to the dimension table.

- **Combining data such as customer data from multiple sources** under a common key. Hopefully you have several rich sources of descriptions of your customers (or your products, or your locations) and you are merging these data sources under a common enterprise-wide customer key in your operational data store.

- **Finding multiply used fields in your legacy data,** where you must interpret the field's value based on the context of the legacy record. In some cases you may not even realize that you have a legacy field that is hiding multiple uses. Your data mining tool will almost certainly figure this out. Perhaps "go crazy" is a better description than "figure this out." A good way to find multiply used fields is to count and perhaps list all the distinct values residing in a field. Our clients have been surprised many times by this exercise.

Data Transformations for all Forms of Data Mining

This group of data transformations may not be needed for standard reporting and analysis functions in a data warehouse but is required for just about every data mining application. Many of these transformations affect the numeric, additive facts in the central fact table of your dimensional data mart:

- **Flag normal, abnormal, out of bounds, or impossible facts.** Marking measured facts with special flags may be extremely helpful. Some measured facts may be correct but highly unusual. Perhaps these facts are based on a small sample or a special circumstance. Other facts may be present in the data but must be regarded as impossible or unexplainable. For each of these circumstances, it is better to mark the data with a status flag so that it can be optionally constrained into or out of the analysis than it is to delete the unusual value. A good way to handle these cases is to create a special data status dimension for the fact record in which the status of each fact in the record can be described and constrained upon. See Figure 11.1.

- **Recognize random or noise values from context and mask out.** A special case of the previous transformation is to recognize when the legacy system has supplied a random number rather than a real fact. This can happen when no value is meant to be delivered by the legacy system, but a number left over in a buffer has been passed down to the data warehouse. When this case can be recognized, the random number should be replaced with a null value. See the next transformation.

- **Apply a uniform treatment to null values.** Null values can often cause a data mining tool to hiccup. In many cases the null value is represented by a special value of what should be a legitimate fact.

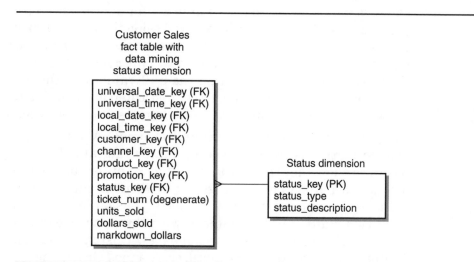

FIGURE 11.1   Using a Data Status Dimension

Perhaps the special value of −1 is understood to represent null. Null dates are often represented by some agreed-upon date like January 1, 1900. Hopefully you haven't been using January 1, 2000. The first step in cleaning up nulls is to use a DBMS that represents nulls explicitly. Replace the specific data values with true nulls in the database. The second step is to use a data mining tool that has specific options for processing null data.

You may have a substantial additional complication if your fact table records contain date fields being used as foreign keys to date dimension tables. In this case you have no good way to represent null dates in your fact table record. You cannot use a null-valued foreign key in the fact table because null in SQL is never equal to itself. In other words, you cannot use a null value in a join between a fact table and a dimension table. What you should do instead is implement the join with an anonymous integer key and then have a special record in the dimension table to represent the null date.

Null values in data are tricky because philosophically there are at least two kinds of nulls. A null value in the data may mean that at the time of the measurement, the value literally did not exist and could not exist. In other words, any data value at all is wrong. Conversely, a null value in the data may mean that the measurement process failed to deliver the data, but that the value certainly existed at some point. In this second case, you might argue that an estimate value would be better to use than to disqualify the fact record from the analysis. Some data mining professionals assign a most probable or median value in this case so that the rest of the fact table record can participate in the analysis. This could either be done in the original data by overwriting the null value with the estimated value, or it could be handled by a sophisticated data mining tool that knows how to process null data with various analysis options.

- **Flag fact records with changed status.** A very helpful data transformation is to add a special status indicator to a fact table record to show that the status of that account (or customer or product or location) has just changed or is about to change. The status indicator is implemented as a status dimension in the star join design. This status can be combined with the status we developed in Figure 11.1. Useful statuses include New Customer, Customer Defaulted, Customer About to Cancel, or Changed Order. The Customer About to Cancel status is especially valuable because without this flag the only evidence that the customer canceled may be the absence of account records beginning the next billing period. Finding such an absence by noticing records that don't exist is impractical in most database applications.

- **Aggregate the data.**   In some cases it may be necessary to aggregate the data before performing data mining. Aggregations may be tempting either to reduce the sheer volume of data being analyzed or to provide analysis buckets that are statistically significant. For instance, it may be desirable to analyze sales of garment products at a brand level rather than to perform the analysis at the color-size level for both of these reasons.

Special Data Transformations Depending on the Data Mining Tool

- **Divide data into training, test, and evaluation sets.**   Nearly all data mining applications require that the raw input data be separated into three groups. Perhaps the data should be separated randomly into three control groups, or perhaps the data should be separated by time. The first data group is used for training the data mining tool. A clustering tool or a neural network tool or a decision tree tool absorbs this first data set and establishes parameters from which future classifications and predictions can be made. The second data set is then used to test these parameters to see how well the model performs. An interesting problem that is discussed in Berry and Linoff's book occurs when the data mining tool has been trained too intensively on the first set. In this case the data is said to be "over fitted" because it predicts results from the first data set too well and does poorly on the test data set. This is the reason for having a fresh second set of data for testing.

  When the data mining tool has been properly tuned on the first and second data sets, it is then applied to the third evaluation data set, where it is assumed that the clusters, classifications, and predictions coming from the tool are to be trusted and used.

- **Adding computed fields as inputs or as targets.**   A data mining exercise can be greatly leveraged by letting the data mining tool operate on computed values as well as base data. For instance, a computed field such as profit or customer satisfaction that represents the value of a set of customer transactions may be required as a target for the data mining tool to pick out the best customers, or to pick out behavior that you want to encourage. You may not have to modify your base schemas with these computed values if you can present the data mining tool with a view containing these computed values. However, in other cases where the added information is too complicated to compute at query time in a view, then you have to add the values to the base data itself before you can perform data mining.

- **Mapping continuous values into ranges.** Some data mining tools like decision trees encourage you to "band" continuous values into discrete ranges. You may be able to do this by joining your fact table to a little "band values" dimension table, but this may be an expensive join against millions or billions of unindexed numeric facts. In such a case, you may have to add a textual bucket fact or even a bucket dimension to your fact table if the fact in question is important enough to be used as a frequent data mining target. See Figure 11.2.

- **Normalizing values between 0 and 1.** Neural network data mining tools usually require that all numeric values be mapped into a range of zero to one. Berry and Linoff warn you that you should make your data range be a little larger than the observed data for this normalization calculation so that you can accommodate new values that fall outside the actual data you have on hand in your training set.

- **Converting from textual to numeric or numeral category.** Some data mining tools may operate only on numeric input. In these cases, discrete text values need to be assigned codes. Care should be taken that this process is only done when the data mining tool is smart enough to treat such information categorically, and does not infer an ordering or a magnitude to these numbers that is unwarranted. For instance, you can convert most locations in the United States into a postal zip code. However, you can't compute on these zips!

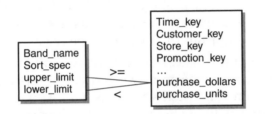

Use Band_name as a row header, sorting on Sort_spec

FIGURE 11.2 Using a Band Value Table

- **Emphasizing the unusual case abnormally to drive recognition.** Many times a data mining tool is used to describe and recognize unusual cases. Perhaps you are looking for fraud in a series of sales transactions. The problem is that your training set data may not contain enough instances of the target fraud behavior to extract meaningful predictive indicators. In this case you may have to artificially replicate or seed the training data with the desired target patterns in order to make the data mining tool create a useful set of parameters.

Although many of the data transformations we have described probably should be done in a general data warehouse environment, the demands of data mining really force the data cleaning issue. The purpose of data mining should be to discover meaningful patterns in your data, not to stumble over data cleanliness problems.

HANDING THE DATA TO THE DATA MINER

The purpose of the Webhouse is to gather, store, and present data in the best possible way to the data mining tool. It is not the purpose of the Webhouse to actually perform the data mining. Data mining is more of an analytic application than it is a database. It is important to separate the responsibilities of the Webhouse and the data mining operation so that the right activities are done in the right places. Historically there has been too much duplicated effort and too many lost opportunities either because data warehouse managers are trying to answer questions that need a data mining tool, or data mining professionals are going around the data warehouse to gather their data.

In the overall flow of data from its original source to the final step of data mining, we recommend the following division of responsibilities.

Webhouse Data Mining Responsibilities

- **Original extraction from all internal legacy sources and third party sources**
- **Data content validation and cleaning**
- Combining of disparate data sources into fact and dimension tables of uniform granularities
- Creation of derived facts and attributes of interest to data mining tools as described in this chapter

- Assignment of all foreign and primary keys in fact and dimension tables
- **Creation of complex drill-across reports which are "ready-to-go observation sets"**
- Storage of the ready-to-go observation sets for high-performance access by the data mining tools
- Optionally accepting and storing the results of data mining tool runs

Data Mining Tool Responsibilities

- **Reading the ready-to-go observation sets, perhaps repetitively, directly into the data mining tools**
- Providing on-the-fly data transformation steps where not provided by the Webhouse
- **Performing the data mining analytic analyses**
- Handing off the results of the data mining tool runs to the Webhouse for storage

The key steps in this process that make the partnership between the Webhouse and the data mining tools successful are highlighted in bold in the preceding list. The creation of the complex drill-across reports is the most valuable step because it uniquely draws upon the strengths of the Webhouse, and it is the step the data miners are least prepared to do.

Many data warehouse developers are inwardly focused on data that is available from production systems in their organizations. These developers may not be aware of the rich sources of data available from third-party data providers. With the increased focus on customer behavior and customer demographics, the Webhouse team needs to become more familiar with the data sources and the companies providing this data. It would be a mistake to turn this data sourcing over to the data mining group because that leaves all the issues of sourcing data, conforming keys, combining tables, representing time series, and providing data access to the end users whose main interests are analyzing the data. These jobs, and hence the acquisition of the demographics data, belong to the Webhouse team. Jesus Mena, in his book, *Data Mining Your Website*, has an excellent discussion of the third-party demographics data industry, which is well worth reading, even if his discussion of the data warehouse is very abbreviated.

A typical ready-to-go observation set is a list of customers together with complex demographic and behavioral measures such as the following:

- Customer Identifier
- Census Tract
- City
- County
- State
- Postal Code
- Demographic Cluster
- Age
- Sex
- Marital Status
- Years of Residency
- Number of Dependents
- Employment Profile
- Education Profile
- Sports Magazine Reader Flag
- Personal Computer Owner Flag
- Cellular Telephone Owner Flag
- Current Credit Rating
- Worst Historical Credit Rating
- Best Historical Credit Rating
- Date of First Purchase
- Date of Last Purchase
- Average Number of Purchases in Last Year
- Change in Average Number of Purchases vs. Previous Year
- Total Number of Purchases, Lifetime
- Total Value of Purchases, Lifetime
- Number of Returned Purchases, Lifetime
- Maximum Debt
- Average Age of Customer's Debt, Lifetime
- Number of Times Late Payment
- Number of Times Fully Paid
- Number of Times Visited Website
- Change in Weekly Frequency of Website Access, Current Quarter To Previous

- Average Number of Pages Visited Per Session
- Average Dwell Time Per Session
- Number of Web Product Orders
- Value of Web Product Orders
- Number of Website Visits to Partner Websites, Current Quarter
- Change in Partner Website Visits, Current Quarter to Previous

Most data miners would love to have this rich set of observations! The Webhouse can provide such a set of observations, but it is a lot of work. The various behavioral measures come from many different Webhouse tables and they are expressed in different granularities. A Webhouse application producing this set of applications might consist of more than a dozen separate queries to different fact tables, all of which are combined under the customer identifier row heading. There is no way the Webhouse could provide this set of observations directly from the original data sources with the speed desired by the data mining tool.

The Webhouse needs to produce this set of observations once and then store it for high-performance, repeated access by the data mining tools. A decision tree or a neural net might only read the data once, but a memory-based reasoning tool may want this set of observations available for repeated reading.

The highest-performance access may well be through a flat file. It would be reasonable for the Webhouse to hand off the ready-to-go observation set as one or more flat files. The Webhouse then steps back and lets the data mining tool process the observations at high speed.

All data mining is a repetitive cycle of cutting and trying. It would be very typical of the data mining project to want more data behavioral measurements or to want numerical or categorical transformations of existing measurements. In some cases, it will be efficient for the data mining tool to provide these final transformations, but it is very likely the Webhouse data delivery environment should be used to augment and extend the observation sets. Most Webhouse tool suites can easily take the flat file outputs described earlier, and augment them with further columns of data, for each customer.

The data warehouse team can work with the data miners to reduce the amount of data handed across. After all, not every demographic indicator provides useful insight or has useful predictive value. Some data inputs provided by the Webhouse may be expensive to compute or expensive to buy. It would be helpful to eliminate these variables. By using a neural network tool in "auto-associative mode," the data miners can literally test to see whether the data inputs describing the customer can predict themselves. Some data elements can be eliminated by this technique because they literally are not consistent with the rest of the customer profile information. Similarly, other variables can be eliminated by a neural network tool when it is configured in the normal mode of predicting or recognizing desired output variables from the input variables. In this case, the data miner compares the changes in neuron weights from the beginning of the neural network training phase to end of the training phase. Input variables whose neuron weights change very little in the training phase clearly have not affected the model very much and can probably be dropped from consideration.

OLAP, DATA MINING, AND THE WEBHOUSE

We have not focused much in this book on the specific advantages of OLAP (on-line analytic processing) technology for the Webhouse. When most people discuss OLAP, they are discussing one or more specific, proprietary implementations such as Microsoft OLAP Services, Hyperion Essbase, or Oracle Express. All OLAP systems are based, both logically and physically, on modeling data as a "cube" with many dimensions. An OLAP dimension is essentially identical to a Webhouse dimension as described in this book and in dimensional modeling circles in general.

OLAP represents the next evolution in decision support systems because OLAP has far more powerful analytic capabilities than SQL. The biggest difference between OLAP analytics and SQL analytics is the ability to perform comparisons and calculations along any dimension in an OLAP system. In SQL, the powerful analytic functions are confined within a single row of the SQL answer set. In SQL it is essentially impossible to perform operations across separate rows. This is why we resort to multipass SQL for most of the complex reports we must produce in the Webhouse.

For most of the 1990s there has been a natural market segmentation between OLAP systems and SQL-based systems based on the size of the database being stored. Even in 1999, OLAP systems do not scale gracefully beyond 10 GB of input data and 500,000 members in any single dimension. This is an awkward cut-point in our data warehouse applications because perhaps half of all applications fall below these points and half fall above (or way above) these points.

At the time of this writing, there are rumors in the marketplace that OLAP systems will finally and decisively remove the size barriers and will be able to scale into the hundreds of GB of input data, and to tens of millions of members in a dimension. When and if this happens, there is likely to be a sea change for many data warehouses as they consider switching to OLAP technologies.

However, at the time of this writing, OLAP systems are not mainline contenders for Webhouse applications and for associated data mining activities, for the following reasons:

- The clickstream data sources are far, far beyond the reach of OLAP systems today. Clickstream sources are extremely granular and must be connected to an individual Web visitor dimension. A responsible designer must anticipate handling a Web visitor dimension with 100 million members and individual fact tables extending up to multiple terabytes.

- OLAP systems are natural analysis platforms for aggregated data. To the extent that the Webhouse is trying to store and analyze disaggregated data representing customer behavior, this is in conflict with OLAP.

- Even if the first versions of expanded OLAP capabilities are released as early as the Year 2000, a conservative deployment of this technology would wait 1 to 2 more years to let the bugs and limitations shake out before putting this technology into a production Webhouse delivery system.

So, our recommendation at this time is to wait hopefully and expectantly for OLAP systems to approach their destiny at the high end of Webhouse applications, but to continue for the next several years with relational-based technologies as the platform of choice.

SUMMARY

The Webhouse and the data mining shop are natural partners. The increased focus on customer behavior in all our Web-driven businesses is a perfect opportunity for us to make sure the Webhouse team and the data mining team are talking to each other. There is a natural handoff between the two teams. The Webhouse sources and prepares the voluminous databases, and makes sure that they are conformed to each other. This is a huge responsibility that most data mining teams cannot take on unilaterally.

The Webhouse hands off the data in the form of ready-to-go observation sets that can be digested immediately by the data mining tools.

In many cases, the data mining tools produce interesting predictions or behavior scores that, themselves, are databases. The Webhouse can then be a good place to store and make available these results from data mining.

CHAPTER 12

Creating an International Data Webhouse

In this chapter and the next one on security, we attack two data warehouse challenges that can seem hopeless to understand and deal with fully. But in both cases we believe that there are some simple guidelines that turn these challenges into manageable problems. In this chapter we gather together a collection of issues that arise from the international nature of the Web. Although each of these "internationalization" issues is interesting and open ended, we will seek a pragmatic course rather than trying for a fully elegant solution. Also, by taking a consistently international perspective in the design of the Webhouse, we can avoid costly system redesigns and we can avoid ignoring or insulting our international users.

Almost all of the international issues in the Webhouse *come from different ways of expressing the same thing*. This is a useful unifying perspective. The same Web page can be presented in multiple languages. The same currency amount can be presented in multiple currencies. The same moment in time can be expressed from the perspective of different time zones. The same report can be sorted with different language-based collating sequences.

Most of the solutions for the above list of problems come from providing parallel alternatives that the user can select among. Each parallel alternative can be driven from a separate cultural or geographic interpretation. We'll just refer to these separate alternatives as *languages* in this chapter, to keep the terminology simple.

The international issues in the Webhouse include:

- Foreign alphabets and character sets
- Names
- Addresses and their extensions to locations and maps
- Numbers
- Telephone numbers
- Currencies
- Time of day
- Calendars
- Handling of unsupported characters
- Reports, printing, and collating sequences

But before digging into each of these topics, we need to look at certain developments on the Web that will affect how we respond to these international issues.

By understanding the language and cultural expectations of international customers we can address several of Patricia Seybold's success factors mentioned in Chapter 1 and described in her book *Customers.com* (Random House, 1998). In particular we can target the right customer when we know something about the cultural preferences and demographic characteristics of international customers. We can streamline business processes for international customers when we understand their names, addresses, currencies, calendars, and reporting expectations. We can deliver personalized service using other techniques described in this book, but only if we can communicate this personalized service in a way that seems to know who these people are.

THE EVOLVING INTERNATIONAL WEB

In this section we describe a number of vigorous new developments on the Web whose aim is to address problems unique to the international perspective.

UNICODE

Many of the international display and printing problems on the Web require being able to represent foreign characters, including not just the accented characters from western European alphabets, but Cyrillic, Arabic, Japanese, Chinese, and dozens of other less familiar writing systems. It is important to understand that this is not a font problem. It is a character set problem. A font is simply an artist's rendering of a set of characters. There are hundreds of fonts available for standard English. But standard English has a relatively small character set that is enough for anyone's use unless you are a professional typographer. This small character set is usually encoded in ASCII (American Standard Code for Information Interchange), which is an 8-bit encoding that has a maximum of 255 possible characters. Only about 100 of these 255 characters have a standard interpretation that can be invoked from a normal English keyboard, but this is usually enough for English-speaking computer users. It should be clear, though, that ASCII is woefully inadequate for representing the thousands of characters needed for non-English writing systems.

An international body of system architects, the UNICODE Consortium, has defined a standard known as UNICODE for representing characters and alphabets in almost all of the world's languages and cultures. Their work can be accessed on the Web at www.unicode.org. UNICODE is a 16-bit encoding that has a maximum of 65,535 possible characters. The UNICODE Standard, version 2.1, which is the published version of UNICODE as of the writing of this book, has defined specific interpretations for 38,887 of the possible characters and now covers the principal written languages of the Americas, Europe, the Middle East, Africa, India, Asia, and Pacifica. Languages (which the UNICODE Consortium call *scripts*) that have been accepted for support in future versions of UNICODE include Burmese, Cherokee, Ethiopic, Khmer, Thaana, Sinhala, and Yi. Modern scripts without a definite commitment for support include Mongolian, Moso, Pahawh Hmong, Rong, Tai Lu, Tai Mau, and Tifinagh. A number of archaic scripts including Egyptian hieroglyphics and Sumerian are not yet supported. At least in the case of Mongolian, you may be relieved to know that it is acceptable to use Cyrillic script as an alternative.

UNICODE is definitely the foundation we will all eventually use for addressing international character sets. But it is important to understand that implementing UNICODE solutions is done in the foundation layers of the Webhouse. First, your operating system must be UNICODE compliant. Fortunately, the most current releases of all of the major operating systems are UNICODE compliant, but you should check the fine print with your vendor.

Above the operating system, all the devices that capture, store, transmit, and print characters must be UNICODE compliant. See Figure 12.1. Data entry terminals, for instance, do not need to be able to enter every UNICODE character, but should provide UNICODE support for the characters they can enter. Text editors likewise must not truncate UNICODE to ASCII. Even if the editor cannot create or display a specific UNICODE character, it must not delete or alter the character. Unrecognized characters should be displayed with a distinctive "blot" character to warn the user to be respectful of whatever-it-is.

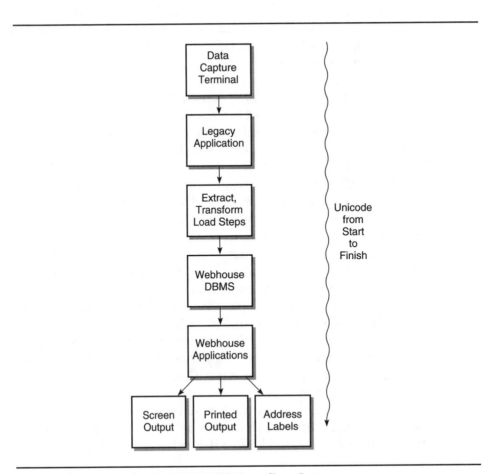

FIGURE 12.1   An End-to-End UNICODE-Compliant System

Webhouse back-room tools must be UNICODE compliant, including sort packages, programming languages, and automated ETL (extract, transform, and load) packages.

Finally, the Webhouse applications, including database engines, application servers, and their applications packages including report writers and query tools, Web servers, and browsers must all be UNICODE compliant. The Webhouse architect should not only talk to the vendors of each package in the Webhouse data pipeline, but should conduct various end-to-end tests. Capture some names and addresses with UNICODE characters at the data capture screens of one of your legacy applications and send them through your system. Get them to print out of a final report or a final browser window from your data Webhouse and see if the special characters are still there. That simple test will cut through a lot of the confusion. At the time of this writing, many existing systems will pass this test. Note that even when you do this, the same character, such as an umlaut, will sort differently in different countries like Norway and Germany. Even though you can't solve all the variations in international collating sequences, at least both the Norwegians and the Germans will agree that the character is an umlaut.

Send a representative set of characters end-to-end through your Webhouse to see if the Webhouse is UNICODE compliant.

Parallel Hypertext and Machine Translation

The Internet Engineering Task Force (IETF) has been working on the definition of an extension to HTML known as Parallel Hypertext Data Structure (PHDS). This would allow a given physical Web page to have parallel pages in other languages. See Figure 12.2. Parallel pages could be actual physical pages that have been carefully translated word for word in another language, or they could be dynamically created pages translated by machine on demand. These parallel pages would not actually be connected to the first page with normal hypertext links, but would be connected by "implicit links" that a browser could compute when an alternate language is requested by the user. A special PHDS header in the Web page instructs the browser where to go look for a requested parallel page. This scheme is intended to simplify the creation and maintenance of multiple-language Websites. For example, many sites in the

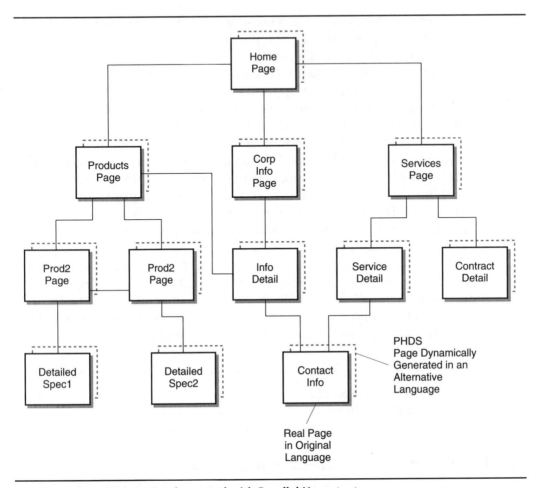

FIGURE 12.2   A Website Implemented with Parallel Hypertext

European Community need to support Web pages simultaneously in the eleven official languages of the community. It would be possible to build such a Website only once physically, but then have the other ten languages available through parallel hypertext, especially if the parallel pages were generated dynamically.

The European Community has addressed the problem of translation among the eleven languages with the Eurovoc thesaurus. The Eurovoc thesaurus is a multilanguage and multidisciplinary thesaurus for the translation of documents of the European Parliament and the Office for Official Publications of the EC. This thesaurus can be used as part of an automatic translation capability.

Machine translation is the name of an expanding field of products, research, and development. At the time of this writing there are more than twenty commercial software products available for automatic translation of documents between languages. These products can be configured in a number of interesting ways in a Webhouse environment. Some of these products already exist as services on the Web that accept URLs and return the requested page, translated to a desired language. Other products are standalone translators that can be configured within a server or at the user's workstation.

Even if we are not probing Websites with parallel hypertext, we must deal with the babel of languages. As non-English sites proliferate and eventually dominate the Web, how do we search the Web?

An automatically translated set of pages for a PHDS implementation should be intended as a convenience for the remote visitor who otherwise could never use your site, because the quality of the translation may not meet your standards for intensive day-to-day commercial use.

Multilingual Search

The ability to conduct Web searches across multiple languages is of intense interest to the Web community. Multilingual search is also called *cross-language information retrieval*. The multilingual search problem can be broken into several related approaches; see Figure 12.3:

- Translating a search specification from the user's original language to one or more foreign languages in order to run the search
- Translating target documents from a foreign language into the user's original language so that the documents can be searched or simply read
- Translating both the search specification and all or part of selected target documents into an intermediate representation so that they can be searched

Like machine translation, cross-language information retrieval can be provided in the Webhouse in several different configurations, corresponding to these approaches.

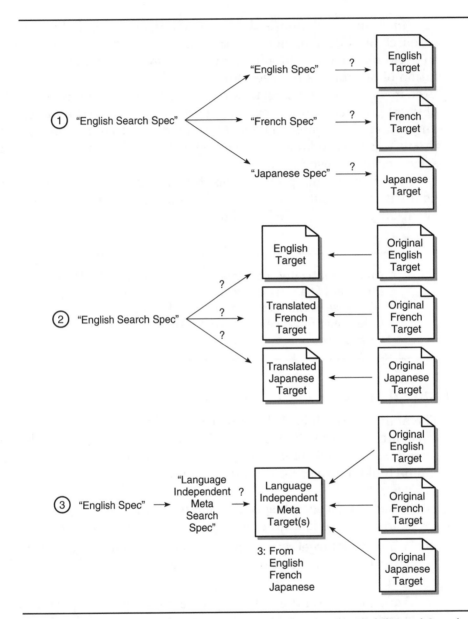

FIGURE 12.3 Three Translation Approaches for Supporting Multilingual Search

Time Zone Converter Services

The calculation of the true wall clock time in a given location around the world is surprisingly complicated. Most people think there are twenty-four time zones, corresponding to the twenty-four "possible" hours per day. But with even a little foreign travel experience, one begins to realize that this situation is much more complex. The entire country of India, for instance, sits in between these hour boundaries, since at different times of the year, it is either 5.5 or 6.5 hours ahead of Greenwich Mean Time. The rules of when various locations go on and off daylight savings time are amazingly intricate. Parts of Indiana, for example, go on daylight savings time, and other parts do not. The dates when daylight savings time goes into effect vary by location. The time difference between London, England and Sydney, Australia can vary by as much as two hours, depending on the time of year. In reality, there are more than 500 time zones in the world, and the list is constantly changing.

The complexity of time zone calculations makes it clear that one cannot embed time zone assumptions in the code of applications or fixed queries. It is also pretty clear that each IT organization should not reinvent the wheel and derive all the time zone rules independently.

The issue of time zone conversions is a data extract issue, not a query and reporting issue.

Fortunately, the Web comes to our rescue. A number of time zone conversion services, such as www.timezoneconverter.com, are available on-line that have up-to-date databases reflecting all the complexities of time zone calculations.

Holiday Lookup Services

Every country has a unique list of holidays. In many cases the holidays do not occur on the same day in successive years. Some holidays, such as Easter, are based on very complex rules that involve the phases of the moon or other events. Some religious holidays are not celebrated on the same day in various parts of the same country.

Holidays are so complicated that it probably does not make sense to try to define them more than ten or twenty years into the future.

Much as with time zones, the technical definition of holidays in the Webhouse needs to be driven from a service. At the time of this writing, one of the best publicly available sources of international holiday definitions can be found on the Web at www.holidayfestival.com.

INTERNATIONAL WEBHOUSE TECHNIQUES

In this section we present a number of techniques for handling situations that come up in an international Webhouse.

Synchronize Multiple Time Zones and Time Formats

In many businesses we measure the exact time of basic transactions. The most common transactions include retail transactions at conventional stores, telephone inquiries at service desks, and financial transactions at bank teller machines. When our business spans multiple time zones we are left with an interesting conflict. Do we record the times of these transactions relative to an absolute point in time, or do we record the times relative to local midnight in each time zone? Both of these perspectives are valid. The absolute time perspective allows us see the true simultaneous nature of the transactions across our entire business, whereas the local time perspective allows us to accurately understand the transaction flow relative to the time of day. In the United States, "everyone" gets off work at 5 P.M., watches the news at 6, and eats dinner at 6:30.

It is tempting to store each underlying transaction with an absolute time stamp, and then leave it up to the application to sort out issues of local times. Somehow this seems to be a conservative and safe thing to do. However, we do not support this design. The database architect has left the downstream application designer with a complicated mess. Doing a coordinated local-time-of-day analysis across multiple time zones is nightmarish if all you have is a single absolute time stamp. Transaction times near midnight will fall on different days. States like Arizona and parts of Indiana do not observe daylight savings time. Reversing the design decision and storing the transaction times as relative to local midnight just recasts the same application problem in a different form. What is needed instead is a more powerful design.

The recommended time stamp design for businesses with multiple time zones is shown in Figure 12.4. The time stamp is simultaneously recorded in both absolute and relative formats. Additionally, we recommend

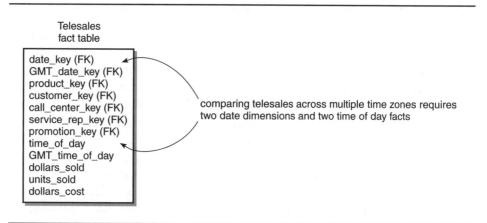

Telesales fact table

date_key (FK)
GMT_date_key (FK)
product_key (FK)
customer_key (FK)
call_center_key (FK)
service_rep_key (FK)
promotion_key (FK)
time_of_day
GMT_time_of_day
dollars_sold
units_sold
dollars_cost

comparing telesales across multiple time zones requires two date dimensions and two time of day facts

FIGURE 12.4   A Schema Design for Comparing Sales Across Multiple Time Zones

separating the calendar day portions of the time stamps off from the time-of-day portions of the time stamps. We thus end up with four fields in a typical transaction fact table. The two calendar day fields should be surrogate keys pointing to two instances of a calendar day dimension table. These key entries in the fact table should *not* be actual SQL date stamps. Rather, these keys should be simple integers that point over to the calendar date dimension table. Using surrogate (integer) keys for the actual join allows us to deal gracefully with corrupted, or unknown, or hasn't-happened-yet dates. We split off the time of day from the calendar date because we don't want to build a dimension table with an entry for every minute over the lifetime of our business. Instead, our calendar day dimension table merely has an entry for every day. In any case, we probably don't have unique textual descriptors for each individual minute, whereas we do have a rich array of unique textual descriptors for each individual day.

The two time-of-day fields are probably not keys that join to dimension tables. Rather, they can simply be numerical facts in the fact table. To constrain such time-of-day facts, we apply *between* constraints to these fields. If we do a lot of these kinds of constraints, it will be helpful to build an index on each of these time-of-day fields.

Although this double-barreled design uses a bit more storage space (three extra fields) in the fact table, the application designers will be delighted. Both absolute and relative time analyses will "fall out" of the database, regardless of how many time zones your business spans.

Support Multiple National Calendars and Date Formats

A multinational business that spans many countries cannot easily keep track of an open-ended number of holidays and seasons across many different countries. As seems to happen so many times in database design, there are two different perspectives that need to be addressed. We need to see the calendar from the perspective of a single country (is today a holiday in Singapore?). But we also need to look across collections of countries all at once (is today a holiday anywhere in Europe?).

The recommended design for an open-ended number of calendars is shown in Figure 12.5. The primary calendar dimension contains generic entries independent of any particular country. These entries include weekday names, month names, and other useful navigational fields like day number, week number, and month number. If your business spans major basic calendar types such as Gregorian, Islamic, and Chinese calendars, then it would make sense to include all three sets of major labels for days, months, and years in this single table.

The calendar dimension just described provides the basic framework for all calendars. But each country has a small number of unique calendar variations. We like to handle this with a supplementary calendar dimension whose key is the combination of the calendar key from the main calendar dimension, together with the country name. This supplementary table is also shown in Figure 12.5. You can join this table to the main calendar dimension or directly to the fact table. If you provide a user interface that requires the country to be specified, then the attributes of the supplementary table can be logically viewed as being

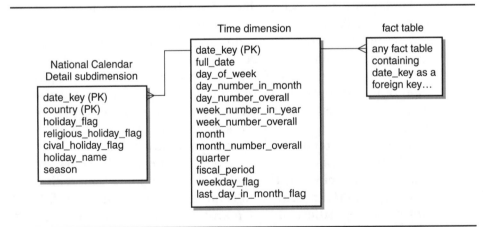

FIGURE 12.5   A Schema Design for Dealing with Multiple National Calendars

appended to the main calendar table. This allows you to view your calendar through the eyes of any single country at a time.

You can use the supplementary calendar table to constrain groups of countries. The grouping can be geographic or by any other affiliation you choose for a country (such as Supplier Business Partners). If you choose a group of countries, you can use the EXISTS clause of SQL to determine if any of the countries has a holiday on a particular date.

Purely numeric versions of dates, such as 2/5/02, have many problems. Is this February 5, 2002 or May 2, 1902? If the Y2K problem has taught us anything, we need to be more careful with date specifications and make them unambiguous. We recommend spelling out the month in some way whenever possible, simply to eliminate the ordering confusion, which is the biggest source of mistakes when interpreting dates. Thus 2/5/02 is revealed as 2 May 2002. If sorting is required on the date field itself, then 2002-05-02 is fairly readable and can serve as the basis for sorting.

Collect Revenue in Multiple Currencies

Multinational businesses often book transactions, collect revenues, and pay expenses in many different currencies. A good basic design for all of these situations is shown in Figure 12.6. The primary amount of the transaction is represented in the local currency. In some sense, this is always the "correct" value of the transaction. For easy reporting purposes, a second field in the transaction fact record expresses the same amount in a single global currency, such as United States dollars. The equivalency between the two amounts is a basic design decision for the fact

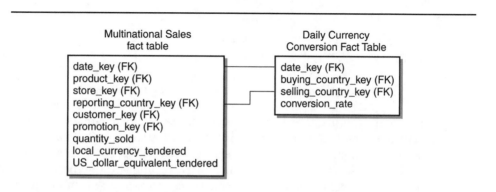

FIGURE 12.6   A Schema Design for Dealing with Multiple Currencies

table, and probably is an agreed-upon daily spot rate for the conversion of the local currency into the global currency. Now all transactions in a single currency can be added up easily from the fact table by constraining in the country dimension to a single currency type. Transactions from around the world can easily be added up by summing the global currency field. Note that the fact table contains a currency dimension separate from the geographic dimension representing the store location.

THE EURO

Many of the European nations (known as the European Union, or EU) have standardized on a single European currency known as the euro. The euro is significant from a data warehouse point of view and should not be viewed as just another currency. The euro brings with it some specific financial reporting and data warehousing requirements. The most significant requirements are the triangulation requirement and carrying all euro amounts with three decimals. The official abbreviation, according to ISO 4217, for "euro" is "EUR" in all languages.

On January 1, 1999, all EU countries adopted a final, fixed permanent conversion rate of their currencies to the euro. One euro permanently equals

40.3399	BEF	(Belgium)
1.95583	DEM	(Germany)
166.386	ESP	(Spain)
6.55957	FRF	(France)
0.787564	IEP	(Ireland)
1936.27	ITL	(Italy)
40.3399	LUF	(Luxembourg)
2.20371	NLG	(Netherlands)
13.7603	ATS	(Austria)
200.482	PTE	(Portugal)
5.94573	FIM	(Finland)

The formal definition of these conversion rates expresses all conversions to exactly six decimal places, and all currency conversions should be performed to six significant digits. Notice that this is not the same as "six decimals." For instance, the reciprocal of the Italian lira exchange rate is $1/1936.27 = 0.000516457$, which requires nine decimals to support the six significant figures. The six significant digit rule is also useful for dealing with countries going through periods of hyperinflation where the denomination of the currency may vary by as much as a factor of 1,000 in the space of a few years.

Currencies and countries are closely correlated, but they are not the same. Countries may change the identity of their currency during periods of severe inflation. Also, the members of the European Monetary Union must be able to express their transactions in both their native currencies and in the euro.

But what happens if we want to express the value of a set of transactions in a third currency? For this we need a currency exchange table,

On January 1, 2002, all original EU member currencies will be extinguished in favor of the single euro currency. Although from that point forward there will literally be no French francs, Spanish pesetas, or German marks, there will still be a need for retrospective views backward before that date that will need to represent the original separate currencies.

Certain currency conversion calculations performed between EU countries require that a currency must first be converted into the euro, and then the euro value is to be converted into the second currency. It is not allowed to convert directly between currencies because there are certain situations where the final converted amount will differ slightly. These conversions in the data warehouse, of course, can be implemented from the design of the previous section, where the global currency is assumed to be the euro.

Triangulation (converting from a source currency to the euro, and then converting from the euro to the destination currency) must be used in the following situations:

EU currency ➜ EU currency (until Jan 1, 2002 when EU currencies vanish)
EU currency ➜ non-EU currency (until Jan 1, 2002 when EU currencies vanish)
non-EU currency ➜ EU currency (until Jan 1, 2002 when EU currencies vanish)

The above table of fixed rates must be used when converting:

EU currency ➜ euro (until Jan 1, 2002 when EU currencies vanish)
euro ➜ EU currency (until Jan 1, 2002 when EU currencies vanish)

Traditional variable rates, determined on a minute-to-minute basis, must still be used when converting:

non-EU currency ➜ non-EU currency
non-EU currency ➜ euro
euro ➜ non-EU currency.

also shown in Figure 12.6. The currency exchange table typically contains the daily exchange rates both to and from each of the local currencies and one or more global currencies. Thus if there are 100 local currencies and 3 global currencies, then we would need 600 exchange rate records each day. It is probably not practical to build a currency exchange table between each possible pair of currencies, because for 100 currencies, there would be 10,000 daily exchange rates. It is not likely, in our opinion, that a meaningful market for every possible pair of exchange rates actually exists.

Handle International Names and Addresses

Names and addresses are the most difficult and far reaching international design problem in the Webhouse. Toby Atkinson has written a remarkable book describing the intricacies of international names and addresses. In his *Merriam Webster's Guide to International Business Communications* (Merriam-Webster, 1996) he gives the following example. Suppose you have a name and address like the following:

Sándor Csilla
Nemzetközi Kiadó Kft
Rákóczi u. 73
7626 PÉCS

Are you prepared to store this in a database? Is this a postally valid address? Does this represent a person or a company? Male or female? Would the recipient be insulted by anything about this? Can your system parse it to determine the precise geographic locale? What salutation would be appropriate if you were greeting this entity in a letter or on the telephone? What is going to happen to the various special characters when it is printed? Can you even enter these characters from your various keyboards?

If your Webhouse contains information about people or businesses located in multiple countries, then you need to plan carefully for a complete system spanning data input, transaction processing, address label and mailing production, real-time customer response systems, and your marketing-oriented data warehouse. Actually, we should remove the "if" at the beginning of the sentence. You can't escape dealing with this problem. Virtually every business has to deal with international names and addresses somewhere, whether the business has actual international suppliers or customers, or whether the human resources department records places of birth or foreign business references.

Before we dive into recommended systems and database structures, let's step back and decide on some goals for our international names and addresses:

- **Universal and consistent.** As they say, in for a penny, in for a pound. If we are going to design a system for representing international names and addresses, we want it to work for every country in the world. Our design must not depend on the idiosyncrasies of any single country, but it should handle even the unusual cases. Our design should have consistency from country to country so that similar data elements appear in predictable, similar places in the database.

- **End to end data quality and downstream compatibility.** The data warehouse cannot be the only step in the data pipeline that worries about the integrity of international names and addresses. A proper design requires support from the first step of capturing the name and the address, through the data cleaning and storage steps, to the final steps of performing geographic and demographic analysis, printing reports, printing letters to customers, and printing postally valid mailing labels. When we hand off a document or report to our foreign subsidiary, we want the names and addresses to be rendered in the correct original form.

- **Cultural correctness.** In many cases, our foreign customers and partners will see the results from our data warehouse in some form. If we don't understand which name is a first name and which name is a last name, and if we don't understand how to refer to a person, we run the risk of insulting these individuals, or at the very least, looking stupid. When our written output is punctuated improperly or misspelled our foreign customers and partners will wish they were doing business with a local company, rather than us.

- **Duplication removal and householding.** It is important to remove duplicates from very large customer lists. Not only do we save money by removing duplicates, but we eliminate redundant communications, and misleading counts of customers. A sophisticated form of duplication removal is householding, where we identify different customers who share the same domestic or commercial household. When we understand the economic unit that is the household, we can plan marketing initiatives more effectively. The secret of duplicate removing and householding is effectively parsing the names and addresses into many, many correctly identified name and address components.

- **Geographic and demographic analysis.**   Geographic and demographic analysis is a kind of "macro householding." Again, to correctly categorize and analyze a large list of customers, we need to parse lists of names and addresses into fine grain detail.

- **Real time customer response.**   Many Webhouses can play an operational role by supporting real-time customer response systems. A customer service representative may answer the telephone and may have five seconds or less to wait for a greeting to appear on the screen that the data warehouse recommends using with the customer. The greeting may include a proper salutation, and a proper use of the customer's title and name. This greeting represents an excellent use of the hot response cache.

- **Foreign mailing, domestic mailing, and package service delivery.**   The Webhouse may play an important role in the production of mailing lists for marketing campaigns, for customer service, or for informational mailings. The Webhouse may have to meet at least three separate requirements. The foreign mailing requirement means that the Webhouse can produce a postally valid mailing address from the country of origin to the destination country. This includes meeting international mailing standards, such as presenting the city and the country in all capital letters, and placing the postal code in the right location within the address. The domestic mailing requirement means that the data warehouse can produce a postally valid mailing address within the destination country. This address format is frequently different from the international format, and may have to be presented in the character set and language of the foreign country. The package service delivery requirement must produce a physical address that a package service can deliver a package to. Such an address cannot be a post office box.

- **Other kinds of addresses.**   We all know that we are in the middle of a revolution in communication and networking. If you are designing a system for identifying international names and addresses, you must anticipate the need to store electronic names, security tokens, and Internet addresses.

The first and most important step is to tackle the language, font and character set problem head on. You simply cannot patch together half-solutions out of ASCII, EBCDIC, incompatible terminals, incompatible word processing packages, and incompatible printers. Your best efforts to capture a name and an address can be thwarted by the next system down the pipe if it remaps your character set or discards all the accents. To solve this problem, as described earlier in this chapter, you must build a UNICODE system from end to end.

The second necessary step is to do a complete job of parsing and storing the names and addresses. Resist the urge to simply cram everything into a few generic fields like Name1, Name2, Name3, and Address1, Address2, and Address3.

For guidance on how to build a robust set of descriptors for international names and addresses, once again Atkinson's book comes to the rescue. By the way, to get the detailed explanation of the example at the beginning of the section, you'll have to read Atkinson's book! Hint: look in the chapter on Hungarian addresses.

Based on studying Atkinson's elaborate examples of name and address variations, we can construct a file layout for names and addresses that will handle nearly every international situation and at the same time serve as a proper target for parsing and duplicate removal. An international name and address to be used in a commercial context could consist of the following fields:

Salutation

First Name

Middle Names

Last Name

Degrees (e.g., MS, Ph.D, and other honorary titles)

Ethnicity

Company Name

Department Name

Job Title

Building

Floor

Mail Stop

Address Type (e.g., headquarters office, secondary field office, parcel delivery address)

Intended Use (e.g., domestic mail, foreign mail)

Street Number

Street Name

Street Direction

Post Office Box

Locality

City

State

Postal Code

Region

Country

Assembled Address Block

Written Greeting

Verbal Greeting

Unique Personal Individual Identifier

Unique Commercial Individual Identifier

Unique Commercial Entity Identifier

A record with this content should be created for each variation of address you have for each individual. We don't recommend trying to cram all the variations of addresses into a single long record. You may have a single address for a customer in some cases, and a half dozen addresses for customers in other cases. Sometimes the same individual may play more than one role with different titles and addresses, and hence the individual needs more than one record.

The Assembled Address Block is a long text field with a complete and correct address for the intended use, rendered in the proper order according to the regulations of the destination country, including the line breaks. Having this field simplifies address list creation applications because they don't have to contain the country-by-country rules for correct address formulation.

The written and verbal greetings resolve the issue of what is the individual's first name and last name and how custom demands that these name parts be used. The unique identifiers at the end of the record provide the means for you to manage duplicate names and roles. It is possible that you may wish to count a given individual multiple times in different commercial roles. The identifiers give you several options for correctly counting and managing such overlapping entries.

Telephone numbers should not be appended to this record layout because there are an open-ended set of such numbers for any given individual. A separate record layout for telephone numbers should have at least the following structure:

Salutation
Title
First Name
Middle Names
Last Name
Country Code
City Code
Telephone Number
Internal Extension
Phone Number Type (e.g., main office, direct line, secretary, home, pager, fax)
Secretary Name
Secondary Dialing Instructions (e.g., for a pager)
Complete Foreign Dialing Sequence
Complete Domestic Dialing Sequence
Complete Local Dialing Sequence
Company Name
Department Name
Job Title
City
State
Country
Verbal Greeting
Unique Personal Individual Identifier
Unique Commercial Individual Identifier
Unique Commercial Entity Identifier

These record designs can be used for foreign and local address labels, real time greetings, duplication removal, householding, and demographic analysis. When combined with end-to-end UNICODE support, you should have a foundation for effectively dealing with international names and addresses well into the next millennium.

Support Variable Number Formats

Numbers are represented differently in different cultures. The number 100.456 is slightly larger than *one hundred* in the United States, but slightly larger than *one hundred thousand* in Germany. In India, a large number may be written as 23 34 789, since they may group the digits by twos after the first group of three. In India, a lakh represents 100,000 and a crore represents 10,000,000. Other countries use periods, commas, and even apostrophes to separate the digits. An international Webhouse must be able to read and write numbers correctly, given an assigned cultural context.

Support International Telephone Numbers

Telephone numbers, like postal addresses, have two basic representations. One is for domestic consumption, and one is for international use. To make matters worse, the international version is often interpreted in a different way by each international observer. A number (randomly created for illustrative purposes) in South Africa for example is written as

021-222-3333

but must be dialed from the United States as

011-27-21-222-3333.

But the leading 011 is the way the United States dials international numbers. This will not be the same in other countries.

Handle Multinational Queries, Reports, and Collating Sequences

Multinational querying faces some of the same problems that multinational searching faces. The user may wish to enter a query in their native language, but the target of the query may be expressed in another language. But a query interface to a Webhouse in many cases will be equipped to let the user browse a set of permissible values. This simplifies the cross-language issues significantly.

An interesting issue in multinational reporting is how to prepare a set of consistent reports for managers across such an organization in different languages. There are three basic issues that must be dealt with simultaneously:

- sorting (collating),
- grouping, and
- conforming.

Many language systems sort their special characters in a unique way. Atkinson's book discusses the specific rules for sorting in Catalan, Czech, Danish, Finnish, German, Hungarian, Norwegian, Polish, Slovenian, Spanish, Swedish, and Turkish. And these are only languages using the Roman alphabet. A report could sort the same set of customer names differently in different languages.

Great care must be taken if a set of attributes in a dimension is translated from one language to another. For instance, if the category and department names for a large number of products are translated into more than one language, then the cardinality and the detailed many-to-many and many-to-one relationships must be identical between the two language versions of the dimension, or else the use of an attribute from the dimension as a row header (grouping criterion) will not produce the same results in the separate languages. Because the maintenance of two language versions of a large dimension table would be so subtle and difficult, we recommend against this approach.

If the same dimension table has several language versions in different countries, then it may be impossible to conform data marts across these versions, because at an SQL query level, the row headers of the separate answer sets in different languages could not be matched.

If we assume that we want a set of reports to span multiple languages, then we probably need to implement a two-layer architecture. In the lower layer, we store all data and produce all reports from a single base language system. This system should be based on the UNICODE character set so that all possible rendering and sorting issues can be dealt with. In the upper layer, the finished report is augmented with translations in auxiliary reporting columns. These auxiliary reporting columns do not affect sorting, grouping, or the ability to conform reports across data marts located in different countries. If we adopt this approach, managers from different countries should be able to sit in the same room with their own versions of the same reports, but be able to understand each other's reports and compare them.

Apply Localization in the Data Webhouse

Localization is a standard software development technique that isolates all of the language content delivered through any user interface into a set of text files separate from the program code itself. In this way, a version of the software for any given language can be produced merely by substituting a new text file in the desired language. Of course, in practice it is not quite so automatic. The entire software release has to be tested with the new language prompts, both to make sure that the text fits in the expected places on the screen, and to make sure that the translations preserve the intended content.

If we think of localization as providing an open ended number of switchable versions of text files in different languages, then this becomes a useful technique for the Webhouse as well. Because of the distributed nature of the Webhouse, localization can be applied in many places. Localization can be applied to:

- Back-room metadata describing the lineage and business rules of Webhouse data.

- The user interfaces of back room extract-transform-load (ETL) tools

- Front-room metadata, especially including auxiliary reporting fields in dimensions, as described in the previous section.

- The user interfaces of front-room query, reporting, and data mining tools, typically implemented in the application server layer.

- The user interfaces provided by the Web server in addition to the content provided by the application server. These user interfaces may include standard button and navigation support on all pages, and may be created by a Web page authoring package, which should be UNICODE compliant and should have the capability to switch languages.

- The user interfaces of the authentication and authorization layers of the Webhouse, which is probably implemented on the firewall machine.

A sophisticated version of localization also allows number, date, currency, and punctuation details to be specified, both for input and output.

SUMMARY

In this chapter we have described all of the international design issues we are aware of that impact the Webhouse. Although many of them are open ended and have no truly complete or elegant solution, in most cases we can reduce the problem to manageable proportions by providing flexible ways to switch among the multiple languages we must support.

The most important architectural step is to provide full UNICODE support throughout the Webhouse.

Next, you should localize all of the language dependent portions of the Webhouse by providing parallel text files and parallel Web pages. In many cases these parallel versions in different languages can be created dynamically with translation software.

Then, you make sure that you correctly handle and interpret the formatting vagaries of numbers, currencies, dates, names, and addresses in each of the language systems you support.

You should use Web-based services on a daily basis in your back room-extract-transform-load operations to access currency conversion rates and time zone definitions. Perhaps you can also translate Web pages dynamically using one of these services.

Finally, you need to provide special extensions to your normal dimensional data mart designs to handle international issues. These extensions include multiple date and time fields to deal with absolute and relative time stamps, very verbose name and address parsing in your customer dimensions to handle international locations and mailing addresses, and special auxiliary fields for showing a report in a foreign language without compromising sorting, grouping, or conforming.

CHAPTER 13

Data Webhouse Security

Security is a topic most data Webhouse managers would probably like to avoid. In a way, this is surprising, because security is an intricate, fascinating puzzle, and data Webhouse people generally like to work on puzzles. Security also involves a lot of interesting hardware and software technology, ranging from biometric scanning devices for identifying users, to virtual private networks based on advanced encryption, to new network servers with interesting names like LDAP. Security has a compelling people angle, because the perpetrators of security problems (the hackers, crackers, and industrial spooks) have varying kinds of pathological personality flaws that make them threats to computer systems and data Webhouses. Finally security also is immensely important commercially, and management is probably willing to spend a lot of money to get security right. So what's the reluctance to make security one of the main design topics in the data Webhouse, and in data warehousing in general?

Maybe the problem with security is that it is fundamentally an issue of control and avoidance of problems. It is not the typical "upside opportunity" kind of topic typical of data warehousing. Good data warehouse managers are really drawn to the business issues illuminated by the data warehouse. They don't like to talk about controlling problems. And maybe the security problem seems so complicated and so diffuse that no one knows where to start attacking it.

It is certainly true that the Web has made security problems more acute. All of us are rapidly joining a fully connected world, where our networks are separated from the chaos of the public Web by just one or two machines. Most of us have no real choice but to connect to the Web, to listen to the Web, and to deploy our services (and our Webhouses) across the Web. So, one possible approach for this chapter is just to say that security is a necessary part of the Webhouse experience, so take your medicine, and keep reading.

But we would like to make this chapter more interesting and more compelling in its own right. We actually think that the Web in some ways has made security easier to think about and easier to manage. In the same way that the Web is finally exerting effective pressure on user interfaces to conform and to improve, the Web is also exerting effective pressure on Web based security to conform and to improve. Certain key architectures have already emerged that are ready to provide the data Webhouse good security.

Rather than providing a complete, broad tutorial on all the components of data Webhouse security, in this chapter we present a single recommended, coherent approach to security that we think addresses all of the main issues confronting the data Webhouse manager. This approach is highly consistent with current product offerings from major vendors, although we will not name those products specifically because we have no commercial ax to grind in this book. Think of this chapter as describing one complete solution that you can either implement verbatim, or can contrast with another solution you prefer. Either way, you will have a solid data point for comparison and discussion.

A good security program is essential to the interests of CRM. The customer needs to be reassured that confidential information about them is not available to unauthorized parties. A customer should never be able to see revealing information about someone else that would create the fear that such information is easy to obtain. The trappings of security, therefore, need to be present in a continuous and subtle way as a reminder.

The creation and administration of roles, described in this chapter, is a very important mechanism for preserving the identity and individuality of the customer.

There are many useful references discussing the technical foundations of security. *The Data Warehouse Lifecycle Toolkit* devoted a "graduate" chapter to these foundations, and to a case-by-case analysis of where the security risks lie, and what the data warehouse's exposure to each of these risks could be. But for a more comprehensive treatment of security, our favorite complete book devoted to this subject is *Security in Computing,* 2nd edition, by Charles Pfleeger (Prentice-Hall, 1997).

RECOMMENDED SECURITY TECHNIQUES

The security framework in this chapter is meant for any user accessing sensitive data in your organization. The framework is meant to cover employees, business partners, and customers, with a single security solution, regardless of their physical location. They can be inside your secure company intranet, or outside on the Web.

We chose the framework we are about to describe because it is simple and yet powerful. In the last section of this chapter we urge you to think of security as a continuous process, not a one-time solution. The security manager in your data Webhouse team will need to continuously visit and revisit the elements of this framework, always adapting and strengthening the security protection. The content of the data changes. The legitimate roles of the users change. Users themselves come and go from the organization, and their personal roles change. Technology changes, and the threats posed by various kinds of hackers and other disaffected individuals changes. So, above all, you must treat security as a dynamic process that is an ongoing part of your Webhouse experience.

Our Webhouse security framework is based on the following four elements:

- Two factor authentication
- A secure connection
- Strong definition of user roles
- Access to all Webhouse objects controlled by the roles

All four of these elements can be seen in Figure 13.1. We can now describe the elements one at a time.

Provide Two-Factor Authentication

The traditional text passwords that we all use are the biggest single source of security breaches.

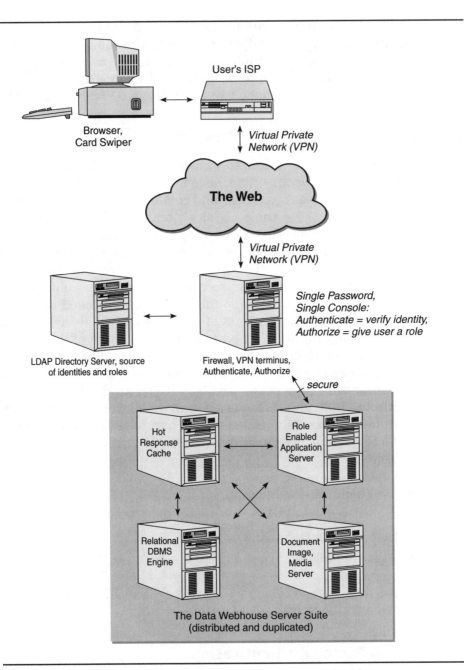

FIGURE 13.1 A Recommended Security Framework for the Webhouse

It is not an exaggeration to say that if we could decisively solve the password problem, most of our security problems would go away.

Passwords are easily guessed. Any password that is directly typed by a human being is too short. Even encrypted lists of these short passwords are easily cracked. Users are notorious for managing their personal passwords poorly. And you can hardly blame them. Passwords are a pain in the neck.

In security parlance, a password represents one-factor authentication, because it is "what-you-know." Unfortunately, with one factor authentication, if someone else knows your password, they become you, with all your rights and privileges.

Security is immensely improved with two factor authentication. The second factor can be "what-you-have" or maybe "what-you-are." With what-you-have authentication, if you possess a unique piece of plastic (a "token") with an encoded magnetic strip and your password, you have a familiar two-factor authentication system. We all use a two-factor authentication system when we present our ATM card to the automated bank teller and withdraw cash. The two factors are the plastic token and our personal identification number (PIN).

Although compromising a two-factor system is certainly possible, it is immensely more difficult than just compromising a password. It takes a determined high-technology attack to create the special plastic cards and to generate the PINs. It seems likely that ATM-style two-factor security is plenty good enough for data warehouse purposes, and we encourage this pragmatic perspective. When evaluating security solutions, it is very important to keep the cost and complexity of the solution in perspective. If we are dealing with an attacker who has access to the technology required to make false security tokens or an attacker who is willing to use violence or blackmail to achieve their ends, then most technical solutions cannot provide very much protection. We detect and deal with these more serious kinds of security violations with a threat detection program, described later in this chapter.

If the data Webhouse end user employs a two-factor authentication system based on a plastic token and a password, then every PC needs to be equipped with a card-swipe device. In Figure 13.1, we assume the user at a PC anywhere in the extended Webhouse system actively swipes a plastic token and supplies a PIN in order to be authenticated. Card swipe devices for PCs are readily available and declining in price. They can be external units connected through one of the I/O ports, or they can be PCMCIA cards. PCMCIA cards are natural for portable PCs, but may not be very convenient for desktop systems. The plastic tokens can contain an embedded microchip, and the more sophisticated "smart cards" are essentially impossible to forge.

The other kind of two-factor authentication combines what-you-know with what-you-are. What-you-are is determined by a biometric scanning device like a fingerprint detector, a signature analyzer, or a retinal scanner. Theoretically, this kind of authentication is better than a plastic card–oriented system, because in this case you can be pretty confident your intended user really is sitting at the PC. The only objection to the what-you-are systems is the cost of the biometric input device and the reliability and hassle of using it in real life. It would be infuriating to not be able to use your PC because for some reason your thumbprint isn't recognized today. Some of the more sophisticated what-you-are authentication systems are good choices for very expensive terminals like bank teller machines, but probably not appropriate for cheap personal computers.

Our bottom line recommendation is to implement two-factor authentication based on passwords and plastic tokens for all users of your Webhouse, regardless of location. Choose a technology that allows the card swipe device to be attached to portable and fixed PCs. Make sure that the administration of the cards and the passwords is practical. Understand what it takes to create a new card, invalidate an old card, whether the cards are valid forever, and what the renewal scenario is.

Secure the Connection

So far we have discussed only the user's view of authentication. But the real act of authentication is complete only when a secure authentication server located in your organization's intranet recognizes and validates the remote user. See Figure 13.1. This authentication server must have a detailed and up-to-date list of all possible users. This detailed and up-to-date list resides on a directory server, shown in Figure 13.1. The directory server contains the information required to authenticate anyone claiming to be a legitimate user.

It is very important that the connection from the remote user to the authentication server be secure. In other words, no one should be able to watch the interaction between the user and the authentication server and glean any compromising information. Let's discuss two cases where the user-to-server interaction must be protected.

The Virtual Private Network (VPN)

When the user connects to the Webhouse through the Web, it must be assumed that the connection is through an inherently insecure network and that eavesdropping may occur. In this case, a virtual private network connection must be established. See Figure 13.2. A VPN connection encrypts all the communication between the user's PC and the authentication server. Anyone eavesdropping on the communication is unable to make sense out of it.

Encrypted Local Communications

Unfortunately, local communications on a company intranet are not nearly as secure as we would wish. Any PC connected to the local Ethernet can be equipped with a "promiscuous packet sniffer" that will decipher and print out all plain text communications between machines on the same segment of the Ethernet. See Figure 13.3. Any end user

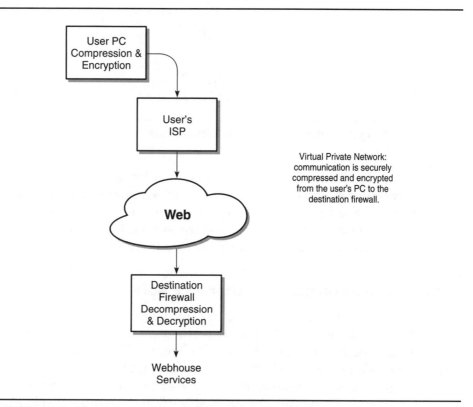

FIGURE 13.2   The Components of a Virtual Private Network

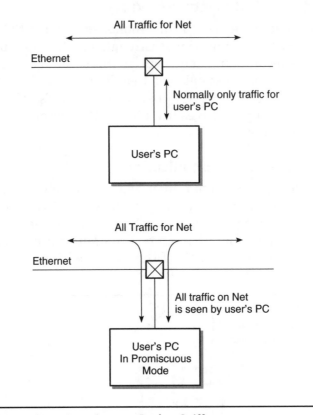

FIGURE 13.3   Using a Promiscuous Packet Sniffer

connected to the local area network can install such a sniffer and rapidly collect passwords and other sensitive communication flowing across the net. For this reason we recommend that the authentication handshaking between the end user and the authentication server be encrypted, even on a supposedly secure corporate intranet.

Connect the Authenticated User to a Role

Once the user has been securely authenticated, and we are willing to trust their identity, then we need to grant them rights to accessing information resources on the data Webhouse. We want to base these rights on *single-password, single-console* administration. Single-password administration means that once the user has supplied everything that is needed for authentication (a password and a physical token), then no further authentication is required. Single-console administration means that the security administrator only needs one interface for defining the security privileges of all possible end users. In a large, complex environment, single-password, single-console administration is essential for keeping security under control. The more complicated and more multi-layered the security, the more likely it is that serious gaps in security will appear, so we are motivated to keep it simple.

Figure 13.1 should make clear our recommendation that every user must pass through the same, centralized security gate. Everyone must run the same gauntlet, regardless of whether they are located remotely on the Web, or whether they are sitting in a cubicle connected to the company intranet. The rare special administrative console that can override this authenticated, role-based security must be physically connected to a special network isolated by packet-filtering gateways to eliminate packet sniffing, and must be physically located behind locked doors requiring some form of access security.

Every user must be assigned to one or more roles. A big organization may have dozens or even hundreds of roles. But the goal with roles is to reduce the number of complex decisions that must be made in matching users to the appropriate uses of data. Each kind of internal employee (secretary, knowledge worker, marketing analyst, executive, finance clerk, CFO, etc.) should have a separate role. All business partners should have separate roles. All customers should have separate roles. In this way you can make sure that each role can be partitioned so that data doesn't spill over the boundaries inappropriately.

Roles should be inheritable so that a "marketing analyst" dynamically inherits all the privileges of "marketing employee." Inheritance of privileges greatly simplifies the administration of roles.

You must manage the roles fanatically. Individual end users must constantly be matched against the role definitions to make sure that the assignments are sensible and correct. The data Webhouse security manager must cultivate a regular relationship with the human resources department. All changes in status of employees and contractors must be communicated in a timely way from human resources to the Webhouse security manager. It would even be appropriate for human resources to notify the Webhouse security manager if an employee was going to be terminated, so that the role definitions could literally be adjusted during the exit interview. A similar kind of communication should take place defining the status of business partners and customers, but perhaps the organizations you must collaborate with in these cases are the business relations department and the sales department.

Access All Webhouse Objects Through the Roles

Now that we have an authenticated user attached to one or more proper roles, all that is left is to use these roles whenever information is requested. This is the step where the growing use of Web interfaces potentially makes life simpler. If we take the view that every screen showing remote information is delivered through a Web browser, then we know that behind every Web browser is a Web server, which in turn is controlled by an application server to determine what is painted on the screen.

The key to our Webhouse security framework is to require that all access to remote information be controlled by *role-enabled application servers*. In other words, every application server is modified so that a page image is associated with a role, and the application server will deliver the page only if the connected user possesses that role.

The role-enabled application server is the only place where you won't be able to connect off-the-shelf products together to build your security system. Each application server must potentially be modified to support role-enabled delivery. Although this sounds like a daunting task, this is still the best place to get control of security. Application servers all have a roughly similar architecture. They all are responsible for defining a page image to be rendered by the Web server. Increasingly, these page images will be generated dynamically, rather than being simple static pages. We must remember to associate Webhouse page attributes with these dynamically created pages so that we can understand what kind of page the Web visitor was using. Most application servers can access and combine information from many sources and many formats. This is why we don't dare try to apply a uniform security solution *below* the application server. The individual sources of data are too granular and too varied in format to control in a single comprehensive security solution.

A big bonus of the role-enabled application server approach is that it is just as easy to define access rights to a complex multimedia report, such as a PowerPoint presentation, as it is to define access rights to a traditional low level database table. This higher-level view of security control is much more appropriate in today's modern, multimedia information environment. Security at the low-level data objects themselves doesn't work.

A corollary to using role-enabled application servers is not to let anyone connect to the database machine directly. If any users on the company intranet can connect directly to the database and gain access by only supplying a password, then the whole system is defeated. At least two showstoppers arise. First, these same users will argue persuasively that they need the same kind of direct access to the data regardless of their location. They will claim they need it from a remote location within the company, and they will claim they need it from home. Of course, their connection from these remote locations is likely to be over the Web. Second, a direct connection to the database using only a password is likely to be implemented in clear text on the local area network, making the entire interaction vulnerable to packet sniffers.

Administrative users, including DBAs and system administrators, who obviously need to interact directly with the primary data sources, must conduct their business from PCs connected to special isolated networks that sit behind packet-filtering gateways. These isolated networks cannot be sniffed from the regular company intranet. Additionally, the PCs used by the DBAs and system administrators must be physically secure.

MANAGE A SECURITY PROCESS, NOT A SOLUTION

We have described a framework for implementing security that can provide a very high degree of control. But no security framework and no technology can be a solution by itself. The security challenge is dynamic and continuously evolving. The data Webhouse security manager must manage an ongoing process that never ends.

A good security program continuously educates and motivates users to be aware of security, to be proud of security, and to guard security. It is essential to have executive involvement in promoting security and creating an example where the impositions created by security are understood to be part of doing business in the real world. Most people are quite tolerant of airport security because they can see that their safety is enhanced by the security procedures. So in the same way, company employees and other users of the Webhouse should be glad that the security mechanisms make themselves obvious, up to a point.

A good security program is updated continuously. We have already talked about working closely with human resources to update employee

	User1 (roleA)	User2 (roleB)	User3 (roleC)	User4 (roleD)
Table1	y	y	n	n
Table2	y	n	y	n
Table3	n	n	n	y
Report7	y	y	y	y
Report8	n	n	y	y
Report9	y	n	n	n

FIGURE 13.4   A Horizontal and Vertical View of Object Access

and contractor access rights. The security manager also keeps abreast of security threats and new kinds of exploits aimed at Websites and data warehouses. Virus definitions should be updated very frequently.

A good security program constantly scans the entire system for possible vulnerabilities and actual intrusions. There are many utilities that can profile a Website for vulnerabilities to known attacks. Consulting firms can periodically analyze a company's information infrastructure for weak points. This may not need to be done frequently, but at least one such analysis is sure to be eye opening.

A simple horizontal and vertical matrix, as shown in Figure 13.4, is a good way to start analyzing security patterns and coverage. Two such matrices should be built, one for assigned access rights and one for actual accesses performed. A glance along a row shows what the security settings for a given information object are. Conversely, a column shows what objects are accessible from a given role. Studying the two matrices is a useful way to think about security and to detect situations where security is not being properly applied.

SUMMARY

With a security framework in place, as described in this chapter, the only other ingredient needed for the data Webhouse team is a dedicated security manager. This person should be assigned to the team and take directions from the overall data Webhouse manager. The role of the security manager and the relationship of this person to the rest of the team are explored in Chapter 15.

CHAPTER 14

Scaling the Webhouse

In this chapter we discuss Webhouse architecture. We examine performance requirements for systems that will handle the enormous volume of transactions produced by a busy Website, and how these volumes can be extracted, transformed, and loaded into the Webhouse. Hardware and operating system implications will also be discussed. We try to identify some of the critical bottlenecks in scaling hardware, software, and operations, and discuss tradeoffs that can be made in areas such as granularity to reduce the Webhouse scale while still providing adequate analytical flexibility.

This chapter is important to CRM because it describes some of the technical requirements for building a big, serious data Webhouse that can serve both the real-time query and longer-term analytic needs of customers, business partners, and employees.

We are especially sensitive to "success disasters" that arise from explosive surges in demand. Although the Web server bears the brunt of such surges, the Web log extract pipeline and ultimately, the Webhouse itself must respond to these unexpected levels of demand.

The Webhouse is also becoming more and more operational as its recommendations drive customer interfacing decisions. These decisions can be automatically "dispensed" by computer or can be the background for a customer service representative understanding the current state of the customer's account.

THE WEBHOUSE IS NOT THE WEB SERVER

The Web server(s) that comprise your Website have extraordinary performance demands placed on them. They must be able to respond to hundreds or even thousands of information requests each second and to deliver the requested data back into the Web. The bandwidth of data flowing from the net into the Website may be small but the bandwidth required to deliver information from the Website to the net is huge. A commercial Website must be designed to handle peak loads with acceptable user response time, and users are notoriously impatient. The Web server is like a sprinter—it must deliver at peak performance for an instant but can rest in between requests, if only for a few milliseconds. In general, commercial Web servers will be transaction-intensive with large communication bandwidths and modest data storage needs. Above all, Web servers must be reliable, even to the point of employing redundant processors, hot standby databases, RAID disk storage, and diverse network routing.

Unlike the Web server with its extraordinary *peak performance* needs, the Webhouse has extraordinary *capacity* demands placed on it. It's more like a marathon runner, working at a constant rate for hour after hour capturing and digesting data for the complex queries that will eventually be asked of it. We usually don't have to be concerned with the Webhouse's ability to handle a peak time of day in the same way that demand may peak for the primary Web server. See Figure 14.1, which shows the diurnal load on a typical high-volume Web server. Look carefully at these graphs. In most commercial IT applications peak hours extend for the duration of the business day, typically eight hours, including time-zone effects. In Figure 14.1 we see peak load lasting about sixteen hours a day. This effect is a result of the Web's ability to provide access from home at any time of the day or night.

If we are willing to allow the Webhouse's data currency to lag several hours behind Web server activity, we can buffer clickstream data from the Web server in a FIFO cache. Although the Web server must be scaled to handle peak loads, the Webhouse's computation capacity is determined largely by the need to serve the ETL load generated by the buffered clickstream from the enterprise's Web servers and by the query load placed on the Webhouse by analytical activities. The Webhouse's network load will be very small compared to the Web servers, but the disk storage needs will be enormous, easily in the terabyte arena, if a fine granularity is required. We estimated the size of the largest clickstream fact tables in Chapter 6.

'Daily' Graph (5 Minute Average)

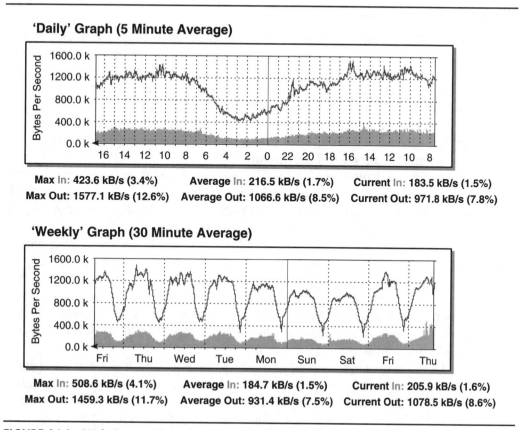

Max In: 423.6 kB/s (3.4%)   Average In: 216.5 kB/s (1.7%)   Current In: 183.5 kB/s (1.5%)
Max Out: 1577.1 kB/s (12.6%) Average Out: 1066.6 kB/s (8.5%) Current Out: 971.8 kB/s (7.8%)

'Weekly' Graph (30 Minute Average)

Max In: 508.6 kB/s (4.1%)   Average In: 184.7 kB/s (1.5%)   Current In: 205.9 kB/s (1.6%)
Max Out: 1459.3 kB/s (11.7%) Average Out: 931.4 kB/s (7.5%)   Current Out: 1078.5 kB/s (8.6%)

FIGURE 14.1   Web Server Diurnal Load Characteristics

EXPLOSIVE CHANGES IN CLICKSTREAM ACTIVITY

If you have a popular Website up and running, you already are facing a daunting flow of clickstream and transaction data headed in the direction of your Webhouse. You might even believe that, given today's volumes, things couldn't get much worse. Trust us, they will get worse—much worse. The clickstream volumes you're seeing today are just the beginning of what the next few years will bring. In this section we'll explore some additional Web developments that will bring explosive increases to clickstream volumes. Keep these trends in mind when you're sizing today's Webhouse. Plan your initial implementation to accommodate the volumes you anticipate in the next one to two years, but make sure you are considering scalability. Web usage and technology is in its infancy. Consider the following.

Web-Enabled Population Growth

Basic Web access today is enjoyed by about a third of the U.S. population and by a miniscule percentage of the world's population. But having Web access isn't a guarantee that any particular person will actually access the Web. Individuals need time to become familiar with the tools and the navigation paradigms of the Web before they can begin using it in their day-to-day work or recreation activities. They also need time to begin to trust the Web, with initial concerns over confidentiality, reliability, and security to be overcome.

In the workplace, there is a distrust of the Web as a potential time-waster. As justifiable as this concern may be, there is also the inevitability that Web- (or intranet-) based applications will be a part of most jobs within the first five years of the new millennium.

We also believe that many of the linguistic barriers to Web access will dissolve over the next few years. Your Website may today only be accessible by a few hundred million English speakers worldwide. Advances in computer-based language translation will change this. Even if your Website is available only in English, it will be readable by billions of non-English speakers as Web-based automatic translation services become universally available.

In summary, we see the number of people who have access to your Website from their homes or workplaces growing by orders of magnitude over the next few years. See Figure 14.2. If your content has broad appeal, a much, much larger Web-enabled populace will access it.

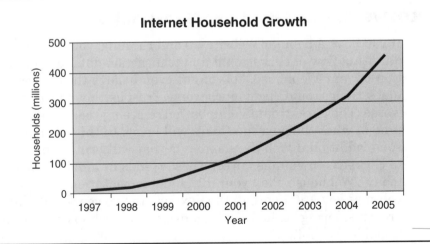

Internet Household Growth

FIGURE 14.2 Predicted Web Usage Growth

Increasing Click Rates

Before the invention of remote controls, a television viewer had to get up from his beloved couch every time he wanted to change channels. Because of this, he would dwell on a single channel or network for a long time—perhaps an entire evening if the couch was particularly comfortable. The invention and deployment of TV remote controls changed this basic behavior pattern, and actually contributed significantly to the loss in power of the "Big Three" TV networks. Instead of leaving the channel knob set, the viewer began surfing. He was able and willing to change channels in response to a momentary lapse of interest in a program or because of a particularly disagreeable advertisement.

We see a similar phenomenon at work on the Web today. As shown in Figure 14.3, the painfully slow download speeds of dial-up modems have imposed an artificial limit to the frequency of a typical user's clicks while they surf the Web. As wider-band access channels are deployed, the typical time-between-clicks will decrease significantly and click volumes will rise, especially if dwell time is relatively short. We can see this happening in rollouts of DSL (digital subscriber line) and cable modems. Because download times are much shorter, the time between clicks is also shorter. For inveterate channel-surfers, click rates become much higher, and Web server loads increase proportionally.

Technology	Download Secs	Clicks per min. Dwell = 20 Secs	Clicks per min. Dwell = 10 Secs
28.8 Modem	35.7	1.0	1.3
56K Modem	17.9	1.5	2.0
128 Kbit ISDN	7.8	2.0	3.0
192 Kbit DSL	5.2	2.2	3.5
256 Kbit DSL	3.9	2.3	3.8
384 Kbit DSL	2.6	2.4	4.1
768 Kbit DSL	1.3	2.6	4.5
5 Mbit Cable Modem*	0.2	2.7	4.9

Assumptions:
1. Content size is 1 Mbyte broken into 20 HTTP GETs
2. Server GET overhead is 0.1 second

*Note: Cable modem speed varies considerably depending on the number of modems distributed along a given cable trunk.

FIGURE 14.3   The Relationship Between Bandwidth and Click Rate

User-Level Auto-Search

Another factor contributing to clickstream growth is the rollout of individualized auto-search applications. These applications have the ability to look for sites or articles of particular interest to an individual, and run as a background process on PC or on a corporate or portal host. Such applications can place a heavy load on information-intensive sites as they search, for example, for all articles that cite a particular corporation or business sector. We can expect these auto-search programs to find their way into the consumer marketplace where they will be searching for specific auction items, hobby news, and favorite movie stars.

We expect that the majority of these individualized search bots will operate in off-peak hours and will contribute more to overall clickstream volume than to instantaneous peak volume.

Deeper Economic Penetration

The economics of Web access continue to change rapidly. Home computers are well below the $1,000 price point and show every indication of continuing their price declines for a number of reasons. Net access is similarly becoming cheaper, with access being offered free in Great Britain. Telcos in Europe are coming under intense pressure to drop their current practice of charging local calls by the minute. As this practice goes away, there will be a big surge of usage from European locations. We expect to see free Web access being used as an incentive to sell services such as cable TV in the immediate future. TV-based Web portals will also contribute to increased Website traffic, though not nearly to the extent that dropping PC prices will.

Taken together, the continuing drop in hardware and access costs means a penetration into lower-income families and into institutional settings that can't today justify Web access.

Sudden Fame

When planning the capacity of your Web-enabled data warehouse you need to consider the possibility that your Website may become the victim of some kind of overnight fame. Many, many sites have found themselves being the "site of the day" due to unexpected publicity, the only source of a suddenly very hot new product, or even a chance mention on CNN or other national media. This can lead to a kind of "success disaster" in which hit counts are suddenly many times the normal levels. If the Website keeps up with these volumes then it's up to the Webhouse to handle them as well. If, on the other hand, the Website collapses under an unanticipated load, then the back-end data warehouse won't see huge transaction volume increases and will survive relatively unscathed.

IP as a Universal Transport Protocol

When the Internet protocol (IP) was first invented three decades ago, it was conceived primarily as a transport layer for exchanging text packets within a network. We have seen an explosive growth not only in IP-based traffic but in the types of content now carried on the Web. What started as a text-only network layer is now carrying audio and full-motion video. The latest standard for the Internet protocol, IPv6, extends the IP address space from its current 32 bits to 128 bits, making it theoretically possible to assign a unique IP address to every individual and even to every electronic device on earth. Some analysts believe that within the next few years virtually *all* information will be sent encapsulated in IP packets and that the protocols used today for voice and video will cede to IP as well because of its universal addressing capability. Although this trend doesn't directly affect clickstream volume growth, it certainly indicates an acceptance of the core technology underlying the Web, and indirectly leads to the continued explosive growth of the Web and similar application layers simply because of its ubiquitous deployment.

XML—Universal Transfer

In the next three to four years we expect to see a universal rollout of XML-enabled server and browser applications. XML will enable thousands of as-yet untapped Web-based applications that today are confined to client/server architectures. XML provides a very rich set of tags below the Web's basic HTML language, which can be used for almost any kind of data transfer. One of the benefits of XML is to provide a way of penetrating firewalls so that peer-to-peer applications can be enabled via Web protocols and not be blocked by current security mechanisms.

We expect an explosive growth in XML applications and a corresponding growth of corporate Web server traffic. As XML-enabled applications are rolled out the demand for processing their associated clickstreams and log transactions will grow significantly. The widespread use of XML will also increase the granularity of the clickstream because a low-level record could now consist of an action taken against an individual named field on a page rather than the whole page.

EXPLOSIVE CHANGES IN DEMAND FOR DATA WAREHOUSE SERVICES

Until recently, data warehouse technology has been employed only by selected large corporations that could afford to explore an emerging technology, with its very high entrance costs in terms of staff, hardware and software, and custom ETL subsystems. This profile is rapidly changing.

We believe that, particularly in the field of Website clickstream analysis, we will see a mainstream acceptance of data warehouse technology and that over time, most commercial Web-hosting software will contain an embedded data warehouse component for clickstream analysis. The economics of data warehousing are changing rapidly. Hardware costs continue to drop, and there appears to be no end in sight for this trend. Databases capable of supporting very large data warehouses are now available from many vendors, and software costs are dropping rapidly as mass-market software companies embrace the data warehouse marketplace.

As we have discussed earlier, the explosion of Web-based services is continuing unabated and is expected to do so for the foreseeable future. It's not unreasonable to predict that every business will have a Web presence of some kind within the next five years, and that Web-based commerce will account for a large portion of our economy within the first few years of this new millennium.

Certain new technologies have the potential for vastly increasing the number of page events measured by our Web servers. Current Web user sessions are mostly manually driven. That is, each page event is a mouse click triggered by a human user. But new ubiquitous wireless devices and TCP/IP appliances may well generate trillions of automatic page events. It seems likely that the growth of such data will take place faster than our ability to process such large volumes, at least in the short term. We will be forced to discard or aggregate much of this data in order to stay ahead of the wave.

CRITICAL BOTTLENECKS IN HARDWARE AND SOFTWARE

In planning your Web-enabled data warehouse you need to be aware of the performance limitations imposed by hardware and software, and to avoid common pitfalls that will ultimately limit the scalability of your system to accommodate the inevitable growths in Website traffic and warehouse use. Most of the suggestions in this section aren't unique to data warehouse applications; they apply to high-volume applications that must provide for future scalability.

Avoiding the Single Bottleneck

The common mantra that runs through most advice on avoiding bottle-necks is: Keep it parallel! Providing multiple parallel paths and devices provides several benefits. First, it enables parallel processing for the current load. There is no single bottleneck through which all transactions must pass. Second, parallelism provides an upgrade path to handle growth. Instead of replacing overloaded components with a bigger or faster device, you simply add more of them. Finally, parallel designs provide an ideal basis for failure mitigation. If one part of a parallel system suffers a hardware or software failure, the remaining components might be able to pick up the full load.

Parallelism can be achieved in a number of ways, including tightly coupled symmetrical multiprocessing (SMP), CPU clustering, and shared disk. See Figure 14.4. The top configuration in the illustration shows the components of an SMP machine. This approach permits a great deal of parallel processing but meets a limit when the ultimate capacity of the machine in terms of allowable processors is met. The middle configuration shows a clustered arrangement. This has the advantage that any number of machines may be clustered, even dissimilar machines and operating systems. However it is difficult to synchronize their operations except in the case of highly modified applications such as DBMSs. The bottom illustration shows independent processors with a Network File System (NFS) mounted shared disk. This is an attractive way of running multiple copies of the same application that can deal with their disk needs asynchronously. Any of these architectures can be considered as long as they meet the goals of reliability and scalability.

The Web-enabled data warehouse has three distinct components with high capacity needs, all of which are candidates for parallel implementation:

- **Log transaction cache.** The transaction cache is a FIFO queue that accepts Web server and application server log records in real time as they are produced by the Website's on-line application(s). These are queued for eventual processing by the clickstream post-processor that we have described in detail in Chapter 8. The cache can be distributed. It need not be in a single place, and in fact, each individual server in your Web complex—whether a Web server or an application server—can have its own transaction cache, with the queue contents being gathered periodically by a clickstream post-processor task.

- **Clickstream post-processor.** The clickstream post-processor is, in data warehouse terminology, the extract/transform/load (ETL)

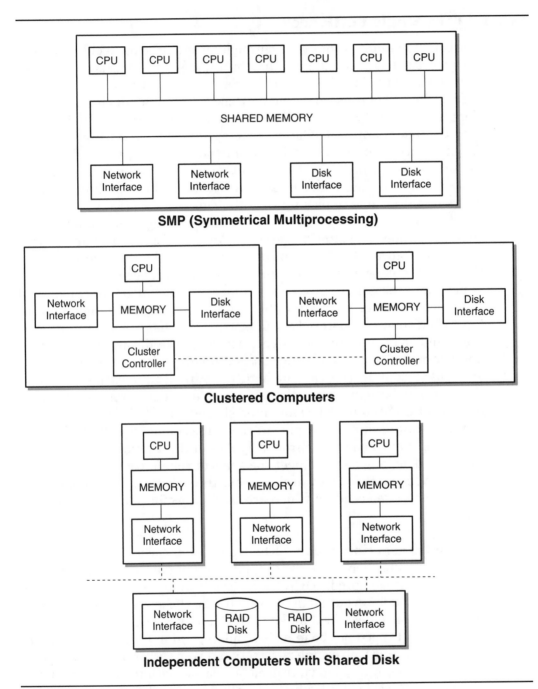

FIGURE 14.4 Alternatives for Shared Memory Parallelism

application for the Web-enabled data warehouse. This compute-intensive application takes records from the log transaction cache, merges related events by session, and creates load batches for the Webhouse database's dimension and fact tables. From its inception, the post-processor should be designed for parallel implementation. The post-processor should be designed in such a way that a post-processor thread handles extract and transformation tasks for a specific user session. The thread identifies and extracts the log records for a specific user session, computes fact and dimension values, and transforms these into dimensional database load records.

■ **Webhouse database.**   The Webhouse database itself will probably be a commercial OLAP- or ROLAP-enabled database. In choosing the database platform, keep in mind the need for parallel loading capabilities. All currently available commercial systems offer parallel query, and most permit parallel loading.

Avoiding Process Duplication

A good parallel system architecture spreads a single type of process across multiple machines but at the same time avoids unnecessary process duplication. Within each machine in a parallel architecture, computational processes should be shared rather than duplicated. Many existing CGI server processes suffer from not being able to share their code in a re-entrant way. Ten identical processes on the same machine therefore load and execute ten instances of the code. This consumes unnecessary program memory and buffer space and invokes unnecessary I/O. Many of these issues can be addressed with the new generation of reentrant CGI compilers.

The same sharing and pooling techniques can be applied to application threads, data, and connectivity within each server machine. Key software modules, buffers, and system resources can be locked in memory and made persistent. This approach minimizes resource creation costs, process startup delays, memory usage, and I/O. In many ways, these techniques hark back to the terminate-and-stay-ready (TSR) routines in early versions of DOS.

Physical Considerations: Co-Location

Because of the large volume of clickstream transactions and intimate connections between the clickstream preprocessor and the Website application server databases, you will probably physically locate your Webhouse equipment in the same facility as your primary Web servers. Before beginning the Webhouse project, it is advisable to make sure that there is space available to locate your equipment.

Over the last few years a significant trend has developed to put Web servers in commercial third-party co-location facilities such as those provided by above.net and Verio, rather than into a corporate data center. These new co-location facilities are usually able to provide extremely high-bandwidth Web connectivity through physically diverse fiber optic links to multiple network access points (NAPs), as well as private network peering arrangements with Tier I Internet carriers that bypass already crowded public NAPs. Commercial co-location facilities are staffed with administrators with expertise in Internet network administration and have tools available to detect and fix latency and routing problems that might otherwise significantly impair Website performance. These facilities also usually have extensive physical security and uninterruptable power backup systems.

Rented co-location space is usually very expensive compared to corporate data center space. If space isn't available in the same facility as your primary Web servers, you will have to plan on wide-band network capacity between the co-location facility and wherever your Webhouse equipment is located.

Operating Systems

Unless there is a strong enterprise motive to do otherwise, we recommend that the Webhouse and its ETL applications be coded for a UNIX operating system. UNIX has shown its scalability and versatility across a wide variety of platforms and processor topologies, and it is inherently capable of supporting the multithreading parallel architecture we recommend for both ETL and OLAP applications.

We believe that Linux or NT should be considered for the clickstream post-processor only for independent parallel processor architectures. Neither Linux nor NT have established strong track records for SMP or clustered system support, although both are candidates for use in architectures that employ uncoupled independent CPUs. One advantage of Linux and NT systems is that if you need to include an OLTP staging database as part of your post-processor architecture, RDBMS software licenses for Linux and NT tend to be considerably less expensive than for similar-capacity UNIX systems.

Programming Languages

The specific programming languages used for developing the Webhouse ETL components are not important, but it is essential to avoid the use of interpreted languages or languages that don't support multithreading. C or C++ are suitable for program development. Graphical-based tool suites dedicated to the ETL process are available from more than half a dozen vendors and offer the promise of end-to-end applications development, significant metadata support, component reusability, and high performance modules for parsing the clickstream itself.

Databases

For the foreseeable future, the large granular fact tables such as we have designed in Chapter 7 will only be able to be manipulated in relational databases. The dimensional approach, which we believe is essential, means that the particular relational database must be extremely adept at handling the characteristic pattern of joins between dimension tables and fact tables. Additionally, a consistent characteristic of clickstream schemas is that the customer dimension is really huge, in many cases exceeding 100 million members (customers).

The relational database used for the Webhouse absolutely must have a flexible file and indexing partitioning capability so that distinct physical subsets of the mammoth fact tables can be moved between media, or taken on-line and off-line. Such a partition should be coupled with its indexes so that if the partition is taken off line and then later restored, no index builds are necessary. Similarly, the index of the most current partition should be able to be dropped, so that high-speed loading can occur. Then the index of this current partition should be able to be rebuilt quickly.

The relational database used for the dimensional clickstream schemas should be singularly resistant to "ad hoc attacks." In other words, if the fact table has nine dimensions, it should make almost no difference which subset of the dimensions are constrained. Given a nine-dimension design, it is impossible for a DBA to use the old approach of building specially planned composite indexes of the keys on the fact table that anticipate user queries. Rather, the database should have a completely symmetric key indexing strategy that is capable of using any random subset of the keys at query time. One promising approach taken by some vendors is to build bit-mapped indexes on each of the separate foreign keys. Clickstream fact tables have a predictable asymmetry since they all have one monster dimension (customer) and a host of medium and small dimensions. Perhaps the monster dimension is indexed with a B-Tree index and the rest are indexed with bitmaps. You should carefully investigate whether these options are possible in the database you are considering, and whether the database optimizer acts coherently when faced with these schemas. Make sure you ask for detailed references from the vendor!

We are very impressed with OLAP databases, and we think that in the long run their superior analytic capabilities may make them be the future of all data warehousing. But as of this writing, all OLAP systems still cannot scale to the hundreds of gigabytes and to the terabytes *of raw input data* required to directly support the big clickstream schemas. The other scalability problem faced by today's OLAP systems is the inability to handle more than about 500,000 members in a dimension. This is a showstopper problem when you have a customer dimension with many millions of members.

Query and Reporting Software

The beauty of the dimensional approach is that all query tools look good. The simple schema is reflected in simple user interfaces. But there are a number of specific features we think you should insist on for your Webhouse analysis tools:

- **Full Web deployment.** Don't forget this one! Every screen of your tools should be available via a Web browser. This includes the expert developer interfaces, the ad hoc end user interfaces, and the final delivered answer sets and reports.

- **Driven from a role-enabled application server.** If your query tool expects to make direct private connections to the DBMS, you will circumvent our recommended security strategy, and you will be back in the password and security nightmare. Make sure that your tools rely on an intermediate application server, and make sure that this server participates in LDAP directory-driven role definitions of security.

- **Drill-across and complex comparisons implemented with multipass SQL.** The Webhouse has no center. You cannot put all your data in one table, one OLAP cube, one table space, one machine, or even one city. Yet we have given you an architecture for tying all the diverse distributed data marts together, so that you can query all the parts simultaneously. In this way you implement your enterprise (or cross-enterprise) data warehouse. Make sure that both your ad hoc query tools and customer report writers are capable of multipass SQL so that you can tie your data marts together. Of course, multipass SQL also gives you the added bonus of being able to decompose very complex analytical requests into discrete queries that can be managed separately and then combined in the application server.

- **Aggregate awareness.**   You cannot survive in a world of mammoth fact tables without an automatic aggregate navigation capability. As of this writing, the aggregate navigation capability is being subsumed by the database engines, and we support that strongly. In this way all applications get transparently navigated, just as all applications get the use of database indexes. It is not appropriate or efficient for a single end user tool to control aggregate navigation, and we think the era of end user tool aggregate navigation is coming to an end.

Balance the Use of E-Mail and Links

Often a report can be distributed automatically via e-mail. This is a good mechanism for widespread distribution. But make sure that you e-mail a link to the report, not the report itself. Better yet, make the link be an interface that allows the user to select or scroll through pages on demand. This approach should minimize the actual pages transmitted and stored across the Web.

Hardware Characteristics

For systems coming on-line in the first two or three years of the twenty-first century you can safely assume that reasonably priced SMP machines with two to four 1,000-MHz processors will be commonly available. Machines with 16 to 128 of these processors will be available, but at a much greater cost. These machines will be available with either Intel or RISC-type CPUs. Shared memory capacities of 1 to 4 GB will be common and affordable in low-to-mid-range systems. Systems with these speeds, and especially a move to 64-bit system architectures, will provide adequate capacity real-time clickstream post-processing and will allow the use of ROLAP queries in support of real-time applications.

We anticipate that in the same timeframe, 100-GB disk drives will become commonly available and that these will lead to mirrored and

RAID storage systems with terabyte capacities at prices under $100,000. These, too, will make real-time OLAP queries attractive. Current ultra-wide SCSI controllers support transfer rates up to 40 MB/second and high-end fiber-channel disk controllers with much higher transfer rates are available today in higher-end machines.

Tape backup systems with 20- to 100-TB capacity will be available in the same timeframe, making backup of terabyte databases relatively fast and straightforward.

THE GRANULARITY TRADEOFF

In any data warehouse system, the size of the database and concomitant load and backup issues is extremely sensitive to the granularity of non-sparse dimensions.

If business analytical needs allow it, you can reduce granularity in order to cut down the size of the data warehouse, lower its cost, and simplify its maintenance. Remember, however, if you are tempted to do this that you cannot at a later date regain lost information. If business needs dictate that the granularity of a dimension be increased you have lost all prior data at the increased granularity so you won't be able to make "this year versus last" comparisons that rely on the existence of older data.

Candidates for granularity reduction in the Web-enabled data warehouse include the following:

- **Eliminate ancillary download requests, such as images, audio, and video.** If everything except HTML downloads are removed from the clickstream, then you can expect a 2:1 to a 5:1 reduction in the number of click events reaching the warehouse. Your warehouse will still contain click events but will be considerably reduced in size. It is important, however, to retain the dimension data that might have originally been found only in the ancillary download requests.

- **Use canonical hosts, not unique IP addresses.** A large service provider like AOL or Earthlink can have tens of thousands of individual IP addresses that are assigned dynamically to client sessions. Except for their role in tying together diverse session elements, these dynamically assigned IP addresses provide little additional information. By considering only the address range "AOL" or "Earthlink" you can cut down your IP dimension by a factor of at least 100:1. This produces a significant reduction in granularity with little loss of meaningful data. Eliminating hosts altogether and retaining only domain postfixes such as .com and .org, and international postfixes such as .au and .uk can reduce the host dimension even further.

SUMMARY

In this chapter we have reviewed the significant issues raised by the volume of clickstream data and the large dimension tables that clickstream analysis demands. We have looked at some of the hardware and software implications of this. We conclude that technology available now and in the first few years of the next century will provide sufficient increases in capacity to handle this load at reasonable costs.

CHAPTER 15

Managing the Webhouse Project

A good Webhouse project manager balances all the separate tasks that must be completed in order to build and support the complete Webhouse system. A good project manager also understands all the people and roles involved in the project. Above all, a good project manager must have perspective, judgment, and flexibility, because no project will ever proceed according to the original plan.

In this chapter we don't try to introduce general project management skills or treat data warehouse project management exhaustively. The project planning and management chapter in *The Data Warehouse Lifecycle Toolkit* ran 54 pages, and that would be a reasonable background for this chapter. Instead, we more briefly summarize the main components of data warehouse project management, and we pause at various points to pay special attention to the tasks and responsibilities that are unique to the Webhouse. This chapter follows a typical lifecycle development for a data warehouse, starting with project definition and business requirements gathering, followed by design and implementation, then followed by rollout and sustaining efforts, and finishing with preparing to do it all over again. Welcome to the data warehouse, and to the Webhouse.

In this chapter we try to frame the project management responsibilities for building a serious data Webhouse. Perhaps the biggest risk to CRM interests is the gulf that separates the Webmaster and his or her colleagues from the data warehouse project leader and his or her colleagues. Chief among the responsibilities shared jointly between these two groups is making the Web server logs more expressive and making these logs tie to other customer-oriented data sources.

All the pages available through the Website need to be tagged with marketing-defined categories and descriptions. Ultimately this is a joint project for the two aforementioned groups and their clients.

The Webmaster and colleagues need to go to considerable length to support "cookieing" of customers across all the Web servers of your enterprise and to align the separate time clocks of all servers very accurately so that the logs can be reassembled in the right order. In other words, the Web server folks must really pay attention to a set of business requirements that go beyond the basic delivery of Web pages.

DEFINE THE PROJECT

A data Webhouse project is any data warehouse activity that aligns with one or both of the main themes of this book. Either you are bringing the Web clickstream to the data warehouse, or you are deploying mainline data warehouse services over the Web. In all likelihood, you are doing both.

At the very beginning of the Webhouse project, you need to understand why the organization wants a data Webhouse, and how deeply that need is felt in the organization. If you are bringing the clickstream data into the data warehouse for analysis of your customers' behavior on your Website, then you should make a list of the various executives and departments you suspect recognize the potential of this data. Later in the project you will interview these executives and departments to get a detailed understanding of their needs, and to make sure that they really have an interest. If you are deploying data warehouse services over the Web to employees, business partners, or selected customers, then you should similarly make a list of who these interested parties are and why you think they want access to your data warehouse.

As you begin to assess the depth of support in your organization for the Webhouse, you hope to find broad-based support. You don't want to depend on a single zealot as the sole sponsor for your project. If only one person can be found who is willing to articulate the benefits of the Webhouse, that is a clear danger signal. Even if your lone zealot sponsor is a powerful business manager with a qualified budget, the project may crash and burn if business conditions change, or if the zealot manager takes another job assignment.

A much better scenario is consistent support across the organization and clear statements of the anticipated benefits of the Webhouse from multiple executives in multiple departments. Again, you begin the project-definition process by guessing that this support exists. Early in the project, before budgets, deadlines, and technology choices are made, you must go verify with the suspected executives and departments that this support is really there.

We recommend that you look at five key indicators for the readiness of your Webhouse project:

- Strong business management sponsorship, as described earlier.
- A compelling business motivation, where the end users can visualize what nuggets of wisdom and insight the data is likely to contain.
- A good partnership between IT and the business, where IT understands the business and is involved with the business users, and where these same end users are respectful and appreciative of the skills IT brings to the party.
- A supportive analytic culture, where there is an existing tradition of managing by the numbers, and trusting in data to reveal important trends and developments in the business.
- The existence of real data from a real operational system, that contains enough quality-assured content to be the basis of your Webhouse. This is a requirement for either sense of the Webhouse, whether it is clickstream data coming in from the Web or internal operational data being published to selected end users over the Web.

Once you are confident that these key Webhouse indicators are positive, then you need to identify a committed business sponsor and a committed IT sponsor. The committed business sponsor is the most important single individual for the whole project. This manager will provide the justification, the motivation, and ultimately the end users for the project. The committed IT sponsor also plays a crucial role at various points, when expectations in the organization for the delivery of the Webhouse need to be set, and when the discussions of conformed dimensions and conformed facts get really serious.

Perhaps you will be asked to provide an *a priori* financial justification of the Webhouse before you begin. Although all projects need a rational justification, you should be cautious if this justification looms as the biggest hurdle for the project. Maybe you don't have the broadly based support you think you have. By its nature, a data Webhouse is a decision support system. The true outputs from the Webhouse will be insights that will lead to decisions being made. The Webhouse will never make a decision all by itself, nor will it ever supplant human business instinct and experience. But the Webhouse, if it is designed effectively, should consistently provide the insights that are key ingredients of decisions. By taking this perspective, paradoxically one can calculate a fairly unambiguous return on investment (ROI) for the Webhouse itself, but it is all done retrospectively, because the impact of the decisions takes a while to measure.

IDENTIFY THE ROLES

As with any data warehouse project, building a Webhouse requires the involvement of more than a dozen separate roles. We show all of these roles in their nominal organization settings in Figure 15.1. Some of the roles are permanent and central to the project, and some of the roles are only needed for a finite period of time. In a modest project, a small number of people will fulfill all of the roles. Each person will wear a number of hats. In a large, enterprise sized project, the key manager roles will be filled by separate individuals, and some of the development and support roles will be staffed by entire groups.

It is immensely helpful to list all the roles at the beginning of the Webhouse project and to begin planning when and how to staff these roles. In this section we list all of the roles we think are required for the Webhouse project. *Italicized* roles are familiar roles required for just about any data warehousing effort. **Bold-faced** roles are new roles necessitated by the unique requirements of the Webhouse.

Front Office: Sponsors and Drivers

- *Business sponsor.* We have already said that the business sponsor is the pivotal role in a data warehouse project. The business sponsor is the ultimate client. A good business sponsor provides the demand and the resources for the project. The business sponsor for a Webhouse needs to be committed to doing business on the Web, whether this sponsor is watching customer behavior through the clickstream, or is depending on the Web as an access mechanism to get at the data warehouse. In both cases, this executive must believe in the Web as a primary way of doing business.
- *IT sponsor.* We also described the importance of the senior IT sponsor. This executive makes IT resources available to complete the

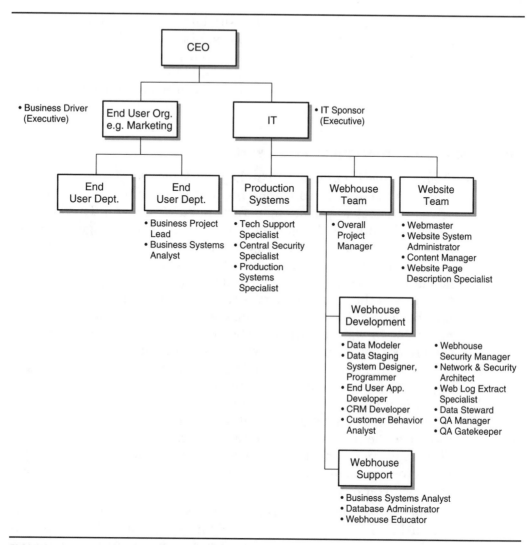

FIGURE 15.1   Webhouse Roles and Organizations

Webhouse project. The IT sponsor needs to understand the rhythms of the Webhouse and what makes the project easy and what makes the project hard. The IT sponsor, more than anyone else, sets the expectations of the other senior management in organization for the delivery of the Webhouse project. The IT sponsor needs to know that extracting the data is hard and always takes more time than expected. Tuning the database for good query performance is hard. Being truly sensitive to end user needs is hard.

- *Business driver.*   When the ultimate business sponsor executive is not continuously available, many organizations will appoint a mid-level manager to serve as a proxy for the business sponsor. The goal of this appointment is to have an available, dedicated manager on the business side with authority to make decisions, resolve disputes, and provide motivation.

Coaches: Project Managers and Leads

- *Overall project manager.*   The key working role in the Webhouse project is the project manager. This person probably thinks of themselves as a data warehousing person, not a Webmaster. This is a full-time position in IT. As we have said, the project manager needs to have multiple skills. The project manager needs to be good with people, good with technology, and good with managing a project. It is not necessary to be encumbered by a lot of project management structure, unless the structure serves the project manager's needs. Some project managers, especially on smaller projects, are comfortable with managing by walking around. They have an intuitive sense of what the project needs, and they spend their time communicating. Other project managers, especially on big projects, rely on the use of tracking tools for documenting dependencies and status. But above all, the project manager needs to keep perspective on the whole project. If the project gets behind schedule, the project manager needs to recognize the reality and begin communicating expectations to both IT management and the business sponsors. The project manager needs to be good at acquiring resources at various times from various organizations.

- *Business project lead.*   The overall project manager's counterpart is the business project lead. This person must be available on a day-to-day basis to coordinate with the project manager. At the beginning of the project, the business project lead will be instrumental in arranging the end user interviews. During development, this person will interpret questions about data content as well as query and reporting tool features. This person will drive end user tool selection. When the project approaches rollout status, the business project lead will make sure that the end users are available for training. When the Webhouse is up and running, the business project lead makes sure that communication channels to IT are being used and are effective. It is not absolutely necessary that the business project lead be a full-time responsibility, but this person needs to be highly responsive to the needs of the project. It is possible that this person is also the business driver described earlier.

Regular Lineup: Core Project Team

- *Business systems analyst.* The business systems analyst is a technical person who understands the business questions in detail. A successful business systems analyst can be an IT person with a lot of credibility in the end user business environment or an end user analyst with good technical skills. The business systems analyst will lead the business requirements definitions phase at the beginning of the project, and later will be responsible for the architecture of the standard queries and reports built for the end user community. The business systems analyst is the ultimate power user, but it is important that a major part of their responsibility be the overall success of the Webhouse, not just a particular business analysis.

- *Data modeler.* Modelers for a data warehouse project need to understand both entity-relationship (E/R) and dimensional modeling. The E/R models will often come from the transaction processing environment and may also be used for data cleaning in the back room of the Webhouse. Dimensional models are needed for effective delivery of the data to the end users. Data modelers also need to have a fine appreciation for the difference between modeling real data and modeling abstract data relationships. In the final analysis, real data is what gets delivered to the end users, and most of the modeling effort needs to be spent on the practical concerns of dealing with what is actually there. A large Webhouse project will have a whole group of data modelers. The most senior data modelers may carry the title of *data architect*.

- *Database administrator.* The database administrator (DBA) is responsible for actually implementing the database. He accepts database designs from the data modeler and creates the database in the enterprise standard DBMS. He is responsible for performance, space utilization, backup, and recovery. A senior DBA may be responsible for determining the software and hardware platforms on which the OLTP and OLAP databases run. After implementation, the DBA often continues in an operational role, watching and shepherding the company's day-to-day database operations to ensure that the performance and backup goals are being met. A database administrator must be highly sensitive to capacity and performance issues and be able to put together systems that meet initial goals and have the ability to be upscaled for both size and load.

- **Website system administrator.**   The system administrator (SA) handles all operational aspects of Web hosting. He is responsible for hardware selection and overall hosting architecture. He also handles the intricacies of connecting the Website to the Internet, providing reliable and secure wide-band communication pipelines for this purpose. The system administrator will choose the hardware and software platforms for Web hosting and will maintain a constant 24-by-7 watch over Web hosting operations to ensure that Website performance meets the expected standards. The SA may be responsible for site security, maintaining firewalls, and monitoring system activity for evidence of intrusion. The system administrator will jealously guard his turf. With his responsibilities for maintaining system uptime in a hostile Internet environment, he is likely to resist any changes that will tax the security or the capacity of his installed systems. It is essential for the Webhouse project manager to engage the system administrator at the outset of the project because many of the issues of hardware capacity and software security may take a long time to resolve within the purview of the system administration group.

- *Data staging system designer.*   This team member is responsible for the extract-transform-load (ETL) systems that feed the Webhouse. Ideally, this person holds a senior technical staff position in the IT department and will be on loan to the project from its inception through initial implementation. This person should have hands-on experience with a broad range of technologies including Web servers, databases, client/server architecture, and UNIX. The data staging system designer will write specifications for various ETL components and must understand the technical nuances of the challenges of the clickstream post-processor.

- ***End user application developer.***   The end user application developer has a healthy interest in both the business issues and the technical issues. The full scope of this person's activities is more than application coding. The application developer needs to spend time with end users to understand what they are trying to do, and what is easy and hard for them when using the system. The application developer must spend time in pure support activities, including helping users with their queries and reports, and in conducting training.

Only with this intimate involvement with end user issues can the application developer have the full judgment needed to produce a library of useful parameterized reports. We have made the heading for this role both italic and bold because the application developer role has always been central to the data warehouse project, but there is no question that application development has been affected strongly by the Web. In many cases, the application developer must forego the traditional client/sever development packages in favor of a Web page development environment in which the developer places data-aware objects.

- **CRM developer.**   The CRM developer is part of the team that implements the CRM system itself. The CRM developer is potentially responsible both for production aspects of the CRM system as well as the data warehouse aspects. A CRM developer is concerned with delivering the most effective user interface in real time to the customer knocking on the door of the Website. The CRM developer is almost certainly using data warehouse facilities to deliver a customized experience. As we described in Chapter 1, responses that can be generated in advance are often stored in a hot cache server that directly supports the Website. But in other cases, the Website may let the customer pose queries that go to the underlying data warehouse itself. This, of course, is an example of bringing the warehouse to the Web. The CRM developer is also very interested in the results from analyzing the clickstream because that affects the design decisions in the CRM system. The CRM developer works closely with the Web page developers, as described later in this chapter.

- **Customer behavior analyst.**   Another member of the CRM team is the customer behavior analyst. This person is directly responsible for understanding the clickstream, and the relationship of the clickstream to the transactions captured by other systems, such as the order entry system. This person works with the Website designers to propose labels for Web pages so that their functions can be understood when the clickstream is analyzed. The customer behavior analyst works with the Web log extract specialists, described shortly, to diagnose user sessions so that the session dimension can be more expressive and useful.

- *Webhouse educator.*   The Webhouse educator is someone who also works in end user application development. This person needs to understand and teach the content of the data as well as the use of the tools. The balance between teaching data content and tool content should be close to 50/50. Even more than the application developer, this role, although a familiar one from the pre-Web data warehouse era, is profoundly affected by the Web. Nearly all the detailed user interface training must be recast in terms of the Web user interfaces.

- **Webmaster.** The Webmaster is responsible for the overall look and feel of the Website, for ensuring that common tools such as search facilities are available within the hosting architecture, and that all of the enterprise's Internet activities hang together with common links and a unified front to the Web user. The Webmaster will often choose the Web development and maintenance tools to be used for Website development throughout the enterprise (e.g., FrontPage, Cold Fusion). The Webmaster may have responsibility for supplying overall site statistics in terms of hits, response times, and the like, but this person will not normally be concerned with the fine-detail analysis that the Webhouse is intended to service.

- **Content manager.** The Website content manager is key to the Webhouse project and may, in fact, be a primary consumer of Webhouse output. The content manager will usually be a departmental or divisional manager with the responsibility of getting the organization's message out onto the corporate Website. Content managers are frequently found within marketing organizations, and may have a title like Managing Editor. A content department will have one or more Web page developers who create actual page contents at an HTML level. The content manager should be a strong advocate of the benefits of data gathering. If the content manager's enthusiasm for quantitative analysis is absent, then the likelihood of project success is small. If the content manager recognizes the value of quantitative analysis, your project will have a strong and active team member.

- **Webhouse security manager.** The Webhouse security manager role is tactical. In Chapter 13 we described a recommended Webhouse security architecture. That design concentrated and simplified the management of security. The main responsibility for the Webhouse security manager is to define and administer the user role definitions. A large Webhouse environment could have dozens or even hundreds of separate role definitions. Trusted customers or business partners who have access to the data warehouse may each have their own security role. Half of the security manager's responsibility is defining the roles. The other half is applying those roles appropriately to all the information objects in the Webhouse. In the architecture described in Chapter 13, we applied the roles at the application server layer of the Webhouse because that is where the final information delivery is being assembled. This allows us to apply security to the high-level report, which may even be a multimedia object. As we remarked, it is not sufficient to apply security at the lowest level of the DBMS because in many cases, the application server is actually accessing the data, not the end user. In addition to the role definitions, the Webhouse security manager also needs to monitor the Webhouse for security intrusions and security weaknesses. In this capacity, the Webhouse security manager can work with the IT central security team.

- **Website page description specialist.** The page description specialist assists the Webhouse by defining attributes for Web pages that make the pages understandable in a database sense. Each page needs one or more descriptive attributes that can serve as the basis for constraining or grouping. For example, a page can be a navigation page, an ordering page, or a product information page. The page description specialist also needs to work with the CRM development team so that dynamic pages generated in the application servers possess useful attributes.

Special Teams

- **Network and security architect.** The security architect's role is strategic. This person is responsible for the overall security architecture of the Webhouse. The decisions made by the security architect include the choice of technologies for implementing security, the places in the system at which security is invoked, the location of packet filtering gateways and other security isolation devices, and the design of the disaster recovery system. The security architect may be the same person as the security manager (if they have any spare time!), but does not really need to be a full-time, dedicated resource to the Webhouse. The security architect does not need to make the tactical decisions about which users get to see which data.

- *Technical support specialist.* Technical support specialists are IT personnel responsible for various parts of the infrastructure the Webhouse depends upon. This infrastructure includes the mainframe, the inventory of personal computers, and the physical plant including the network.

- *Data staging programmer.* Data staging programmers are responsible for implementing the back room extract, transform, and load (ETL) systems. They may program directly in a conventional programming language, or they may use an integrated, graphically oriented tool that allows the ETL logic to be assembled and rearranged on the screen. Data staging is one of the most lengthy and unpredictable phases of any data warehouse project. A good data staging programmer spends equal time with primary logic development, unit testing, system testing, and documentation. A decent rule of thumb is that each new production source of data requires six months of a dedicated data staging programmer to work through all four of these phases.

- **Web log extract specialist.** The Web log extract specialist is a special kind of data staging programmer, unique to the Webhouse environment. The Web log extract specialist works with the Webmaster to provide Web logs that are as verbose and meaningful as possible. In some cases the Web servers can be configured to provide optional, more useful information. The Web log extract specialist needs to understand all the vagaries of the separate Web log formats the organization must deal with. The Web log specialist needs to keep up to date with the many formats of search string specifications that arrive in the referral information. The Web log specialist will work with the CRM team, and the operational system teams to define and make available XML tags that give insight into sub-page behavior.

- *Data steward.*   The data steward is responsible for defining the conformed dimensions and conformed facts in the Webhouse. The data steward plays the central role in defining the business-oriented metadata, and making this metadata available in a useful way to application developers and end users.

- *Production system support specialist.*   Production system support specialists are personnel normally assigned to the production legacy systems of the enterprise. They are invaluable resources for the Webhouse team, when the original data audits are being conducted in the early planning stages, and when the Webhouse ETL systems are being built.

- *Quality assurance manager.*   The quality assurance manager has the strategic role of defining acceptable data quality for the Webhouse. The quality assurance manager defines the procedures used by the quality assurance gatekeeper each "morning" when the data is loaded into the Webhouse. The quality assurance manager alerts senior management to meaningful data quality issues, since most of these data quality problems are symptoms of pathology in the organization, not just technical problems. For instance, if the master list of customer addresses contains thousands of corrupt or unmailable addresses, the organization has a major issue because it is obvious that no one is seriously using the list.

- *Quality assurance gatekeeper.* The quality assurance gatekeeper makes the final human judgment as to whether the data is fit to be published. This usually occurs as the last step of the ETL pipeline. Even if the load ran to completion with no errors, there can be missing data, and there can be out-of-bounds data. The decision to publish ultimately must rest in a human being, just as the decision to publish a magazine or a newspaper rests with a human being. The quality assurance gatekeeper uses a number of auditing tools, including special end user reports, to determine if the data is complete and sensible. The quality assurance gatekeeper, then communicates directly with the end user community, probably via e-mail, with the status of each release of the Webhouse data.

GATHER BUSINESS REQUIREMENTS AND AUDIT DATA

After identifying all the Webhouse roles and verifying that these skills will be available when they are needed, the next step is to interview the end users and conduct the data audit. This should be regarded as a single step, because the business requirements and the available data interact with each other so profoundly that they need to be understood at the same time. The essence of the Webhouse project leader's job is to choose the right data to answer the right business questions.

In *The Data Warehouse Lifecycle Toolkit*, we described a comprehensive framework for gathering the business requirements and performing the data audit. We broke it down into four phases:

1. **Preparing for the interviews.** Careful preparation is required for an effective interview process. You need a team of interviewers with specific roles. The lead interviewer is responsible for asking the questions and guiding the progress of the interview. The scribe takes comprehensive notes and listens for gaps and inconsistencies in the interview that can be clarified before the interview is finished. Before the interviews take place, significant research should be done to understand as much as possible about the activities of the groups being interviewed. Any earlier attempts to provide a data warehouse to these groups should be thoroughly understood.

   The business interviewees and the IT data audit interviewees need to be selected. Preliminary interview questionnaires need to be prepared, although it is an axiom of these kinds of interviews that the discussion will go in unexpected directions.

The interviews need to be scheduled, and the interviewees prepared. Perhaps the most important concept for the end user interviews is that the interview is meant to listen to them talk about what they do, *not* to discuss the technical content of the Webhouse. In the data audit interviews, the objective is to focus on the main production sources of data, to understand them, and to get a realistic feeling for the quality of the data.

2. **Conducting the interviews.** The lead interviewer's job is to get the end user to talk. The questions should be open-ended why, what-if, and what-then kinds of questions, rather than leading questions that telegraph a desired answer. Terminology must be defined, especially when jargon or acronyms fly by in the interview. We do not recommend taping the interviews. Taping is intimidating and adds an undesirable formality to the interview. Taping is notoriously inefficient for any kind of later use; it is much better to take copious notes, preferably by hand. The end of the interview is an ideal time to ask the end users for sample reports they regularly depend on. By that time a level of personal trust has been established and the end users will often hand over much more than they might have at the beginning of the interview.

3. **Assimilating the interview results.** Immediately after the interview, the written notes should be scanned to fill in incomplete sentences, cryptic comments, and half-sketched diagrams. The half-life for remembering incomplete thoughts from an interview is measured in one or two hours, so it is best to schedule a full hour between interviews for this process. This also makes the schedule more rational. There is a natural tendency to over-schedule interviews. More than four interviews per day is not advised.

When all the interviews have been completed, the interview team should assimilate all the notes as soon as possible. All the major business findings should be highlighted and organized into categories. The categories can be arranged from the most important to the least important. Then, the data audit findings can be matched against the business findings. For each category of business finding, a data availability statement should be generated that, in one paragraph, summarizes whether the data resources exist to address the business findings, what the quality of those sources are, and roughly how difficult it will be to use that source of data.

4. **Publishing the interview results.**   The results of the interviews, organized by matching the business findings and the data audit results, should be published to the interviewees, to end user management, and to IT management. These interview results will serve as a very valuable context for all the decisions that need to be made next.

PLAN AND MANAGE THE IMPLEMENTATION

Data warehouse development projects are difficult to plan precisely at the outset. Several things will develop or change in unexpected ways between the beginning of a project and the end of a project. The data will be harder to extract than was initially planned. Perhaps the data will be more complex and the source may contain complicated subcases that make the extraction programs significantly harder to write or debug. The end users may think of new issues they want to explore, and they may ask for additional data, such as cost drivers, to be sourced that were not on the original plan. Vendors may introduce delays with the delivery of hardware, software, promised features, or bug fixes. The entire end user organization or IT organization may be distracted by an acquisition or an emergency project. Thus the data warehouse project leader must be prepared to adjust the schedule and communicate with all affected parties on a regular basis. Since schedules rarely are shortened, and are often lengthened, we recommend not being extremely aggressive in promising delivery of a big project at the outset. Even part-way though a project, you will have a much better idea where the difficulties will be. A good mid-course correction can be considerably more accurate.

The Webhouse project leader must control scope creep, especially in the second half of the project, where many of the systems have begun to work, and the project is being tested for completeness and correctness. It is at this stage that a change of scope, perhaps introduced by the end user clients, can cause real management headaches. It is all too easy to agree in the spirit of accommodation to add one or two more features, but this kind of incrementalism is famous for doubling the size or time scale of projects. Toward the end of the implementation phase, the wise project leader will recognize these extra requests and gracefully put them on a "deferred" or "hopefully" list.

A good project leader is a good communicator. A project leader who walks around talking to people may be a better project leader than one who stays in their office adjusting dependency graphs in a PC-based project management program. The project leader educates the business partners, end users, and senior management continuously about the needs and the deliverables of the project.

LAUNCH THE SYSTEM

It is very important to assess the readiness of Webhouse before launching the system. It is far better to delay user training and especially rollout if the system is not ready, than it is to declare a milestone to be met when the system cannot perform or cannot deliver reliable data. A lot of pick and shovel items need to be in place before a system can be rolled out. Some of these items include:

- Completing hardware and software configurations, and arranging for database connectivity, and net connectivity. This may mean a systematic audit of the hardware situations for all affected end users.
- Completing hardware and software procurements, including final contracts, and final delivery of upgrades or releases.
- Defining all of the end user security roles and tying the end user authentication scheme to these roles.
- Testing and rehearsing the installation procedures on a variety of machines.
- Scheduling the installation with users, and aligning this installation with end user training.
- Making sure that the education courses and materials are ready.

End user training should strive for approximately a 50/50 balance between training the user interfaces to the Webhouse with training the content of the data. Often only the product user interfaces are thought of in the training development plan. If the data content is not taught in a systematic way up front, the users will effectively cause the training to occur as they barrage the Webhouse team with questions about the content of the data and how to build applications. A corollary of this is that if the user has not received training, then the user does not get access to the system. This is easy to control if each user is assigned to a role. One role is "untrained user" and another is "trained user."

Once the rollout has occurred, it is very important to maintain a significant support presence as users make their first cautious forays into using the system. The first one or two experiences are pivotal in determining whether they will expand their use of the system or give up. This is also a great time for the IT support staff to bond effectively with the end users. When the users move past initial training, they will begin to probe the true content of the Webhouse, and that is a great time for both IT and the end users to be studying the same issues and challenges.

Finally, it is important for IT to be constantly looking for evidence of insights gained from looking at the Webhouse data. These insights, even if they are anecdotal, can be accumulated in a kind of diary. Since some of these insights will support major multimillion dollar decisions made by the end user management, it is enormously valuable to record the link between the decisions and the original content of the Webhouse.

LOOP BACK AND DO IT AGAIN

As soon as the Webhouse is up and running and the initial objectives have been satisfied, it is time to plan the next iteration. Data Webhouses are never done. The next level of granularity of the data can be exposed. Hopefully, Chapter 7 made it obvious what additional questions can be answered as the data granularity evolves from monthly session summaries by demographic cluster, to individual sessions by user, and finally to individual page events by user. At the same time that granularity is being deepened, other data marts can be added to the suite because, hopefully, you have implemented conformed dimensions and conformed facts. The second, third, and subsequent data marts should plug gracefully into the data warehouse bus.

At the same time the pool of data is being expanded, other groups in the organization can begin to use the Webhouse. Perhaps marketing began by looking at the clickstream data. Another natural group would be the Website design staff. Other product or service groups in the enterprise may want to match their customer files with the clickstream files to see if their customers are also coming to the Website.

SUMMARY

As we said at the beginning of this chapter, if you are pretty good with people, pretty good with technology, and pretty good at managing a project, then by following the user interface, security architecture, and scaling architecture recommendations in this book, your project has a high chance of success. In the long run, your mission boils down to four carefully chosen words: *Publish the Right Data.*

In this chapter we have described the myriad roles that are needed to pull off a full data Webhouse project. Remember that you don't necessarily need a separate person for each role. Some of the roles are transient and some can be overlapped to a degree. But the list of roles is useful because it clearly defines the scope of the Webhouse management task.

Before leaving you to manage your project, in the final chapter of this book, we want to give you a glimpse of what we think lies in the future for data Webhousing. We are at the very beginning of the Web revolution. Paradoxically, our predictions will on the one hand sound like extravagant blue-sky fantasies, but on the other hand, will almost certainly be more conservative than the reality that lies ahead.

CHAPTER 16

The Future of Webhousing

If there is one thing we have learned during the age of the Web, it is that the pace of change is accelerating. We have all become change junkies. If something hasn't changed since the last time we saw it, we get bored. We want Web pages to be different each time we visit them. Or, at least we want the last-updated-date to be *very* recent so we know we are getting "current stuff."

Product cycles are now measured in three-month increments rather than one-year increments. We write off our hardware in two to three years because we know we will buy a new generation soon. And that new generation will be astoundingly faster and larger in capacity and throughput. In fact, as the sidebar "Predicting the Future" illustrates, we anticipate laughing at our limited expectations.

Since we yearn for evermore rapid change, we will be increasingly fickle in our on-line relationships. We may buy from Amazon today, but how deep is our loyalty, and what must Amazon do to really lock in that loyalty? The answer to on-line loyalty may be found in today's Yahoo and eBay. Both of them have critical mass, and that critical mass makes it harder for their competitors to ever be successful. Yahoo gets so many Web sessions that it is almost the only e-business that can stay profitable on 1999's version of Web advertising. eBay has created the world's biggest flea market, and the depth of that market is irresistible to both buyers and sellers. Who would want to sell in a place with very few

PREDICTING THE FUTURE

In 1987, one of the authors (Kimball) was asked to write a speech for an industry executive predicting the state of personal computer technology at the end of the 1990s. When the draft of the speech predicted 1 GB disk drives and 50 MB RAM memories, the executive demanded that the predictions be toned down because they were outlandish and unrealistic. He didn't believe them. Well, this chapter is being written on a 1998-era *laptop* with an 8 GB disk drive and 128 MB of RAM. So much for predictions.

buyers? Who wants to visit a market where there is almost nothing for sale? But please, eBay, give us a better search engine for finding things.

CRM WILL CONTINUE TO DRIVE DATA WEBHOUSING

Occasionally in this book we have touched on the larger changes going on in our society and how they impact data Webhousing. We have swept up a lot of these trends under the label "CRM." For instance, partly because of the Web, the fundamental relationship between the manufacturer and the end consumer is changing. The manufacturer is touching the end consumer directly, and the roles of middlemen are changing dramatically. These big shifts in the ways we communicate are, of course, fundamental themes in this book. The Webhouse is implicated repeatedly. If CRM was only concerned with bringing up the status of the most recent order, we wouldn't need a Webhouse. But CRM seeks a much broader perspective on the customer relationship. Many of the real-time decisions made in the customer facing business processes need something from the Webhouse, whether it is showing the lifetime growth in purchases or collaborative hints about what other similar customers want.

The Webhouse needs new and more efficient kinds of query processing that are better suited to the needs of CRM. SQL and even MDX were not designed with the needs of 2010 in mind. A reasonable checklist for the next generation of Webhouse query languages would include:

- Data pattern searching, so that the analyst could look for "unexpected increases or decreases in revenue over a three-month period compared to the combined experience of the previous two years."
- Sequential behavior querying, so that the analyst could look for and classify distinct patterns in the way people traversed Websites.

- Case-based reasoning built directly into query engines so that the analyst could ask "based on similar Web visitors, what opt-in offer should we make to this visitor that he or she would be most likely to accept?" The implication is that the profile of the current Web visitor would be matched against the known profiles of a large number of existing customer visitors. Of course, this kind of technology is available today in specialized data mining tools, but we need these specialized tools to go "mainstream" so that these kinds of matching analyses can be done just as easily as a Web text search. The underlying technology may be very sophisticated, but the user interface should be extremely simple and obvious.

- Context matching query capabilities that would do a much better job than current search engines in finding text documents related to a chosen topic.

DESCRIBING BEHAVIOR BETTER

Today's browsers provide very little feedback to define the user's actual actions. Most of what we learn about user actions is learned by deduction, using the faint trails left in the clickstream to deduce what the user was actually doing.

It would be trivial, for example, to instrument a browser to measure dwell time accurately (e.g., excluding the time a browser window was obscured by other windows), and return XML-coded information to the Website. This could certainly be done without compromising the user's privacy or security and be made a feature that could be turned off if the user wished. However, we don't see this being done in the near future. There is little incentive for the remaining browser builders to incorporate such feedback features. In fact there is a disincentive because of the, perhaps correct, perception by the public that any feedback about individual actions is an invasion of privacy.

There is one major exception to the browser instrumentation issue: In the case of "free" or almost-free computer deals there is clearly an intent by the seller and a contractual obligation by the purchaser to provide more detailed feedback of network activity than is normally given. An instrumented browser capable of collecting and returning this data to the seller or his agent can provide such information. Although the demographics of "free" computer purchasers are undoubtedly biased, the same bias exists in the selection of target families for TV tracking by firms such as A. C. Nielsen.

We don't ignore the fact that the public is notoriously cavalier about giving up privacy for a *quid quo pro*. In the case of supermarket discount cards, the purchasing public has agreed to provide intimate information about themselves and their families with hardly a whimper of dissent. With the proper incentives, browser-level tracking could probably be obtained in a similar way. (See the accompanying sidebar, "Giving Up Cherished Notions of Privacy.")

A more positive spin of this *quid pro quo* is provided by Seth Godin in his *Permissions Marketing* book, referenced in the bibliography. Godin argues that by offering something of significant intrinsic value, such as a product discount, or a customized newsletter, a Website can induce visitors to "opt in." Godin contrasts permissions marketing with interruption marketing, where an enterprise interrupts the viewer or the Website visitor with unwanted and possibly gratuitous advertising. One of Godin's creative perspectives is that interruption marketing more or less works on television, but television is a different medium than the Web. On the Web, TV-style interruption marketing does not work. Godin cites survey response statistics from Web visitors who have opted in to a relationship with an enterprise, and shows that although the pool of target individuals is smaller than television might be used to, the response rates for surveys and promotions can be as high as 50 percent, which is unheard of in interruption marketing circles.

Without any modification to current browsers a great deal of feedback can be obtained using sandboxed tracking applications. These sandboxed applications will scrupulously sanitize the statistics to not compromise the user's sensitivities. We expect to see common browser-level tracking applications developed by data syndicators that can be delivered by diverse Websites to provide accurate, independent user tracking to these syndicators for resale. The developers of such applications will undoubtedly request PC operating system vendors to make as much system-level data as possible available through the sandbox API so that actions such as bookmarking, saving a print-screen, or saving a browser image can be tracked.

WE WILL FINALLY NEED DATA MINING

The next decade will be the coming of age for data mining, although it's unclear that the current set of data mining vendors will be smart enough to catch the wave. The name of the game is behavior. Our ever-more-detailed data sources are increasingly describing customer behavior, citizen behavior, and Website visitor behavior. The Web has introduced enormous urgency to capture and understand this behavior. Frankly, most businesses don't care which data mining algorithm is used. Any vendor caught describing the difference between neural networks and genetic algorithms is going to get left behind. What is important is effective results. What is behavior? Can we identify happy customers? Loyal customers? High-value customers? Customers likely to default? The data mining shakeout has not yet occurred, but it is likely to in the next decade.

In Chapter 11, we described the "perfect handoff" between the Webhouse, which contains the evidence of behavior, and data mining tools, which make sense out of the behavior. During the next ten years, we can expect to see the deployment of powerful hybrid systems, consisting of relational data Webhouses, matched with data mining–oriented behavior analysis engines. The Webhouse will hand the evidence of behavior to the data mining tool, which will often hand back a database to be stored in the Webhouse. This database could be a time stamped set of behavior scores for every Website visitor. This large database, with time and customer dimensions, is then used by the Webhouse to make further customization decisions. Maybe the Webhouse computes several million custom greetings or custom recommendations and then stores them in the hot response cache so they can be instantly displayed when the specific Web visitor arrives.

GIVING UP CHERISHED NOTIONS OF PRIVACY

Technology is so far ahead of the legislators that even if they passed a new law every month, they could not cope with the robust energy of the Web economy and Web community. This is a bit of a cop-out, but let's face it: Our trusted Website partners are going to know a lot about each of us. Certainly, if you never go on-line, you may avoid much of the upcoming privacy degradation, but one-to-one marketing is simply intimate. If they can see your every gesture, then they know a lot about you.

At the same time, Website owners are terrified by the ephemeral loyalty of Web visitors. No entity will stay in business if they churn their customers constantly. A key issue is trust. If a Website abuses a visitor's trust, then they may never get that business back. We predict that Websites will pay a lot of attention to the promises they make to preserve confidentiality and privacy. In most cases, this economic pressure to preserve privacy should be more responsive to a Web visitor's fears than any laws created by our legislators.

ISPS OWN A GOLD MINE

Internet service providers have a unique perspective on their customers' Web activities. The ISPs of the world sit on top of a gold mine of behavioral data because they have two huge advantages that a normal Website does not have. An ISP sees every click emanating from a connected customer, so there is no uncertainty about what constitutes a complete trajectory though Webspace. Also, an ISP always knows precisely who owns the computer producing the clicks. The ISP may not know who the human is at the keyboard, but there is no hiding the owner and location of each computer.

In a word, they see everything that the customer does on the Web because they can see packets going both to and from the customers. Information is available at three levels. At the topmost level is the information contained in the packet headers—the to- and from- addresses in the IP datagram. This information tells where a packet is coming from and where it is going. A Web transaction (HTTP request, image download) may span multiple packets and probably will if the content is more than a few kilobytes. So, counting IP packets doesn't give much information about Web traffic other than raw traffic estimates.

At the second level, the reconstructed packet content can be examined independent of the application or Website, and individual HTTP requests can be parsed. These will give more detailed information about what's going on between the browser and Website, but there is still a critical key missing. There is no easy way of determining what the traffic means unless the characteristics of the application itself is known. We expect a very significant expansion of the Web log contents to tell the Website what the visitor is actually doing with the application. This, of course, will be greatly facilitated by XML, which provides a context for the objects and actions on a page.

Consequently, the third level is essential to detailed tracking. In order to understand the meaning of a packet stream you must have an intimate understanding of the application being supported. We believe that data gathered at an ISP level will, at best, support high-level traffic analysis. Two factors lead to this conclusion. First is the restriction we stated earlier on what an ISP can track because that detailed tracking requires intimate application knowledge. Second is the question of privacy: To whom does this information belong?

Who owns Internet traffic data? The answer to this question may be found in each individual ISP's Terms of Service, the contract under which Internet access is provided. We feel that this information belongs to the customer if not elsewhere stated, but the resolution of this is certainly a legal question and probably has not yet been adequately addressed by either the courts or by legislative bodies. We might be able to draw on an analogous issue from the telephone industry. Although the detail of a customer's calling records is private information, some summarization is publicly available, even down to the customer level, in order to promote potential long-distance competition. At no time, however, is the caller's data content (the conversation) public without a court order.

WANTED: BETTER SEARCH ENGINES

The Web has made us choice junkies. We want dozens, if not hundreds, of alternatives, whether we are looking for hotels to stay in, or software products to help us with extract, transform, and load. But there is clearly a limit to our tolerance for manually scanning undifferentiated alternatives. We want the alternatives, but a major focus in the upcoming decade will be better search engines that filter the myriad choices down to a few really good ones. It is worth remembering that too many choices is a cousin of too many opinions. A fascinating recent study relating to medical information searching on the Web is that some people are learning much more than they need to about diseases and symptoms. If you worry too much that your toe hurts, pretty soon it will hurt. One can only hope that Web users will learn to stand back from the babble of opinions and exercise some judgment.

The 1999 era of Web search engines will surely be regarded as primitive a few years in the future. There is immense value in better context searching, and many interesting new technologies will appear to support such searches. A better context search will allow the user's needs to be expressed more clearly and with fewer crazy "hits". Some of the original ideas in the Wide Area Information Servers (WAIS) search engine were on a creative track. The WAIS engine would match all the words in a paragraph to the candidate target. The total weight of all the words defined a context that seemed to be more discerning than many of the short token based searches we perform with popular search engines.

We are in a position to create huge archives of business results that could be searched with text search engines. A first step in bridging Web search engines and business results would be to have the report author manually create a significant textual context for each searchable business report that would then be the target for a search engine. One might write "This report shows the growth in revenue, growth in market share, and number of Website visits for the ABC division of the XYZ Corporation, from January 2000 to December 2001." Even this little explanation would be useful context for a search engine. In Chapter 12 we briefly described some progress that is being made in automatic translation and multi-lingual search technologies. Again, the Web will exert effective pressure for rapid development in this area. By 2010, we can expect to see the entire Web through a filter that translates everything to our own lan-guage and to be able to search every site in useful ways. We appreciate how difficult automatic translation is, and we expect that in 2010, it will still easily be possible to tell if a site has been translated, but we are certain that language barriers will be much lower than they are today. Perhaps the Web should adopt a text highlighting standard for automatically translated text, similar to the standard blue underline for links. . . .

IS DATA WINNING THE WAR OVER STORAGE AND SPEED?

In the early part of the 1990s it seemed like disk drives and CPUs were gaining ground on the masses of data we were collecting. We graduated from megabytes to gigabytes, and we are now becoming more comfort-able with terabytes. It seemed as if we were reaching a kind of final summit of the mountain when we succeeded in capturing and storing in our data warehouses every atomic transaction in really big businesses like retail, telco, and insurance.

But then along came the Web. The clickstream gives us a very reveal-ing look into the future. There is no upper limit to the amount of data we can collect. The clickstream contains every gesture made by every visitor on a Website. There may be hundreds of low-level gestures made before a single purchase transaction! By the middle of the next decade, click-stream databases will dwarf all the other conventional data warehouse examples. And the worst part is that the clickstream is really interesting.

During the next decade we will be hooking more and more devices to the Web. Not only will we record every page event, but we will record every sub-page event, such as a parameter change in a query. We will also have hundreds of nano-computers in our cars, our homes, and our offices that will record every mile driven, every turn taken, every light bulb turned on, and every keystroke. All these nano-computers will merge to produce a biblical flood of data.

And we are still talking about text and number records. Although we have romanced with multimedia "data blades" for a number of years, maybe this time it is real, because the Web is relentlessly pushing audio, video, and cartographic media in our direction. The only retarding factor in this surge to higher bandwidth media is the lack of high-performance wiring across our country.

Even though the latest clickstream battle has gone in favor of data, maybe our disk drives, CPUs, and communication channels will eventually prevail in the overall war. Within two years, 500 GB disk drives will appear in the consumer marketplace. At the end of the next decade, it will be possible to buy a laptop with a terabyte of writable storage, and many of our desktop PCs will have 10 terabytes of storage. A terabyte of storage is enough for three solid days of compressed video. Ten terabytes will be enough to hold a picture of every citizen of the United States.

FULL INVERSION OF DATABASES

In *The Data Warehouse Toolkit,* one of the authors of this book (Kimball) argued that the future belonged to software, and that the really large gains in query power and speed would come from advances in software technique. Smaller gains would come from hardware power. In the four years since the *Toolkit* was written, in many ways we think that software, not hardware, has provided the biggest advances. Frankly, these gains have been somewhat masked by the out-of-control growth of the data sets we are being asked to analyze. But we feel strongly enough about this issue that we will state it again in 2000: The future belongs to software techniques. All of our decision-support databases still have the potential to answer queries in the future 100 times as fast as they do now, if we aggressively index and invert these databases to be organized for lookup, not for update. We need to use the advances in CPU power and disk storage size to let us do more during the extract-transform-load phase of the Webhouse operations. We trade off huge back-room computational tasks like full database inversion for the promise of rapid querying once the inversion is finished.

We can also trade off storage for applications simplicity with "heterogeneous products" and "transaction-snapshot schemas," which produce alternate versions of the same database that support different query modes. We trade off storage for aggregations, which provide an immediate performance boost, often with improvements of 100 or more in query speed.

WEBSITE APPLICATION LOGS

Commercial Website applications such as e-commerce packages and search engines are potentially an excellent source of meaningful transaction log data. As the marketing practices for such packages evolve beyond the "feature-war" stage, the vendors will begin to meet demands for providing rich transaction logs for downstream processing. We expect that log entries will be available at the session level, the application action level, and the click event level.

In selecting Web applications it is prudent to determine whether the vendor is aware of the need for downstream analysis and data warehousing and is willing to make APIs available to customers for implementing special purpose logging. In many instances a user's group can share applications that will exploit the capabilities of such APIs.

Remember that most Web servers permit adding application-generated log records to their common log files. Using this facility for merging application logs with server logs is tempting and desirable, but should be used with caution; system administrators may want to change the server software to provide new features or efficiencies, and the interfaces will have to be tested and perhaps rewritten.

EVERYTHING IS A MODULE

From the perspective of a computer scientist growing up in the 1960s, the trend toward software bloat is pretty dismaying. Does anyone still read Donald Knuth's wonderful books on how to write really tight algorithms? Does anyone program in Assembler any more? Certainly, one of

THE CD-ROM CONTENT INDUSTRY AT RISK

Earlier in the 1990s it seemed as if the CD-ROM content providers had an interesting future. Encyclopedias and maps seemed like promising applications that would require a CD-ROM to deliver the data. The Web has erased that hope. There is no reason to send a CD-ROM to someone if you can download the same data over the Web.

Maybe this prediction is still arguable, if only because the prediction depends on the widespread deployment of very high bandwidth communications. It will be an interesting race to see whether the highest bandwidth communication channel in 2010 will be (a) 17 GB DVD-ROM sent through the United States mail, or (b) an on-line Internet connection available in most major U.S. cities. Even if the DVD-ROM wins in 2010, it seems clear that when we get properly "wired," the on-line option will be the big winner.

Of course, if the rules got changed and we were told that a DVD-ROM in 2010 will hold a terabyte of data, then maybe we would change our minds. . . .

the amazing successful bets that Microsoft has made is that CPU power is more effective than tight low-level coding over the long run. Microsoft has been very successful in concentrating on adding functionality to their systems, not making them smaller or faster.

Actually, the message is more subtle than "hardware has won over software." The real message is that modern systems are horribly complex by necessity, and the only way to build these systems is from modules. The high level designers of both hardware and software don't need to descend to lowest bit-twiddling levels. They can't descend to the lowest bit-twiddling levels.

The technique of building systems from modules pervades every level of our computing environments. CPU and memory chips are built from modules. Operating systems and applications are built from modules. Data warehouses and Webhouses will be built from modules almost exclusively during the next decade. Rather than programming in C or Visual Basic, IT shops will be connecting icons with "visual pipes" and filling in screens of parameters. Rather than typing in hundreds of CREATES and GRANTS, we will transfer major applications from prototype to production by dragging a master application icon from a picture of the test machine to a picture of the production machine. If you open the master application icon, inside you will find a maze of sub-icons (modules, actually).

A corollary of building systems out of modules is that most IT shops will buy, not make. They will buy suites of modules that can be rapidly configured into the final system. It's crucially important to customize each system, but an IT shop only wants to customize the topmost layer.

It seems likely that the "best-of-breed" software strategy for data warehouse implementers will give way to "end to end solutions." A best-of-breed approach is attractive at the early experimental stages of a technology like data warehousing has been in the mid-1990s. IT shops got experience with many of the extract, transform, load, query, analyze, and presentation modules that are needed in a full warehouse. But having twenty tools is undesirable. As the market evolves, the tools don't necessarily stay in synchrony. Eventually, we think the tools market will shake out to a smaller number of players offering end to end tool suites where all the components are guaranteed to work together.

SUMMARY

Even if we are working on Internet time, we still need to deliver a Webhouse system to our clients that shares many of the characteristics of a normal operational system. The Webhouse must be available, responsive, and accurate. Webhouses may even have service level agreements.

Yet at the same time, the Webhouse designer must ride the Web wave and be responsive to the rapid changes in this marketplace. This chapter tries to hint at some of the big changes we expect, but it is guaranteed that there is something really *big* that we just can't imagine in 1999.

The last thought we want to leave you with is: commit to a flexible architecture that lets you adapt gracefully to new end user queries, new dimensions, new attributes within those dimensions, and new facts. Anticipate the demand for unexpected new data marts, subject areas, and data sources. Make your Webhouse out of lots of little pieces in response to your end user's needs. But don't forget to conform, conform, conform. Good luck. We'll see you in the next book.

Glossary of Abbreviations and Terms

3NF Third Normal Form, a database design approach that eliminates redundancy and facilitates insertion of new rows into tables without introducing excessive data locking problems. See **Entity-Relation modeling.**

404 HTTP code returned to a browser when a page (or URL) cannot be found. See **linkrot.**

A. C. Nielsen Supplier of syndicated summaries of grocery and drug store scanner data, principally to manufacturers and retailers. Nielsen, together with IRI, developed the foundations of dimensional modeling, including facts, dimensions, and conforming.

ACF Automated Collaborative Filtering, where a system modifies or customizes the user interface and the content offered based on understanding the preferences and usage patterns of other users with similar demographic and behavioral characteristics. A similar concept, Active Collaborative Filtering, is based on voluntary inputs from the community of users. The community, in effect, pushes content to the members.

ACID properties Atomicity, Consistency, Isolation, and Durability, the requirements for a serious OLTP system defined by the Transaction Processing Performance Council.

ActiveX Control A Microsoft-defined software module, part of the COM (Component Object Model) family. ActiveX controls are typically passed from a server to a client in order to allow the client to execute special application functions. ActiveX controls can be digitally signed so that the client system can decide whether to trust them and allow them to be executed.

Activity-based Costs   Costs that are reported on the basis of the true incremental activity required, rather than on an unchanging standard value. See also **Allocations.**

Additive (Facts)   Measurements in a fact table that are able to be added across all of the dimensions.

Ad Hoc Queries   Queries that are formulated by the user on the spur of the moment. The Ad Hoc Attack refers to difficulty a database has in anticipating the pattern of queries. The more that queries are ad hoc, the more symmetrical the database model must be so that all queries look the same. This is one of the strengths of the dimensional model.

Aggregate   A physical record in a database created from other records in the database for the purpose of improving query performance. See **Aggregate Navigator.**

Aggregate Navigator   A layer of software in between the client and the relational DBMS that intercepts the client's SQL, and transforms that SQL, if it can, to use aggregates that are present somewhere in the data warehouse. The aggregate navigator should shield the end user application from needing to know if an aggregate is present. In that sense, an aggregate behaves like an index.

Algorithm   A standard method for computing something; essentially, a mathematical recipe.

Alias (SQL)   A short identifier in an SQL expression that stands for a physical table name.

Allocated Inventory   Inventory that has been assigned for shipment to a particular customer before it has actually been shipped.

Allocations   The assignment or proration of a measured value (usually a cost) to several accounts. For instance, the overhead costs in a factory are often allocated to the various product lines made in the factory.

Allowance   An amount subtracted from the list price of a product, typically as a result of a promotion or a deal. Usually shown on the invoice, but called an "off-invoice" allowance.

ANSI   The American National Standards Institute, the recognized standards publishing body for a wide range of businesses, professions, and industries.

Answer Set   The set of rows returned to the end user as a result of an SQL expression presented to a relational DBMS.

AOL   America Online is the largest online service provider in the United States. AOL does not provide full Internet connectivity in the sense that a customer's computer has access to only a limited subset of TCP/IP protocols.

Apache   An open source Web server that dominates the World Wide Web. There are more Apache servers running than all other Web server systems combined.

API   Application Program Interface, an operating system facility that can be used by applications in order to access or use specific features of the operating system.

Application Constraint (SQL)   A portion of the WHERE clause in SQL that defines a constraint on values usually within a dimension table. To be contrasted with a join constraint.

Application Server   The layer of software responsible for interpreting the content of the user's requests and putting together the response delivered to the user. The application server typically has a high-bandwidth, fully enabled connection to the database engines. The application server in a Webhouse provides the screen contents to the Web server, which actually communicates with the end user. The application server is where security decisions must be made, since only the application server has the perspective to judge the full content of the information payload, at the same time being aware of who the end user is.

ASCII   American Standard Code for Information Interchange. An 8-bit character set encoding. ASCII can only support 127 characters, which is not enough for international usage. See **UNICODE.**

ASP   Active Server Pages is Microsoft's proprietary architecture for developing NT-based dynamic Web server pages.

Asset   An item that appears on the balance sheet of a company that represents something owned by the company or something owed to the company by someone else. Bank loans are assets from the bank's point of view because they are owed to the bank.

ATM   Automatic Teller Machine. Also, less commonly, Asynchronous Transfer Mode, a communications protocol.

Attribute   A field in a dimension table.

Authentication   The step of determining the identity of the requesting client. Single factor authentication is usually based on a simple password and is the least secure authentication scheme. Two factor authentication may involve What-You-Know (a password) with What-You-Possess (a plastic card), and is secure enough for banks' automated teller machines. Other two factor authentication schemes involve What-You-Know with What-You-Are, using biometric scanning devices, such as fingerprint-, eyeball-, or voice-based systems.

Average Order Backlog   The average length of time that orders have been waiting.

Back End Tool   A software application that assists in the production data extract process. Contrasted with front end tool.

Banner Ad   An advertisment placed on a Web page (often at the top) which by convention, is 60 pixels high and 468 pixels wide. Other shapes and forms of advertisements are also called banner ads.

Baseline Sales of a Promotion   The level of sales that would have occurred if there had been only regular sales.

BDI   Brand Development Index, the ratio of the percentage of households purchasing a brand in a local market to the percentage of households purchasing the brand in a larger market, such as Total U.S.

Behavior Score   Figure of merit that is assigned to a customer, often based on purchase patterns or credit patterns.

Behavioral Group   A large group of customers or products that is used in an end user analysis or report, but which cannot be defined by constraining on dimensional attributes, and is too large to be defined by an SQL "IN" clause. The behavioral group is often defined from an original analysis that isolates interesting purchase behavior or credit behavior.

BI   Business Intelligence, a generic term for information assets of all kinds that are used by organizations for making business decisions.

Brand Development Index   See **BDI.**

Brick-and-Mortar   A physically tangible business such as a store, as opposed to "virtual" or Web-based business.

Browse Query   A SELECT DISTINCT query on a single dimension table to enumerate the values of an attribute.

Browser   PC client software that communicates with Web servers and displays Web content (text, image, audio, video) on the PC. Certain claims notwithstanding, the browser is a standalone application, not an integral part of an operating system.

BSD Berkeley Software Distribution, an implementation of UNIX developed at the University of California, Berkeley.

BSDI A commercial version of BSD.

Business Reengineering An organizational restructuring based on a fundamental reexamination of why an organization exists.

CA Certificate Authority, an organization that is trusted to dispense certificates containing public keys.

Cache In a Web browser, disk space set aside to store temporary copies of Web objects so that if they are requested again they need not be fetched from the Web but can be obtained locally.

Cannibalization The growth of sales of one product causing the slowing of sales of another product. Usually referring to two products made by the same manufacturer.

Category Development Index See **CDI.**

Causal Something that is thought to be the cause of something else. Causal factors in sales usually refer to ads, displays, coupons, and price reductions.

CDI Category Development Index, the ratio of the percentage of households purchasing a category in a local market to the percentage of households purchasing the category in a larger market, such as Total U.S.

Certificate Usually a so-called X.509 certificate that contains the public key for a named individual or organization. Certificates are obtained from Certificate Authorities (CAs), such as Verisign, who are trusted sources.

CGI Common Gateway Interface is a standard application program interface in Web servers for interfacing with specific computer applications.

Churn In a subscription service, the ratio of customers lost to customers gained.

CLF The Common Log Format is a format for Web server log files.

Clickstream The composite body of actions taken by a user at a Web browser. The clickstream can include both the actual clicks (browser requests) and the server responses to those requests. The clickstream exists tangibly in the form of Web server logs, where each Web server log record relates to a single page event.

Clickthrough The action of arriving at a URL (Web page) by clicking on a button or link, usually located on a different Website.

CLOG   See **CLF.**

COM   Component Object Model, a software architecture, supported by Microsoft, that allows applications to be built from binary software components. See also **DCOM.**

Composite Key   A key in a database table made up of several fields. Same as concatenated key. The overall key in a typical fact table is a subset of the foreign keys in the fact table. In other words, it usually does not require every foreign key to guarantee uniqueness of a fact table record.

Concatenated Key   See **Composite Key.**

Conformed Dimensions   Dimensions are conformed when they are either exactly the same (including the keys) or one is a perfect subset of the other. Most important, the row headers produced in answer sets from two different conformed dimensions must be able to be matched perfectly.

Conformed Facts   Facts from multiple fact tables are conformed when the technical definition of the facts are equivalent. Conformed facts are allowed to have the same name in separate tables, and can be combined and compared mathematically.

Constraint   A phrase in the SQL WHERE clause. A constraint is either a join constraint or is an application constraint.

Continuously Valued (Facts)   A numeric measurement that is usually different every time it is measured. Continuously valued measurements should be facts in the fact table.

Contribution (P&L)   The profit in a business measured by subtracting the allowances, discounts, costs of manufacturing, and costs of sales from the list price.

Cookie   A record placed on a user's PC by a Web browser in response to a request from a Web server. The cookie contents are specified by the Web server and can only be read from the domain that is specified in the cookie.

Copy Book   The traditional COBOL header file that describes all the fields in the file.

CORBA   Common Object Request Broker Architecture, an open architecture for the exchange of software components. Used by systems programmers, not end users. An alternative to Microsoft's DCOM.

Core Table   The fact table or the dimension table in a heterogeneous product situation that is meant to span all of the products at once. Contrasted with the custom tables(s).

Cost-Based Optimizer   The software in a relational database that tries to determine how to process the query by assigning estimated "costs" to various table lookup alternatives.

Coverage Table for a Promotion   A fact table, typically factless, that records all of the products that are on a promotion in a given store, regardless of whether they sold or not.

CRC   Cyclic Redundancy Checksum, the name of an algorithm that is useful for checking two complex items, such as customer records, to see if anything has changed. The CRC can be stored with an existing record, and then the CRC can be computed on an incoming record. If there are any differences, the CRCs will be different. This eliminates the requirement to check each constituent field in the record.

CRM   Customer Relationship Management.

Cross-Selling   The technique of growing sales by selling existing customers a new product line.

Cube   A name for a dimensional database, usually referring to the simple case of Product, Market, and Time dimensions.

Custom Table   The fact table or the dimension table in a heterogeneous product situation that contains facts or attributes specific to one set of products, where those facts or attributes are incompatible with the other sets of products. See **Core Table.**

Customer Master File   A company's master list of customers, usually maintained by the Order Processing legacy application.

Customer Tracking (Financial Services)   The effort to identify an individual human customer across multiple financial accounts, by social security number, address, or some other indicator.

Daily Item Movement   The total of sales of each item in each store at the end of each day.

Data Cube   See **Cube.**

Data Dependencies Model   A bottoms up data design methodology that enumerates every logical relationship amongst all the possible data elements.

Data Extract   The process of copying data from a legacy system in order to load it into a data warehouse.

Data Mart   A data mart is a logical and physical subset of the overall data warehouse. Originally, data marts were defined as highly aggregated subsets of data, often chosen to answer a specific business question. This definition was unworkable because it led to stovepipe data marts that were inflexible and could not be combined with each other. This first definition has been replaced, and the data mart is now defined as a flexible set of data, often based on the most atomic (granular) data possible to extract from an original source, and presented in a symmetric (dimensional) model that is most resilient when faced with unexpected user queries. Data marts can be tied together using drill across techniques when their dimensions are conformed.

Data Mining   A class of undirected queries, often against the most atomic data, seeking to find unexpected patterns in the data. The most valuable results from data mining are clustering, classifying, estimating, predicting, and finding things that occur together. There are many kinds of tools that play a role in data mining. The principal tools include decision trees, neural networks, memory-based and case-based reasoning tools, visualization tools, genetic algorithms, fuzzy logic, and classical statistics. Generally, data mining is a client of the data warehouse.

Data Presentation Server   The target physical machine on which the data warehouse data is organized and stored for direct querying by end users, report writers, and other applications. All querying takes place on the data presentation server. Contrast with the **Data Staging Area.**

Data Quality Assurance   The step during the production data extract process where the data is tested for consistency, completeness, and fitness to publish to the user community.

Data Staging Area   A storage area and a set of processes that clean, transform, combine, de-duplicate, household, archive, and prepare source data for use in the data warehouse. The data staging area is everything in between the source system and the data presentation server. No querying should be done in the data staging area, because the data staging area normally is not set up to handle fine-grained security, indexing or aggregations for performance, or broad data integration across multiple data sources. The data-staging area makes no guarantees to be available for end user data access.

Data Warehouse (the Webhouse)   The queryable presentation resource for an enterprise's data. The data warehouse is usually nothing more than the union of its constituent data marts, because Web-oriented data warehouses frequently have no single center. We recommend the Webhouse not be organized around an entity-relation model because if you use entity-relation modeling for query and presentation you will lose understandability and performance. Also, the data warehouse is frequently updated on a controlled load basis, as data is corrected, as snapshots are accumulated, and as statuses and labels are changed.

Days Supply (Inventory)   The number of days the current inventory level would last at the current rate of sales.

DB2   The IBM relational database system, first developed on the MVS operating system.

DBA   Database administrator.

DBMS   A Database Management System is a computer application whose sole purpose is to store, retrieve, and modify data in a highly structured way. Data in a DBMS is usually shared by a variety of applications.

DCOM   Distributed Component Object Model, a protocol, supported by Microsoft, that enables software components to communicate directly over a network in a reliable, secure, and efficient manner.

DDW   A dimensional data warehouse.

Decision Support   The activity of using data to make decisions in an organization.

Deep Link   A link to a page in a Website hierarchy lower than the site's home page. Website owners do not always favor deep links because they bypass home pages or other pages that might be critical to the Website's revenue stream.

Degenerate Dimension   A dimension key, such as an invoice number, a ticket number, or a bill of lading number, that has no attributes, and hence does not require an actual dimension table.

Demand Side   The flow of processes in a business starting with finished goods inventory and progressing through to customer sales. Contrast with the **Supply Side.**

Demographic Mini-Dimensions   Subsets of the customer (or store) dimension that are made into a separate artificial little dimension to facilitate rapid browsing and the handling of slowly changing dimensions.

Denormalize   The allowing of redundancy in a table in order that the table can remain flat, rather than snowflaked or normalized.

Depletions   Same as shipments. Usually refers to a warehouse drawing down inventory in response to customer orders.

Descriptive Model   A model of an organization that as much as possible is based on what actually takes place rather than what should take place. Contrast with normative model.

Dimension   An independent entity in the model of an organization that serves as an entry point, or as a mechanism for slicing the additive measures of the organization.

Dimension Table   A table in a dimensional model (star join schema) with a single part primary key.

Dimensional Data Warehouse   A set of databases for decision support designed as star-joined schemas.

Dimensional Model   A methodology for modeling data that starts from a set of base measurement events and constructs a table called the fact table, generally with one record for each discrete measurement. This fact table is then surrounded by a set of dimension tables, describing precisely what is known in the context of each measurement record. Because of the characteristic structure of a dimensional model, it is often called a star schema. Dimensional models have proved to be understandable, predictable, extendable, and highly resistant to the "ad hoc attack" from groups of business users. Dimensional models are the basis of many DBMS performance enhancements, including powerful indexing approaches, and aggregations. Dimensional models are the basis for the incremental and distributed development of data warehouses through the use of conformed dimensions and conformed facts. Dimensional models are the logical foundation for all OLAP systems.

Directory Server   A server, which can be viewed as a little data warehouse, that keeps track of all the users of a system as well as all the resources available on the system, such as database servers, file servers, printers, and communications resources. The industry standard way to communicate with a directory server is LDAP (Lightweight Directory Access Protocol).

Dirty Customer Dimension   A customer dimension in which the same person can appear multiple times, probably not with exactly the same name spellings or other attributes.

Discrete (Dimension Attributes)   Data, usually textual, that takes on a fixed set of values, like the flavor of a product.

DNS Domain Name Service is an Internet protocol that matches domain names to their IP addresses. DNS Lookup is the action taken to look up an IP address corresponding to a domain name. Reverse DNS returns a domain name, given an IP address.

Domain A specific range of Internet addresses assigned to a single Internet user.

Domain Name The unique text name of a domain, often ending in .com, .org, .gov, or .net.

Download Loading data into a computer from another source. Also see **Upload**.

Drill Across The act of requesting data from two or more fact tables in a value chain in a single report.

Drill Down The act of adding a row header or replacing a row header in a report to break down the rows of the answer set more finely.

Drill Up The act of removing a row header or replacing a row header in a report to break down the rows of the answer set less finely.

DSS Decision Support System, the original name for a data warehouse. It is still the best name because it describes what a data warehouse is used for. During the 1980s, the term DSS was often interpreted in a highly technical and analytic way, which led the term to be used less frequently.

Dwell Time The length of time that a specific Web page is available for viewing on a user's browser.

Earned Income The income that a company is allowed to report in a given time period based on providing a service during that time period. Money paid in advance cannot be reported as income until it is earned.

ECLF Extended Common Log Format is an enhanced version of the common log format. See also **CLF**.

EDI Electronic Data Interchange, a set of ISO standards for the exchange of structured data between businesses, and less formally, any exchange of data between business partners for operational purposes.

End Aisle Displays A form of promotion in grocery and drug stores. The display racks are often provided by the product manufacturers.

Entity Relation Modeling A model of an organization's data in which the objective has been to remove all repeated values by creating more tables. Entity relation modeling is important for transaction processing and for defining certain data rules (inappropriately called business rules). Entity relation modeling produces complex schemas that are hard to query and hard to understand. A minor change in the structure of an entity relation model may necessitate a significant rewrite of a query application because of a change in the way the tables are joined and because of the multiple possible join paths between tables that cannot be chosen automatically. Entity-relation models are neither unique nor complete. That is, more than one entity-relation model can represent the same data, and no entity relation model claims to represent all relationships within the data.

Equal Access   The original promise of relational databases: the ability to retrieve data based on any criteria present in the data.

ERP   Enterprise Resource Planning, a class of applications aimed at spanning some or all of the business functions of a complete enterprise. ERP applications are often deployed on relational databases, and the data dictionaries for these applications may contain thousands of tables. An organization acquiring a major ERP application usually must shut down existing legacy applications and restructure fundamental business processes around the ERP system. ERP systems often contain the equivalent of an ODS since they usually are capable of real time, or near real time, operational reporting, but ERP systems up until now have not made good data warehouses, because they have not provided acceptable end user query performance, or a flexible environment for importing third party data.

ETL   Extract, Transform, and Load. The primary processes of the back room of a data warehouse, prior to any form of querying. The back room is also called the data staging area.

Event Tracking Table   A fact table, frequently factless, where the dimensions of the table define a description of an event, such as an insurance description of an automobile accident.

EXISTS   A logical expression type in SQL.

Exploit   An act of penetrating or compromising security.

Extended Cost   The unit cost multiplied by a quantity to give an additive value.

Fact   A measurement, typically numeric and additive, that is stored in a fact table.

Fact Table   The central table in a dimensional model (star join schema), characterized by a composite key, each of whose elements is a foreign key drawn from a dimension table.

Factless Fact Table   A fact table that happens to have no facts.

FAQ   Frequently-Asked-Questions are a help mechanism consisting of real or hypothetical questions matched to answers. It is hoped that a user seeking technical help will refer first to a FAQ document before calling a technical support hotline.

FIFO   First-In-First-Out refers to a caching methodology in which the oldest item in a queue is the first to be retrieved. See **LIFO.**

Filter on Fact Records   A type of application constraint that constrains on the numeric values of one or more facts.

Firewall   A firewall is a computer placed between the Internet and a group of computers (a subnet) to protect them from malicious access by remote, unauthorized users. A firewall can also serve to prevent information from inside a protected subnet from reaching the Internet. A firewall may also provide authentication of the user's identity.

Flash Total   A summary total reported from an operational system, such as orders or shipments, usually reported on a daily basis, that can be used to check the integrity of the current data warehouse data load.

Flat File Database   An application, usually implemented on a mainframe computer, that relies on non-relational flat files, such as IBM VSAM files.

Foreign Key   A field in a relational database table whose values are drawn from the values of a primary key in another table. In a star join schema the components of a composite fact table key are foreign keys with respect to each of the dimension tables.

Frame   A frame is a space reserved in a Web page for displaying other Web pages. Essentially, it is a page within a page.

From Clause (SQL)   The SQL clause that lists the tables required by the query.

Front End Tool   A client tool that fetches or manipulates data stored on a relational database. Contrasted with a back end tool.

FTP   File Transfer Protocol is a TCP/IP protocol that, as the name implies, is used for transferring files between computers. Most Web browsers support FTP as well as HTTP.

GB   GB, or one billion bytes. Because megabytes and gigabytes are normally expressed as a power of 2, a GB actually contains exactly 1,073,741,824 bytes.

Generalized Key A dimension table primary key that has been created by generalizing an original production key such as a product number or a customer, usually by creating a surrogate key. Generalized keys are required to handle slowly changing dimensions as well as aggregates.

GET A request for Website data, in the HTTP protocol.

GIF The Graphical Interchange Format is one standard for compressing images when transferring them across a network or storing them. The GIF format is especially suited to images with a limited color range and straight object boundaries. Unfortunately, even though millions of GIF images have been used for more than 10 years on the Web, the Unisys Corporation believes it has a patent on the GIF format, and it is trying to extract royalties after the fact from everyone who is using GIF images. We recommend using some other graphic format than GIF for this reason.

GIS Geographic Information System, a hybrid application combining database and mapping technology. Typically in a GIS, queries can be constructed from maps and maps can be delivered as a result of a query.

Gigabyte One billion bytes. See **GB**.

GMROI Gross margin return on inventory, equal to the number of turns of inventory multiplied by the gross margin percent. A measure of the return on each dollar invested in inventory.

GMT Greenwich Mean Time is the local standard time at zero degrees longitude, which runs through the Royal Navy Observatory near London. See **UTC**.

GPS The Global Positioning System is a system of satellites belonging to the Department of Defense, used to determine a precise geographic location or time.

Grain The meaning of a single record in a fact table. The determination of the grain of a fact table is the second of four key steps in the design of a star join schema.

Gross Margin The gross profit expressed as a percentage of gross revenue.

Gross Profit The gross revenue less the cost of the goods.

Gross Revenue The total revenue paid to a company by its customers.

Group By Clause (SQL) The SQL clause that uniquely lists the unaggregated facts in the SELECT list, i.e., everything that is not a SUM, COUNT, MIN, MAX, or AVG.

Growing the Market in a Promotion   A desirable outcome of a promotion that causes overall sales of a product category to grow, instead of causing cannibalization.

GUI   Graphical User Interface. A style of computer interface characterized by windows, icons, the use of graphics, and the use of a mouse pointing device.

GUID   A Global Unique IDentifier is an identification number that can be used to uniquely identify a specific computing device.

Heterogeneous Products   A set of products with some incompatible attributes and facts. A characteristic design challenge in financial service environments.

Hierarchical Database   An older style of database, typified by IBM's IMS database, that does not allow equal access.

HL7   The Health Level Seven group is an organization that sets data interchange standards for healthcare information systems.

HOLAP   Hybrid OLAP, which combines ROLAP and MOLAP technologies. The relational DBMS provides support for the lower atomic levels of data, and the MOLAP systems support aggregated, smaller levels of data. The best HOLAP systems offer seamless switching between the technologies, and claim to support MDX language capabilities across the entire spectrum.

Host   A host is any computer on the Internet with a domain name, however the term is often applied only to a server, to distinguish it from a client.

Householding (Financial Services)   The effort to assign an account or an individual to a household of accounts or individuals for marketing purposes.

HTML   The HyperText Markup Language is a standard markup language for defining the presentation characteristics of Web documents. HTML is not a programming language.

HTTP   The HyperText Transfer Protocol is the communications protocol of the Web. HTTP specifies the way in which a browser and Website exchange information.

IANA   The Internet Assigned Number Authority is a government-sponsored body that assigns numeric Internet addresses.

ICANN   The Internet Corporation for Assigned Names and Numbers is (or will be) a government-sponsored corporation that assumes the responsibility for IANA's tasks and also determines the method by which domain names are assigned.

ICQ   Literally, I Seek You. ICQ is a Web tool that alerts you whenever a named friend or acquaintance is logged on to their computer, so that you can interrupt them with a greeting or a message or transfer a file.

Impression   A single instance of a graphic image (usually an ad) displayed on a given user's browser display.

IMS   (1) the IBM hierarchical database used by many companies for legacy systems. Criticized for not providing equal access for decision support. (2) IMS, a leading supplier of syndicated pharmaceutical data.

Internet   The Internet is the worldwide collection of communication links and services that are tied together using the Internet protocol (IP).

InterNIC   is the former name for the organization which assigned domain names to the public. It is often referred to by its corporate identity, Network Solutions.

IP   Internet protocol is the communication protocol and associated standards which permit packets of data to be transported and routed by the Internet. It is important to understand that IP mandates the existence of multiple ports for different purposes on host machines. The existence of multiple ports is one of the sources of security headaches.

IP Address   The numeric address of a particular host or subnet on the Internet.

IPSEC   IP Security, a protocol for encrypting IP traffic, such as on a local area network, securely.

IPv6   A standard that defines an extension of the Internet protocol, notable for its substantial extension of IP Address Space. IPv6 addresses are extendable to cover virtually every electronic device on earth.

IRI   Information Resources, Incorporated. One of the two leading suppliers, along with A.C. Nielsen, of syndicated scanner data from grocery stores and drug stores.

ISBN   The International Standard Book Number (ISBN) is a ten-digit number that uniquely identifies books and book-like products published internationally. The purpose of the ISBN is to establish and identify one title or edition of a title from one specific publisher and is unique to that edition, allowing for more efficient marketing of products by booksellers, libraries, universities, wholesalers, and distributors.

ISP   An Internet service provider is a company or organization that provides Internet connectivity to the public through the use of telephone lines, cable TV links, or satellites. ISPs often offer a range of services, like e-mail, Website hosting, and application access, and provide connectivity to the customer's PC using TCP/IP protocols.

IT   Information Technology, the name of the organization responsible for the information assets of the organization. Originally, DP, or Data Processing. Then, MIS, or Management Information Systems, and then IS, or Information Systems.

Java   Java is a programming language and "sandboxed" code interpreter which permits programs to be downloaded to PCs from the Web, but isolates these applications from access to other applications running on the PC.

JavaScript   JavaScript is a programming language whose source code can be carried in HTML documents for execution by a browser-based interpreter. JavaScript has far fewer features than **Java**, and is much simpler to code.

Join constraint (SQL)   The portion of the SQL WHERE clause that bookkeeps the join relationships between the fact table and the dimension tables.

JPEG   An image compression format standardized by the Joint Photographic Experts Group. It is particularly suited to complex images like photographs. A JPEG image can be adjusted by the user to offer high compression with resulting loss of image quality, or low compression with high image quality.

Julian day number   A representation of a calendar date as the simple count of days from the beginning of an epoch, such as January 1, 1900. True Julian dates are numbered in the millions and are not often used as the literal basis of date values.

KM   Knowledge Management, a set of products and processes that enable the knowledge worker to access structured and unstructured corporate information. Corporate information portals are supposed to be the ultimate technological articulation of KM's goals.

LAN   A local area network connects the computers within a physically-contiguous area like a workgroup or small office.

LDAP   Lightweight Directory Access Protocol, a standard, currently agreed to by most of the major systems vendors, for describing the users of a network and the resources available on a network. See **Directory Server**.

Legacy System   An operational system for entering data about the company's operations. Usually a transaction-based system, but may not be a transaction system or a relational system. Usually resides on a mainframe computer.

Liability   An item that appears on the balance sheet of a company that represents money the company owes to someone else. Bank deposits are liabilities from a bank's point of view because they must be paid back.

LIFO   Last in, first out. A queuing methodology in which the most recent item in the queue is the first to be retrieved.

Lift of a Promotion   The increase of sales over the baseline value that can be attributed to the effects of the promotion.

Line Item   An individual line of a control document such as an invoice, usually identifying a single product within the invoice. Most often used as the grain of the associated fact table.

Link   A link is a direction in hypertext from one object to another, usually in the form of a URL.

Linkrot   A Web page whose links are out of date and lead to "page not found" messages is said to be suffering from linkrot.

Linux   An open-source implementation of UNIX which runs on Intel-based PCs.

Logical Design   The phase of a database design concerned with identifying the relationships among the data elements. Contrasted with the physical design.

Loss Party (Insurance)   Any individual or entity associated with a claim (a loss), including injured parties, witnesses, lawyers, and other service providers.

Many-To-Many Relationship   A logical data relationship in which the value of one data element can exist in combination with many values of another data element, and vice versa.

Market Basket Analysis   A kind of analysis in retail environments that seeks to understand all the products purchased by a customer in a single shopping event. Market basket analysis is an example of affinity grouping, which seeks to find things that happen together.

MB   Megabyte, but actually precisely 1,048,576 bytes, or characters of data.

MBA   Master of Business Administration. A graduate college or university degree requiring extensive understanding of how commercial businesses are organized and managed.

MDX   Multi Dimensional Expressions, a part of Microsoft's OLE DB offering. MDX is a powerful query language, which bears a superficial resemblance to SQL, but contains a far richer set of semantics devoted to OLAP analysis. Although MDX is a Microsoft creation, it is the closest thing to a standard OLAP language, and the other OLAP vendors will surely offer significant levels of MDX support.

Merchandise Hierarchy   A set of attributes in the product dimension that define an ascending many to one relationship. Common to all manufacturing and retail environments.

Metadata   Any data maintained to support the operations or use of a data warehouse. Nearly all back end tools and front end tools require some private metadata in the form of specifications or status. Often the metadata is outside the relational database. There are few coherent standards for metadata viewed in the broader sense. Distinguished from the primary data in the dimension tables and the fact tables.

Metatag   A metatag is a special HTML tag used to describe keywords or titles for Web search engines. Metatags in an HTML document are invisible but can be seen using a "view source" feature.

Migrate   The step of moving data from one computer to another.

MIME   Multipurpose Internet Mail Extensions are a set of protocols that permit attaching binary images to email messages or to HTTP documents.

Mirrored Database   A physical organization of data where the entire database is duplicated on separate disk drives. Mirrored databases offer a number of performance and administrative advantages.

MOLAP   Multi Dimensional OLAP. MOLAP systems are dedicated OLAP implementations not dependent on relational databases. Although MOLAP systems do not scale to the sizes that relational OLAP (ROLAP) systems can, they typically offer far better performance and more tightly integrated tools than their relational counterparts. See also **MDX.**

Mozilla   The open source programming organization that maintains the successors to the browser code originally developed as Mosaic by the National Center for Supercomputer Applications at the University of Illinois and later enhanced by Netscape.

MP3   A non-encrypted compression standard for audio that is particularly suited to stereo digital music. MP3 compressions of audio are sometimes claimed to be as good as an uncompressed CD.

MPP   Massively Parallel Processing, a parallel hardware organization that de-emphasizes the sharing of memory resources. Contrast with **SMP.**

Multi-Table Join Query   One of the two characteristic types of queries in a data warehouse environment. Involves the joining of one or more dimension tables to a single fact table. Contrast with **browse queries.**

NAP   A Network Access Point is an official point of entry for the Internet's wideband backbone in the USA. ISPs often link to NAPs to provide their connectivity with the net.

Nonadditive (Facts)   A fact that cannot logically be added between records. May be numeric and therefore must usually be combined in a computation with other facts before being added across records. If non-numeric, can only be used in constraints, or counts, or groupings.

Normalize   The process of removing redundancy in data by separating the data into multiple tables.

Normative Model   A model of an organization that describes how an organization is supposed to function. Contrast to descriptive model.

NUMA   Non Uniform Memory Access, a variant of shared memory architecture claimed to be inherently more scalable than SMP.

ODS   The Operational Data Store was originally defined as a frequently updated, volatile, integrated copy of data from operational systems that is meant to be accessed by "clerks and executives." Ten years ago, the ODS made sense because it was a "hot reporting" system that sat midway between operational systems that were unable to provide any reporting functions, and data warehouses that originally were based on highly aggregated data presented in a very delayed fashion. This original ODS was specifically defined to lack performance enhancing aggregations and to lack supporting time histories of prior data, although the originators of the concept recommended using dimensional models for the ODS. The ODS as a separate system makes much less sense today, because modern legacy applications, such as ERP systems, provide the hot reporting function, and the data warehouse at the same time is providing a far more granular, and up-to-date reporting capability than before.

Off-Invoice Allowances   Typically deal or promotion related subtractions from the list price shown on the invoice. Part of deriving the net invoice amount which is what the customer is supposed to pay on this line item.

Off-Invoice Discounts   Typically financial terms related subtractions from the list price shown on the invoice. Part of deriving the net invoice amount which is what the customer is supposed to pay on this line item.

OLAP   On Line Analytic Processing, a term meant to contrast with OLTP. OLAP is a set of principles that provide a dimensional framework for decision support. The term OLAP also is used to define a confederation of vendors who offer non-relational, proprietary products aimed at decision support. See **MOLAP, HOLAP,** and **MDX.**

OLTP   On-Line Transaction Processing, the original description for all the activities and systems associated with entering data reliably into a database. Most frequently used with reference to relational databases, although OLTP can be used generically to describe any transaction processing environment.

OPS   The Open Profiling System is a proposed standard that extends the cookie system by offering up a user's personal identity to any Website. In return for this personal exposure, the user is granted some control over the content of his or her OPS profile.

One-To-Many Relationship   A logical data relationship in which the value of one data element can exist in combination with many values of another data element, but not vice versa.

Open Source   Software that is developed and maintained by pro bono contributions of individual developers working in a collaborative environment. The software source code is published for anyone to use or modify. Open source does not necessarily imply either non-profit nor royalty-free.

Operational Data Store   See **ODS.**

Order By Clause (SQL)   The SQL clause that determines the ordering of rows in the answer set.

Outrigger Table   A secondary dimension table attached to a dimension table. An outrigger table is a physical design interpretation of a single logical dimension table. Occurs when a dimension table is snowflaked.

P&L Profit and Loss. Also known as an income statement. The P&L is the classic logical ordering of revenues and costs to represent a progression from gross revenues down to a "bottom line" that represents net profit.

Page A Web page is a document in HTML or SGML format that can be displayed by a browser. The term "page" is also used to describe a compound document consisting of the HTML document itself, and ancillary objects such as images or sounds that are downloaded to the browser as directed by the page's HTML.

Page Event Refers to a page or frame downloaded from a Web server to a browser, exclusive of any ancillary content.

Parent Child Database A hierarchical organization of data typically involving a header and a set of line items. The star join approach strips all the information out of the header (parent) and leaves it as a degenerate dimension.

Partitioning of History The natural correspondence between dimension table entries and fact table records when a Type 2 slowly changing dimension has been implemented. See the discussion in the main text.

PERL A programming language frequently used to code CGI-based Web server applications. PERL has excellent string manipulation features but it is interpreted, not compiled, making it prone to performance problems in heavily-loaded applications. It is mostly used in UNIX systems.

PCMCIA A standard for credit-card size expansion cards for portable PCs developed by the Personal Computer Memory Card International Association.

Peering These arrangements are wideband links between geographically diverse ISPs that are provided by the ISPs themselves independent of the formal Internet and its NAPs. They are a method of providing wideband links between ISPs at a lower cost than would be incurred using the Internet's backbone trunks.

Physical Design The phase of a database design following the logical design that identifies the actual database tables and index structures used to implement the logical design.

PIN Personal Identification Number. Used generically to refer to any secret code a person types in to identify themselves, usually at a bank teller machine or other similar device.

Pixel Picture Element. One dot on a display or in a bitmapped picture. A pixel has an X-Y position, and may have a size and color.

Point of Sale System The cash registers and the associated in-store computers in a retail environment.

Portal A Website designed to be the first point of entry for visitors to the Web. Portal sites usually feature a wide variety of contents and search capabilities in order to entice visitors to use it as their portal site. Portals are often selected as browser home pages. Well-known portals include Yahoo and MSN.

POP Post Office Protocol is a TCP/IP application protocol which defines mail box implementations.

POS See **Point of Sale System.**

POST An HTTP command that advises a Web browser to send the contents of a specific form or query string to a browser application.

PPP The Point-to-Point Protocol is the most common telecommunication protocol for dial-up Web connections. It can service a number of different network protocols, including IP.

Price Point Analysis The breakdown of product sales by each discrete transaction price. Requires a fact table with fine enough grain to represent each price point separately.

Primary Key A field in a database table that is uniquely different for each record in the table.

Processes The primary operational processes in an organization. The identification of the candidate business processes is the first step in a data warehouse design. A business process, in order to be used in a data warehouse, must be supported by one or more production data sources.

Product Master File A company's master list of products, usually maintained by a manufacturing or purchase order legacy application.

Production Data Load The entire process of extracting production data from a legacy application, transforming it, loading and indexing it, quality assuring it, and publishing it.

Profiler A profiler is a company that gathers and sells personal information about a family or an individual, and ties that information to an ID such as a unique cookie ID.

Promotion An event, usually planned by marketing, that features one or more causal items such as ads, displays, or price reductions. Also thought of as a deal or sometimes as a contract.

Proxy   A proxy is a server that caches Web data in order to reduce the load on servers or networks.

Pseudo Transaction   A step needed in some production data extract systems, where a non-transactional legacy system is analyzed to see what changed from the previous extract. These changes are then made into artificial (pseudo) transactions in order to be loaded into the data warehouse.

Public Key Encryption   A method of secure data exchange involving a pair of keys that always must be used together. One key is designated public and the other key is designated private. Contrast with Symmetric Key Encryption.

Publishing Used Data   The most succinct way to describe the overall responsibility of the data warehouse. The data is used because it is almost always copied from a legacy system.

Pull Down List   A user interface effect in a front end tool that displays a list of options for the user. The most interesting pull down lists in a data warehouse come from browse queries on a dimension attribute.

Query   An SQL SELECT statement passed from the front end application or the application server to the relational DBMS.

Query String   A query string is a text string that is transferred from a browser to a Web server in order to direct the server to do something. Query strings are a component of the HTTP protocol.

RAID   A Redundant Array of Inexpensive (or Independent) Disks is a disk memory device on which data is distributed across several disk drives with enough error-correcting code to maintain data integrity in the event of a failure of a single drive.

RAM   Random Access Memory is semiconductor-based computer memory.

Reason Code   A field used in conjunction with a transaction dimension to describe why the transaction took place. Reason codes are valuable for returns and cancellations.

Referential Integrity   A mandatory condition in a data warehouse where all the keys in the fact tables are legitimate foreign keys relative to the dimension tables. In other words, all the fact key components are subsets of the primary keys found in the dimension tables at all times.

Referral   A referral is an executed link from one Website to another. Referrals can be automatically logged by Web servers.

Relational Database   A database system that supports the full range of standard SQL.

Repository   A repository in the data warehouse sense usually is the same as an ODS. See **ODS**.

Reverse DNS   The protocol for looking up a domain name given its IP address.

RFC   A Request for Comment is the conventional method of publishing an Internet or Web standard. RFC's are collaborative works that contain comments and inputs from diverse interest groups and individuals. The RFC mechanism, pioneered on the Internet, has proved to be a remarkably open and rapid way of setting standards and developing architectures.

ROI   Return on Investment, usually expressed as a rate describing the growth of an investment during its lifetime.

ROLAP   Relational OLAP, referring to query and analysis tools that impose a strong dimensional (OLAP) flavor to a conventional relational database.

Row Header   The non-aggregated components of the SQL select list. Will always be listed in the SQL group by clause.

SABRE   American Airlines' reservation system, one of the world's busiest and most successful transaction processing systems.

Sales Invoice   The control document that describes a sale. Usually contains multiple line items that each represent a separate product sold.

Sandbox   A set of restrictions on an executable code module that keep the module from controlling the host machine. Typically a sandbox prohibits reading and writing directly to the file system and from controlling peripheral devices. A good sandbox also protects memory use, in order to eliminate buffer overflow security exploits.

SCD   Slowly Changing Dimension. A type 1 SCD is a dimension whose records are overwritten when the value of an attribute changes. A Type 2 SCD is a dimension where a new record is created when the value of an attribute changes. A Type 3 SCD is a dimension where an alternate "old" field is created when an attribute changes.

Schema   The logical or physical design of a set of database tables, indicating the relationship among the tables.

SCSI   The Small Computer System Interface is a standard which describes wideband mechanisms for attaching peripheral devices like disks to computers.

Search Engine   A search engine is a system which searches the Web or a portion of it, indexing sites by keyword or content.

Select Distinct (SQL)   An SQL statement that suppresses duplicate rows in the answer set.

Select List (SQL)   The list of column specifications that follows SELECT comes before FROM in an SQL query. Each item in the select list generates a column in the answer set.

Semi-Additive (Fact)   A numeric fact that can be added along some dimensions in a fact table but not others. Transaction counts in daily or monthly snapshots typically cannot be added along the product dimension if the definition of transaction is an entire market basket purchase. Inventory levels and balances cannot be added along the time dimension, but can be usefully averaged over the time dimension.

Session   The collection of actions taken by a Website visitor while visiting the Website without leaving it. Also called a visit.

Session Map   A session map is the set of paths or vectors taken by the browser user within a particular Website. A session map is difficult to build because of browsers' abilities to cache pages and return to them without returning to the server.

Session Tree   A session tree is a representation of a user's Website browser actions represented using a hierarchical map of the relationships between Website pages, not by the actual sequence in which the pages were accessed. This is much easier to construct than a session map.

SGML   The Standard Generalized Markup Language is a standard for marking documents which can be parsed by a computer. HTML and XML are markup languages that fall under the SGML umbrella.

Shelf Displays   Tags, racks, or other promotional mechanisms used in a retail environment.

Shell Account   A UNIX user account that allows the user to run command-line–based UNIX programs.

SKU   Stock keeping unit. A standard term in manufacturing and retail environments to describe an individual product, often uniquely represented by a scanable bar code.

Slice and Dice   The standard description of the ability to access a data warehouse through any of its dimensions equally.

Slowly Changing Dimensions   The tendency of dimension records, especially in the product and customer dimensions, to change gradually or occasionally over time. Slowly changing dimensions may be handled with three different techniques, which are described in the text. See **SCD**.

Solaris   Sun Microsystems' implementation of UNIX.

SMP   Symmetric Multi-Processing. A parallel hardware organization that emphasizes the sharing of memory resources. Contrast with MPP. See **NUMA**.

Snapshot   A kind of fact table that represents the status of accounts at the end of each time period. Daily snapshots and monthly snapshots are common. Snapshots are required in a number of businesses such as insurance where the transaction history is too complicated to be used as the basis for computing snapshots on the fly.

Snowflake   A normalized dimension where a flat single table dimension is decomposed into a tree structure with potentially many nesting levels. Although snowflaking can be regarded as an embellishment of the dimensional model, snowflaking generally compromises user understandability and browsing performance.

Source System   An operational system of record whose function it is to capture the transactions of the business. A source system is often called a "legacy system" in a mainframe environment.

Sparse   A fact table that has relatively few of all the possible combinations of key values. A grocery store item movement database is not considered sparse because 5 percent to 10 percent of all the key combinations for SKU, Store, and Day will be present. An airlines frequent flyer database is extremely sparse because very few of the customer, flight number, day combinations actually appear in the database.

Spider   A generic name for a Web program which collects information for search engines.

SQL   The Structured Query Language is the standard language for accessing relational databases.

SSL   Secure Sockets Layer is a protocol for secure handshaking between computers. Usually a public key/private key scheme is used at the outset of an SSL communication episode to establish a secure link between the machines, then a symmetric, high-speed key is agreed to between the machines in the secure context. The remainder of the communication is based on this symmetric key.

Star Join Schema   A specific organization of a database in which a fact table with a composite key is joined to a number of single level dimension tables, each with a single primary key. Successful data warehouses usually are based on star join schemas.

Stock Keeping Unit   See **SKU**.

Streaming Media   Web content that is downloaded to the user continuously while he listens to it or views it. Examples are Real Audio and Real Video.

Subdomain   A subdomain is either a contiguous set of IP addresses that are part of a larger domain, or a domain name qualified by a dot-delimited prefix such as "store.webcom.com"

Subrogation (Insurance)   The act of an insurance company selling the rights remaining in a claim, such as the right to sue someone for damages.

Supply Side   The part of the value chain in a manufacturing company that starts with purchase orders for ingredients and parts and ends with finished goods inventory. Physically the supply side is the manufacturing operation. Contrast with **Demand Side.**

Surrogate Key   An artificial key, usually a consecutively assigned integer, that is used in a dimensional model to connect a dimension table to a fact table. In the dimension table, the surrogate key is the primary key. In the fact table, the surrogate key is a foreign key, and may be part of the fact table's primary key, although that is not required. A surrogate key usually cannot be interpreted by itself. That is, it is not a smart key in any way. Surrogate keys are required in many data warehouse situations to handle slowly changing dimensions, as well as missing or inapplicable data.

Symmetric Key Encryption   A method of secure data exchange involving a single key that can be used both to encrypt and to decrypt the communication. Symmetric key encryption is usually much faster than public key encryption, but symmetric key encryption does not allow for the remote handshaking that public key encryption does. Systems such as SSL (Secure Sockets Layer) implement a hybrid of the two techniques, first setting up the exchange with public key encryption, and then performing the bulk of the communication with symmetric key encryption.

Syndicated Data Suppliers   Companies that collect data, clean it, package it, and resell it. A.C. Nielsen and IRI are the principal syndicated data suppliers for grocery and drug store scanner data, and

IMS and Walsh America are the principal syndicated data suppliers for pharmaceutical data.

SYNONYM (SQL) An SQL statement that creates logical copies of a table that can be used separately in a SELECT statement.

Tag A tag is a HTML construct consisting of a symmetrical pair of delimiters in the form **<tagname>…</tagname>**.

Takeaway Consumer purchases.

TB Terabyte. One trillion bytes, equal to 1 million million bytes.

TCP Transmission Control Protocol is the collection of application-specific layers of TCP/IP. Examples of TCP layers include HTTP (the Web protocol), Telnet (a command-line display protocol) and FTP (file transfer protocol).

TCP/IP The basic communication protocol of the Internet, consisting of a network layer (IP) and an application layer (TCP).

Telnet A TCP/IP protocol for supporting character-oriented terminal applications.

Temporal Inconsistency The tendency of an OLTP database to change its primary data relationships from moment to moment as transactions are processed. This inconsistency impacts end users in two primary ways: 1) the database is changing constantly as they query it, and 2) old history is not necessarily preserved.

Temporary Price Reduction A promotional technique in retail environments.

Terabyte One trillion bytes.

Textual (Dimension Attributes) Dimension attributes that are actually text or behave like text.

Time Shifting of a Promotion The tendency of some promotions to cause the customer to defer purchases until the promotion is on, and then not make purchases after the promotion for a prolonged period. In the most serious cases, the promotion accomplishes nothing except to allow the customer to buy products cheaply.

Top-Down View The perspective of a company based on starting with the most global description of the company and its mission and proceding to subdivide this perspective until the objectives of the analysis have been accomplished. The top down view rarely touches the lowest level of detail in a company. Data warehouse design techniques begin with a top down view.

TPR Temporary price reduction, a form of promotion.

Trans Shipments   Shipments of product that occur between the warehouses belonging to the manufacturer or belonging to the retailer.

Transaction   An indivisible unit of work. A transaction processing system either performs an entire transaction or it doesn't perform any part of the transaction.

Turns (Inventory)   The number of times in a given period (usually a year) that the inventory must be completely replenished in order to keep up with the observed rate of sales.

Twinkling Database   The tendency of a transaction processing database to constantly be changing the data the user is attempting to query.

UNICODE   The UNICODE Worldwide Character Standard is a character coding system designed to support the interchange, processing, and display of the written texts of the diverse languages of the modern world. In addition, it supports classical and historical texts of many written languages. UNICODE is a 16-bit implementation, which means that 65,535 characters can be supported, unlike ASCII which can only support 127.

UNIX is a multitasking operating system, originally created by Bell Laboratories, which has undergone thirty years of enhancements and refinements. It is the most commonly used operating system for Internet servers.

UPC   Universal Product Code, the standard bar-coded value found on most grocery and drug store merchandise.

Upload   Sending data from a computer to another location.

Up-selling   Selling a product or service to an existing customer, where the goal is to get the customer to purchase a more expensive, or higher value version than previously purchased.

URL   A Universal Resource Locator is the text address of a specific object on the Web. It usually consists of three parts: a prefix describing the TCP protocol to use to retrieve it (e.g., HTTP), a domain name (e.g., webcom.com), and a document name (e.g., index)

User   On the Web, one who accesses a Website.

User ID   A unique ID used to log onto a computer or computer service.

UTC   Universal Coordinated Time is the international standard term for Greenwich Mean Time. See **GMT**.

Value Chain   The sequence of processes that describe the movement of products or services through a pipeline from original creation to final sales.

VB   Visual Basic, a Microsoft language for application development, which is an object oriented extension of Basic.

Virgin Territory   The portion of disk storage that is unoccupied prior to a data load. In a static database experiencing no in-place updates or inserts, and with a primary sort order with time as the leading term in the sort, all data loading takes place in virgin territory.

Virtual   Not real. Intangible. Virtual memory is memory that can be accessed by a computer but doesn't really exist on a memory chip. It exists only on disk. A virtual retail store is a retail store that exists only as a Web construct and has no instantiation as a three-dimensional object.

Visit   See **Session.**

Visitor   See **User.**

VPN   Virtual Private Network, a secure link between two machines, based on encryption, that allows sensitive traffic to be transmitted over insecure paths.

Walsh America   A leading supplier of syndicated pharmaceutical data.

Warez   A name for a Website that contains pirated content such as software, audio, and video.

Web   Short for World Wide Web, the collection of servers and browsers that talk to each other using the HTTP protocol. In some lexicons, Web is becoming synonymous with Internet.

Webhouse   The data warehouse, evolved to a new form, because of the existence of the Web.

Website   A Web server, or collection of Web servers, that appear to users as an integrated entity with a well-defined system of hyperlinks connecting its components.

WWW   The World Wide Web is the set of all Websites accessible via the Internet.

W3C   World Wide Web Consortium, a standards making body which formalizes the definition of Web-based objects and protocols.

WYSIWYG   What You See Is What You Get. A user interface term, used since the early 1970s, suggesting that what the user sees on the screen is a very accurate depiction of what would be printed on a piece of paper.

XML   The Extended Markup Language is an emerging extension of SGML that provides structured data exchange, structured queries, and extended presentation options. XML is a flexible framework for assigning tags to fields within a document. XML does not specify what the tags should be. It is up to various organizations or industry groups to define and use consistent sets of tags.

X Window System   A terminal application that supports windows. The X Window System consists of a client program (called a "host" in X-jargon), a host interface, and associated TCP/IP protocols. It is most often used for running a UNIX program interface on a PC. The X Window System is not associated with Microsoft's Windows operating system.

Bibliography

Here are some of the books that have influenced us recently. We have divided them into categories.

Data Mining

The best introductory book on data mining is *Data Mining Techniques for Marketing, Sales, and Customer Support* by Michael Berry and Gordon Linoff, 1997, Wiley Computer Publishing, John Wiley & Sons, Inc., ISBN 0-471-17980-9.

A good book for understanding the structure and content of data required for data mining is *Data Preparation for Data Mining* by Dorian Pyle (Morgan Kaufmann, 1999, ISBN 1-55860-529-0).

Jesus Mena's *Data Mining Your Website* (Digital Press, 1999, ISBN 1-55558-222-2) is a good survey of data mining techniques that can be applied to Webhouse data and the clickstream in particular. This book would be strengthened by a more vigorous attempt to attribute content to each particular Web page, but is otherwise quite useful.

A comprehensive list of data mining tools can be found on *Larry Greenfield's Website* at http://pwp.starnetinc.com/larryg/index.html.

Marketing

Customers.com by Patricia B. Seybold (Times Business/Random House, 1998, ISBN 0-8129-3037-1) is becoming the classic book on what marketing people expect from the Web. Read it as if it were a kind of user interview while building your Webhouse.

Seth Godin's *Permission Marketing* (Simon & Schuster, 1999, 0-684-85636-0) is a very entertaining book that describes an alternative to "interruption marketing" and shows why permission marketing may become the dominant way in which Web companies reach their customers.

Website Designs

Philip and Alex's Guide to Web Publishing by Philip Greenspun (Morgan Kaufmann Publishers, Inc., 1999, ISBN 1-55860-534-7) is the most comprehensive and thoughtful guide to Website design.

Global Solutions for Multilingual Applications by Chris Ott (Wiley Computer Publishing, John Wiley & Sons, Inc., 1999, ISBN 0-471-34827-9) is a good tour of the multi-lingual issue in Website design.

Security

Web Security & Commerce by Simson Garfinkel with Gene Spafford (O'Reilly & Associates, Inc., 1997, ISBN 1-56592-269-7) is a good modern survey of security issues and solutions for the Web.

Maximum Security: A Hacker's Guide to Protecting Your Internet Site and Network by Anonymous (Sams.net Publishing, 1997, ISBN 1-57521-268-4) contains all the tricks and exploits that may be tried against your network.

Security in Computing by Charles P. Pfleeger (Prentice Hall, 1997, ISBN 0-13-337486-6) has the most comprehensive explanation for all of your security exposures. An excellent college-textbook-like treatment of security.

Dimensional Modeling and Data Warehouse Project Management

The Data Warehouse Lifecycle Toolkit by Ralph Kimball, Laura Reeves, Margy Ross, and Warren Thornthwaite (Wiley Computer Publishing, John Wiley & Sons, Inc., 1998, ISBN 0-471-25547-5) is a comprehensive guide for the professional data warehouse manager and his or her technical staff. This book leads you from business requirements gathering to dimensional modeling, and all the way through the lifecycle to deployment and rollout.

The Data Warehouse Toolkit by Ralph Kimball (Wiley Computer Publishing, John Wiley & Sons, Inc., 1996, ISBN 0-471-15337-0) is Ralph's original book on dimensional modeling and designing data warehouses. This book is, by a significant margin, the all-time leading bestseller in data warehousing.

Data Warehouse Design Solutions by Christopher Adamson and Michael Venerable (Wiley Computer Publishing, John Wiley & Sons, Inc., 1998, ISBN 0-471-25195-X) is a very useful and well written guide for dimensional modeling in a number of vertical industries. Highly recommended.

Index

Thank you for purchasing The Data Webhouse Toolkit!

Visit www.ralphkimball.com to register for Data Warehouse Design Tip E-mails.

We invite you to receive a series of Data Warehouse Design Tips from Ralph. Ralph will provide you regular, practical insights about Data Warehouse and Webhouse Design, drawing from his vast experience as a data warehouse architect.

- Visit the Ralph Kimball Associates Website at **www.ralphkimball.com**

- Fill out the registration form to receive the Data Warehouse Design Tips

- Please feel free to submit any questions or insights you may have

- Ralph will frequently select from these questions and insights for his Design Tip E-mails

- Take a few minutes to let us know what you thought of *The Data Webhouse Toolkit* and offer any comments or suggestions

Note: We value your privacy. We will never intentionally distribute information about you to anyone.

KIMBALL
UNIVERSITY

RALPH KIMBALL
ASSOCIATES

Also available from Ralph Kimball:

The Data Warehouse Lifecycle Toolkit
0471-25547-5

The Data Warehouse Toolkit
0471-15337-0